Hidden Harmonies

American Made Music Series

Advisory Board

David Evans, General Editor
Barry Jean Ancelet
Edward A. Berlin
Joyce J. Bolden
Rob Bowman
Susan C. Cook
Curtis Ellison
William Ferris
John Edward Hasse
Kip Lornell
Bill Malone
Eddie S. Meadows
Manuel H. Peña
Wayne D. Shirley
Robert Walser

Hidden Harmonies

Women and Music in Popular Entertainment

Edited by
Paula J. Bishop and Kendra Preston Leonard

University Press of Mississippi / Jackson

The University Press of Mississippi is the scholarly publishing agency of
the Mississippi Institutions of Higher Learning: Alcorn State University,
Delta State University, Jackson State University, Mississippi State University,
Mississippi University for Women, Mississippi Valley State University,
University of Mississippi, and University of Southern Mississippi.

www.upress.state.ms.us

The University Press of Mississippi is a member
of the Association of University Presses.

Copyright © 2023 by University Press of Mississippi
All rights reserved

First printing 2023

∞

Library of Congress Cataloging-in-Publication Data

Names: Bishop, Paula J., editor. | Leonard, Kendra Preston, editor.
Title: Hidden harmonies : women and music in popular entertainment /
edited by Paula J. Bishop and Kendra Preston Leonard.
Other titles: American made music series.
Description: Jackson : University Press of Mississippi, 2023. | Series: American
made music series | Includes bibliographical references and index.
Identifiers: LCCN 2023001505 (print) | LCCN 2023001506 (ebook) | ISBN
9781496845375 (hardback) | ISBN 9781496845382 (trade paperback) | ISBN
9781496845399 (epub) | ISBN 9781496845429 (epub) | ISBN 9781496845405
(pdf) | ISBN 9781496845412 (pdf) Subjects: LCSH: Women musicians. |
Women composers. | Women in the music trade. | Women singers. | Feminism
and music.
Classification: LCC ML82 .H54 2023 (print) | LCC ML82 (ebook) | DDC
780.82—dc23/eng/20230124
LC record available at https://lccn.loc.gov/2023001505
LC ebook record available at https://lccn.loc.gov/2023001506

British Library Cataloging-in-Publication Data available

This book is dedicated to all of the women
whose musical lives have been or remain hidden.

Contents

3   Introduction
—PAULA J. BISHOP AND KENDRA PRESTON LEONARD

11   *Chapter 1*
"She Takes up Music as a Profession": Women Organists in the Nineteenth-Century South
—CANDACE BAILEY

24   *Chapter 2*
Agnes Woodward's Whistling School and White Women's Musical Labor in the United States
—MARIBETH CLARK

53   *Chapter 3*
Women's Compiled Scores in Early Film Music
—KENDRA PRESTON LEONARD

71   *Chapter 4*
Listen to the "Poor Girl Story": (Re)Considering Southern Femininity in Early Old-Time Music
—APRIL L. PRINCE

88   *Chapter 5*
Housewives' Choice? Vera Lynn as Lady DJ in the 1950s and 1960s
—CHRISTINA BAADE

111   *Chapter 6*
"A Belly Full of Spaghetti and Ears Full of Song": Felice Bryant and Country Music Songwriting in the 1950s
—PAULA J. BISHOP

129	*Chapter 7*
	Goldie and the Gingerbreads: A Case Study of the All-Girl Band in 1960s Rock 'n' Roll
	—BRITTANY GREENING

149	*Chapter 8*
	Song and Sentiment in an Appalachian Woman's Private Lyric Notebook
	—TRAVIS D. STIMELING

173	*Chapter 9*
	Finding Hidden Women in the Feminist Narrative: Candie Carawan and Music in the Civil Rights Movement
	—KRISTEN M. TURNER

194	*Chapter 10*
	Come Go with Me to Freedom Land: Black Women Musicians and the Unexplored Sonic History of the March on Washington
	—TAMMY KERNODLE

219	About the Contributors
223	Index

Hidden Harmonies

Introduction
—Paula J. Bishop and Kendra Preston Leonard

In 2013, John Thomas chronicled the work of the mostly unknown, faceless, nameless women of the Gibson guitar factory in Kalamazoo, Michigan. This work of scholarship focused on those responsible for creating the iconic Gibson sound rather than those who exploited that sound in their rise to fame as musicians.[1] Three years later, Phoebe Reilly's long-form piece on bassist Carol Kaye uncovered a similarly anonymized woman, one who had contributed to an estimated 10,000 recordings, including those that made the Beach Boys famous.[2] These are examples of "recovery history," in which scholars who have been marginalized have researched and written about figures like themselves—people of color, women, queer, poor, and/or belonging to other underrepresented groups. This shift away from the "great man" and "great (privileged) woman" approach of the nineteenth and early twentieth centuries to a method of studying history "from below," as described by Albert Mathiez, has led to important and revelatory work on musicians whose work otherwise would be unknown.[3] Scholars are increasingly accepting the need for a model in which the individuals and collective entities doing the everyday work of supporting and creating musical genres, venues, and means of transmission are fully recognized and given the same treatment as individual musical stars. This approach, bolstered by what is now nearly forty years of foundational and advanced work in feminist musicology, queer musicology, and critical race theory in music scholarship, informs each essay in this collection, even as their authors seek to expand the materials and topics we consider crucial to developing a fuller understanding of what women have done for and in music. In developing this book, we were inspired by the "Kalamazoo gals" (as they were called), Carol Kaye, and other women musicians who, individually or collectively, contributed to the sound of the twentieth century—in theaters, in the streets, in churches, on the airwaves, and in performance venues, all before the firm establishment of Second Wave feminism. We wanted to learn their stories, tell their stories, consider their unacknowledged labor, and explore the meaning and lasting importance of that labor. We wanted to delve into what Natasha Korda has termed "feminist counterarchives": the documents in which scholars have overlooked the presence of women and women's music-making, like the book of song titles and lyrics kept by Mary Olivia Smith and written about here in Travis Stimeling's essay, or the recordings by Rosa Lee Carson and Roba Stanley, whose full influence is revealed in April L. Prince's essay.[4]

In many historiographies of women in/and music, scholars have focused on the figures riding the top of the wave but less so on those propelling the bulk of the wave forwards and upwards. This is in part because of the discipline's composer- and "great works"–centric model in which the emphasis has been on select figures and their contributions to a canon that has been comprised of similar pieces by similar composers. Considerable work has been done on the "great (usually privileged) women" who have become static figureheads for women in music: Amy Beach is the quintessential example in American "art" music. In vernacular music, it is stars like Dolly Parton or Beyoncé, who did not have the same privileges as Beach, who have managed to become the "great women" who have received scholarly treatment.[5] But for every star there are hundreds of less-recognized women who contribute to musical communities in ways that influence musical aesthetics and expand the opportunities available to women.

Our collection focuses not on those whose names are the best known nor on the most celebrated but on the many women who had power in collective, subversive, or other ways hidden from standard histories. We define *power* here as the ability to incite or drive change; to begin or support new endeavors; or to alter the status quo and established hierarchies, even if those actions are mostly unknown in a historiographical sense. Certainly, in this manner, the "Kalamazoo gals" wielded power, as did (to draw from this collection) Goldie and the Gingerbreads and professional women whistlers, all of whose labor contributed to the development of new roles for women in music. In this collection, "power" is not the power of breaking down doors à la Carrie Nation or suffragettes chaining themselves to fences, but rather a more subtle power that encompasses driving change from within a recognized hierarchy to shift both the foundations and outer reaches of institutions.

In exploring this power, the authors in this collection engage with several larger topoi of feminist methodologies. We collectively reexamine primary sources in regard to women's work in music, expanding our ideas of what primary sources are, and how we must reengage with those sources using feminist and queer methodologies as well as critical race theory in order to overcome previous, biased readings of such sources. Musicology has always privileged certain kinds of scholarship, sources, and approaches and has assigned valence based on a male-normative view, placing certain types of work above others. This means that the presence—or notable omission—of women in primary sources has often gone unstudied and unaccounted-for. We navigate the conundrum in which work with music and gender has stood under two banners: one that claims women had an advantage in music production because of their scarcity in the industry and another that at the same time deems them dilettantes. Finally, we seek to reveal the work of women who have, by societal pressure, personal circumstance, or preference, operated in the shadows of male stars. As Roxane Prevost and Kimberly Francis have asserted, "Without this kind of interrogation, well-intentioned acts of historical recovery will remain susceptible to devaluation based upon the unspoken rules that police the margins of the canon."[6] Because of the existing power structures within academia that privilege the study of the "great" men and women, these are not subjects that draw the attention of scholarship. The result is that only a small number of scholars are able to devote themselves to working in the margins of culture and history.

Our subjects and the results of their power and labor also fall into one or more specific categories: serving as arbiters of taste; expanding or participating in opportunities often gendered as male; and contributing to or strengthening community, often by creating opportunities that did not previously exist. Each chapter examines the contributions of a woman or group of women whose work in music led to developments within the field, and how our understanding of such contributions alters the traditional narratives associated with women and music in popular entertainment. With all of these methodological approaches in use, we have ordered the chapters chronologically, although there is some overlap between several essays. By returning to primary sources and reading them through feminist, queer, and race-aware lenses, and by repudiating earlier, casually or deliberately biased interpretations, we find an astonishing amount of information ripe for more equitable exegesis and analysis. The contributing authors have uncovered striking and often revelatory materials and information that rewrite the histories of women in music. As Kristen M. Turner writes in her chapter here, rather than wishing for more from our subjects, we seek to uncover all they did.

WOMEN AS ARBITERS OF TASTE

In the scholarship of social psychology, researcher Herbert Kelman has written that the social avenue of identification—when a group of people identify with an individual or other social entity (like a band) and are influenced by it in some way—is one of the most common explanations for understanding how people can be led or guided by others.[7] Robert Cialdini takes Kelman's concept of identification further, developing it into a definition of "social proof," in which we see the tolerance, acceptance, and adoption of new ideas and practices by a group of people after having been exposed to those new practices by individuals.[8] In musical culture, an example of this would be fans of an emerging star dressing like or using language in ways that are similar to the star. This signifies for the fans not only their knowledge of the performer and the performer's habits and performance persona, but also signals to other fans that they are knowledgeable about the star and are potentially open to bonding over the same star. When Madonna first became popular as a pop star, young women began dressing like she did on her album covers, in videos, and in live performances. This demonstrated one way in which they identified with her and signaled that they felt part of a group wherein the communal interest in Madonna was central. As Madonna's styles changed, her fans too changed their looks and interests as well; she was influencing them, and they were influencing one another in a classic case of social proof.

Several of the chapters in this collection deal with—in full or in part—the issue of women serving as arbiters or influencers of cultural taste. Previous scholarship has revealed select women whose fame, fandom, and social standing has secured for them a place in history as influencers, like Jenny Lind or Geraldine Farrar. This existing scholarship on women influencers tends to be very narrow, focusing on figures whose influencing work was undertaken primarily through overtly public actions and performances. There is little on the women who worked behind the scenes or in less glamorous venues and their contributions to musical culture. This book seeks to begin to remedy this by addressing this lacuna and offering scholarship on these women whose work was not as immediately visible to the public.

One way to trace influence is to search for citations of women's work. Such citations illustrate the extent to which less public individuals or small groups of women have been able to serve as arbiters of taste and cultural values. Cecile Chaminade's American fans were so inspired by her that they created more than 200 clubs in her name between 1900 and 1904, dedicated to promoting her work, following her musical aesthetic, and creating spaces for performances of chamber music.[9] While the names of the individual women in each club are not well known today, their actions—sponsoring concerts (including selecting music they determined to be worthy, acceptable, and in good taste), offering grants for musical study, and commissioning works—show signs of undeniable influence through the existence of the careers of those who performed for their events and who were the beneficiaries of their largess for advanced study, those who received commissions, and the establishment of women's philanthropic organizations targeted at the promotion and support of music.

For less well-documented work by women in the arts, it can be difficult to qualify or quantify influence. Nonetheless, we can trace the influence of even mostly unknown women and their work through the study of changing demographics; personal, local, and regional citations of their work; the networks in which such women worked; and the extent to which these women were authorized to conduct that work. Changing demographics can show how much of the labor done in a given field is conducted by women. By exploring the backgrounds, educations, and experiences of the women involved, we can begin to formulate an idea of how those aspects, in combination with the proportional involvement of women in the field, have changed tastes or practices. Citations, such as those appearing in archival documents like newspapers, trade magazines, church bulletins, concert programs, and diaries, all offer proof of influence as well; the women named in these materials were deemed noteworthy enough to have appeared in them. As Leigh Gilmore writes, for unvalued women and their labor in the past, "the title page is frequently the site of necessary evasion. One reads here not the signature but the pseudonym, not the family name but 'anon.' The title page of women's writing presents itself not as a fact but as an extension of the fiction of identity."[10] That women's names can be attached to their work signifies that they and the work they do are worthy of being recognized for that work and authorized as competent or important: it indicates their status as individuals contributing to and thus influencing the culture in which they work. Names constitute social proof.

Several chapters here address women as arbiters of taste based on the criteria outlined above. Candace Bailey, in chapter 1, reveals how women in Reconstruction-era Mobile, Alabama, took on positions as church organists, a traditionally male job, and became cultural leaders regarding creating performances, selecting repertoire, and developing a community for those involved in classical music. Kendra Preston Leonard's work on women musicians for the silent cinema in chapter 3 traces how women became demographically dominant as film accompanists and how their performance practices became recognized in the industry as equal in authority—if not superior—to those by men. In chapter 4, April L. Prince excavates the performance history of Southern femininity in Old-time music by examining the influence of singer-songwriters Rosa Lee Carson and Roba Stanley, finding that their songs offer a nuanced portrayal of women's lives in the American South that changes how we might think about this repertoire. Paula J. Bishop's work on songwriter Felice Bryant illustrates how Bryant's use of the domestic sphere enabled her to bypass many of the gendered constraints of the 1950s and become an enormously successful and influential creator. Writing on the band Goldie and the Gingerbreads, Brittany Greening's research in chapter 8 studies how the band—despite its short life—helped influence the industry in terms of signing all-women bands to major labels.

WOMEN LOWERING GENDER BARRIERS

Serving as influencers and arbiters of taste is one way in which the women considered in this collection break down gender barriers, but several of the studies here discuss in detail more specific ways in which women entered into male-dominated fields and created opportunities for others to follow them. There is already a wealth of scholarship on music and gender that addresses bias and discrimination in art music composition and historiography and in popular music as a whole. The essays here, however, are focused case studies on specific women or kinds of women performers who have been previously overlooked.

For many of the women studied in this collection, whose careers took place before the emergence of second-wave feminism, the lowering of gender barriers often came through oppositional action within established boundaries rather than through rebellion. Transgressions that took place within the confines of traditional women's roles could be viewed as innovative or supportive rather than as challenging or threatening to patriarchal structures and practices. Women could gradually take on roles that were once considered to be essentially masculine, especially once World War I had begun and the need for women to replace male workers had become clear. Women also used the domestic sphere as a kind of conveyance for their professional goals. As Paula J. Bishop documents in chapter 6, songwriter Felice Bryant used her role as a housewife to enter what was primarily a man's world of working with singers, producers, and others to create her career. Bryant cooked dinner for performers and producers and hosted them in her home, where her involvement in conversations and decisions that might once have been left to her husband included her as well.

Both Candace Bailey (chapter 1) and Kendra Preston Leonard (chapter 3) engage with the ways women musicians began to acquire and be recognized for their success in jobs that had been traditionally held by men, as church organists and cinema musicians. In chapter 5, Christina Baade offers an analysis of how famous World War II–era singer Vera Lynn became a radio DJ—a position usually filled by men—and how her work helped normalize female DJs. And Brittany Greening's work on Goldie and the Gingerbreads (chapter 8) documents the band's path to becoming the first all-women group signed to a major label.

WOMEN STRENGTHENING NETWORKS

All of the women whose work is excavated in these essays formed parts of recognized and unrecognized networks, and the connections afforded them by these networks enabled them to develop their own careers and interests while also, in many cases, assisting other women in doing so. One example is that of Maribeth Clark's study of women whistlers in chapter 2. Whistling women were largely taught by a handful of performers who were part of the vaudeville, Chautauqua, and women's club performance circuits of the time, and knew or knew of each other and their work. Agnes Woodward, for example, founded a school and formalized an approach to whistling; her system taught numerous women whistlers, among whom were at least four who went on to professional careers as whistlers.

In doing so, Woodward created a network of women whistlers who entered into the entertainment profession via film and giving recitals. Woodward's development of networks and teaching gave her students the skills and connections to create new kinds of careers for women. In theoretical terms, Woodward created what Bourdieu calls a *habitus*—a collection of abilities, connections, and influence that enables people to use their personal cultural capital in a particular field.

Travis Stimeling's essay (chapter 7) situates Mary Olivia Smith as someone who was eager to cultivate a sense of belonging. Her engagement with music demonstrates her aspirations to be part of something associated with the middle class. Smith's transcriptions of popular songs indicate her awareness of middle-class popular music culture and its role as cultural capital, which she hoped to use as a member of a white, middle-class network of women. Her actions in collecting lyrics are representative of the ways in which many women collected both materials (such as recipes, patterns, or items of home décor) and behaviors (accents, phrases, manners, and gestures) as a way of performing aspiration.

In the final two chapters, Tammy Kernodle and Kristen M. Turner address different facets of women's contributions to the civil rights movements that have long gone unacknowledged. The master narrative of the civil rights movement has historically overlooked the cultural labor of women whose musical activities on behalf of the movement were essential. Kernodle (chapter 10) and Turner (chapter 9) both unpack the work of women musicians in relation to social expectations and codes of conduct and, by tapping into a network of knowledge and experience, find ways to work around those limitations. Kernodle's essay focuses on musicians who were and are well known but whose cultural labor has not been prominent in accounts of the movement. Turner examines the work of Candie Carawan, a lesser-known figure whose music became central even when she herself was overlooked in part because of her marital status.

Ultimately, we hope that this volume will provoke further research into the work, careers, and contributions of those whose participation in music making of all kinds has been ignored, erased, or suppressed. We especially hope that, in these essays, we provide the impetus and frameworks for detailed research on people who have been marginalized in traditional academic studies because of their status and identities as women or nonbinary, people of color, queer, disabled, and others.

NOTES

1. John Thomas, *Kalamazoo Gals: A Story of Extraordinary Women and Gibson's "Banner" Guitars of WWII* (Franklin, TN: American History Press, 2013).

2. Phoebe Reilly, "The Beach Girl Behind the Beach Boys," *Vulture*, April 16, 2016. https://www.vulture.com/2016/04/carol-kaye-sets-record-straight.html. Accessed May 12, 2020.

3. Albert Mathiez, quoted in François Dosse, Patrick Garcia, and Christian Delacroix, *Les courants historiques en France: 19e–20e siècle* (Paris: Armand Colin, 2005).

4. Natasha Korda, "Shakespeare's Laundry: Feminist Futures in the Archives," in Ania Loomba and Melissa E. Sanchez, ed., *Rethinking Feminism in Early Modern Studies: Gender, Race, and Sexuality* (New York: Routledge, 2016), 96.

5. For work on these artists, see Leigh H. Edwards, *Dolly Parton, Gender and Country Music* (Bloomington: Indiana University Press, 2018); and Kinitra D. Brooks, ed., *The Lemonade Reader: Beyoncé, Black Feminism and Spirituality* (New York: Routledge, 2019).

6. Roxane Prevost and Kimberly Francis, "Teaching Silence in the Twenty-First Century," *The Oxford Handbook of Music Censorship*, ed. Patricia Hall (Oxford Handbooks Online, 2017), 10.1093/oxfordhb/9780199733163.013.26.

7. Herbert C. Kelman, "Compliance, Identification, and Internalization: Three Processes of Attitude Change," *Journal of Conflict Resolution* 2, no. 1 (March 1, 1958): 51–60, https://doi.org/10.1177/002200275800200106.

8. Robert Cialdini, "Harnessing the Science of Persuasion," *Harvard Business Review* 79, no. 9 (2001): 72–92.

9. Marcia Citron, *Cécile Chaminade: A Bio-Bibliography* (Westport, CT: Greenwood Press, 1988), 108.

10. Leigh Gilmore, *Autobiographics: A Feminist Theory of Women's Self-Representation* (Ithaca, NY: Cornell University Press, 1994), 81.

BIBLIOGRAPHY

Brooks, Kinitra D., ed. *The Lemonade Reader: Beyoncé, Black Feminism and Spirituality*. New York: Routledge, 2019.

Cialdini, Robert. "Harnessing the Science of Persuasion." *Harvard Business Review* 79, no. 9 (2001): 72–92.

Citron, Marcia. *Cécile Chaminade: A Bio-Bibliography*. Westport, CT: Greenwood Press, 1988.

Edwards, Leigh H. *Dolly Parton, Gender and Country Music*. Bloomington: Indiana University Press, 2018.

Gilmore, Leigh. *Autobiographics: A Feminist Theory of Women's Self-Representation*. Ithaca, NY: Cornell University Press, 1994.

Kelman, Herbert C. "Compliance, Identification, and Internalization: Three Processes of Attitude Change." *Journal of Conflict Resolution* 2, no. 1 (March 1, 1958): 51–60. https://doi.org/10.1177/002200275800200106.

Korda, Natasha. "Shakespeare's Laundry: Feminist Futures in the Archives." In *Rethinking Feminism in Early Modern Studies: Gender, Race, and Sexuality*, edited by Ania Loomba and Melissa E. Sanchez, 93–112. New York: Routledge, 2016.

Mathiez, Albert. In François Dosse, Patrick Garcia, and Christian Delacroix, *Les courants historiques en France: 19e–20e siècle*. Paris: Armand Colin, 2005.

Prevost, Roxane, and Kimberly Francis. "Teaching Silence in the Twenty-First Century." In Patricia Hall, ed., *The Oxford Handbook of Music Censorship*. Oxford Handbooks Online, 2017. 10.1093/oxfordhb/9780199733163.013.26.

Reilly, Phoebe. "The Beach Girl Behind the Beach Boys." *New York*, April 16, 2016. https://www.vulture.com/2016/04/carol-kaye-sets-record-straight.html. Accessed May 12, 2020.

Thomas, John. *Kalamazoo Gals: A Story of Extraordinary Women and Gibson's "Banner" Guitars of WWII*. Franklin, TN: American History Press, 2013.

Chapter 1

"She Takes up Music as a Profession": Women Organists in the Nineteenth-Century South

—Candace Bailey

That the Civil War in the United States marked a watershed moment in the nation's history is common knowledge; one has to look only as far as school textbooks, television documentaries, or even popular films to gain a sense of how impactful the war was, particularly on Southern culture. And yet—in spite of how familiar most readers will be with the war as a turning point for many aspects of US history—few scholars have examined women's musical culture from this perspective. Nonetheless, ample evidence supports the fact that, when the Civil War ended in 1865, Southern women seized new professional opportunities that had been suddenly made available through a paradigmatic shift in social conventions. In *Music and the Southern Belle: From Accomplished Lady to Confederate Composer*, I document how upper-class Southern women developed a new sense of self after the war, one that opened the doors to unexpected prospects.[1] My focus in that book deals primarily with women as composers, but the phenomenon also affected other aspects of musical culture. In this essay I will establish that, even before the war, women worked as remunerated church musicians and, similar to my research on composers, show that Reconstruction women began not only to participate more fully in but also to be in charge of musical organizations and performances that, for the first time, included both women and men.[2] I also document the developing acceptance and even encouragement of professional women musicians in the popular press during this period. The women examined here were all white; Black women, too, performed as church musicians, but they would not have been accorded the opportunity to lead the high-profile productions discussed in this essay.

Perceptions of what women musicians could and should do changed dramatically during the Reconstruction era. Not only were women recognized as having the talent to be professional musicians, which led to opportunities such as directing large groups or civic organizations, but they also were finally allowed to take on such roles without public censure. Women who had worked in music and established themselves before the war were, postwar, able to be much more fully the "architects" of their own fortunes, and their activities opened doors for the women who followed them. The work done by these women challenges our ideas about women's musical activities in the first half of the nineteenth century. As their music-making shifted from the vernacular to the professional, and as they crafted what we would now call careers, such women had significant influence on the music in their cities and towns. By examining the careers of Charleston organist Hermine Barbot and Mobile-based musicians Mariah Kowalewski, Josephine Pillichody, and Fannie Sands, I show how these performers, all organists, developed and maintained previously unknown careers in music—and what that means for our understanding of women's involvement in professional music-making in the postwar South.

WOMEN AND VERNACULAR MUSIC IN THE PREWAR SOUTH

Almost all Southern women of the mid-nineteenth century were vernacular musicians in the sense that *vernacular* means "ordinary, everyday." Before the Civil War, however, such female musicians, regardless of ability, were part of a vernacular tradition in which society did not recognize them as professionals because women—ladies—did not perform in public. Many women participated in literate music culture (what was called "scientific" at the time), but a wide majority of them performed only for their peers. Their music-making was for home and school; this everyday music formed part of the lives of not only elite planters' daughters but also that of poorer farmers' daughters in rural areas.[3] Music often stood as the centerpiece in social rituals: women in the company of other women (and sometimes men) danced in the parlor, sang or played the piano when calling on acquaintances, or performed on the guitar in even more intimate settings. This kind of performance formed a part of Richard Bushman's "vernacular gentility," a term he coined to describe the cultural system that developed in the United States at the end of the eighteenth century that dictated gender roles in various situations. By the mid-nineteenth century, vernacular gentility's principles spread across a larger part of the population, resulting in further systems of codes that reassured social hierarchies and their markers. As Karen Halttunen's scholarship has demonstrated, this widely accepted view of gentility, replete with signifiers of class and social standing, also applied to a growing middle class, particularly in urban areas.[4]

Music served as one of these markers of gentility, and musical ability was a significant part of what contributed to the "accomplished" lady. Musical ability figured as part of parlor "performance," which was not necessarily understood as a strictly musical performance, but the performance of culture. Such private performances emphasized that the music played was music "of the people," and therefore part of a shared social aesthetic that valued the vernacular over the music of the concert stage even if the performers were middle- or even upper-class people. Women who performed in a somewhat more public sphere—such as in multi-performer recitals for school graduations, occasional "oratorio" concerts in which they appeared only as "a lady amateur," or for in-home performances that included all genders—also performed this repertoire of the vernacular gentility. These female vernacular musicians were not singled out for their public artistic contributions to the community but remained behind the scenes in the day-to-day musical life of their communities. In contrast, women such as Jenny Lind, Adelina Patti, and Anna Bishop offered public vocal performances in both metropolitan and rural areas, while instrumentalists like the violinist Aniela Niecewska and flutist Amelia Siminski toured in the manner of Ole Bull and Louis Moreau Gottschalk. Although many of these public performers were celebrated, they were also rare and often judged disapprovingly for displaying their musical talents.[5]

WOMEN AS CHURCH ORGANISTS

Paid women musicians in nineteenth-century worship services have probably remained unnoticed by scholars because, although we are often aware that a woman played the organ or piano (or other keyboard instrument) in small churches, it wasn't understood as her "job." Men who held cathedral positions, such as Lewis Mendelssohn in Raleigh, North Carolina, or Gustavus A. Gnospelius in Savannah, Georgia, fit a societal expectation of classically trained organists. Their arrivals from Europe usually warranted notices in the local newspaper, and frequently they participated in other civic music organizations as well, furthering their reputations as performers. If they also taught, and they often did, they garnered the title "Professor of Music," taking leading roles in the musical lives of the cities in which they lived. Women were rarely heralded for their church work, and until the war was over, almost never adopted the title of "Professor" for their work in music instruction. However, numerous women are documented as having held formal positions in both small and large churches: North Carolina native Eliza Adam Jones (1839–1911) played at the Episcopal St. Matthew's Church in Hillsborough; London-born Marian Halton Verdier (1796–1877) was employed by St. Helena's Episcopal Church in Beaufort, South Carolina; Elizabeth Robertson Sully was the organist of the Monumental Church in Richmond, Virginia; and Sully's daughter Sally played professionally at St. John's Episcopal Church in the same city. Even more surprisingly, perhaps, given the gendered environments of both the time and that of the Catholic Church, is that women occupied organist positions in cathedrals as well, including those in Charleston, South Carolina, and Mobile, Alabama.[6]

CHARLESTON, SOUTH CAROLINA: HERMINIE BARBOT

Belgian-born pianist Blanche Herminie Petit Barbot (1842–1919) was one of the most prominent woman musicians in Charleston in the second half of the nineteenth century, and her career illustrates how a woman musician might develop a considerable reputation over the course of several decades both prior to and after the Civil War. Barbot's mother, Marie Petit, ran a school for young ladies in Charleston during the 1850s, and her father, Victor, was a music instructor there, teaching solfeggi and other classes starting in 1853.[7] A child prodigy whose debut took place before royalty when she was just seven, Barbot performed in such venues as Brussels's Theatre Italien-Français (1851); the court of William II, the King of Holland (1851); and, as part of an American tour, Niblo's Garden in New York (1852). At age ten, Barbot reportedly accompanied Adeline Patti, and her playing was commended by both Marie Pleyel and Sigismund Thalberg. Letters from Thalberg to Barbot's mother indicate that Barbot had been destined for a career as a concert pianist until her father's premature death in 1856, at which time she and her mother settled permanently in Charleston.[8] At this point, Barbot gave up her planned career as a concert pianist to teach music at her father's school and at Charleston's Orphan House School.[9]

Barbot also performed as a church organist. Barbot quickly became a fixture in Charleston's sacred music scene, playing the organ at the Cathedral of St. John the Baptist and at St. Mary's Catholic Church on Hasell Street. In 1879 she became organist at St. Michael's Episcopal Church, a position she held for three years.[10] Barbot's sacred performances, especially those she gave on Christmas Day, were frequently lauded in the *Charleston Daily News*. In 1868 she accompanied Haydn's Imperial Mass in D, in which, a reviewer wrote, "the organ accompaniments were played by Mrs. Barbot, the organist of the church, who showed her management of her instrument as much good taste and judgment as musical knowledge and skill." The reviewer continued: "no music, sacred or secular, has ever been performed in Charleston in a more satisfactory manner than was the grand Mass at St. Mary's Church."[11] In the spring of 1873, Barbot accompanied "the beautiful music of Maillard with fine effect" during a special Grand Vespers service.[12] The following year, the *Charleston Daily News* reported that St. Mary's musicians and especially Barbot had once again performed exceptionally well: "The music was superb. Haydn's first mass, a *salutaris* and an *adeste fidelis*, were sung in a manner that would have reflected credit upon any choir in the country. This church has always good music, but Madame Barbot and her assistants on Christmas day excelled themselves."[13] It is significant that the other musicians, some of whom were presumably male orchestra members, were placed lower in the performance hierarchy as Barbot's "assistants," indicating that it was becoming more conventional for women to direct men in performance, at least in church settings.

Barbot was married for the duration of her career, but "her marriage in no way interfered with her musical work," as Frances Elizabeth Willard wrote in 1897, suggesting that music was her primary focus in life. Her obituary describes her dedication to her career in a like manner, noting "her marriage did not interrupt her music and her home has always been one of the city's musical centers." Nonetheless, Barbot's sex was routinely noted; she was "the best of wives [and] mothers," and a "brilliant pianist with fine technique and great force and delicacy of expression."[14] Willard emphasized her femininity, or at least prewar gendered conventions in that, as would have been in keeping with ladylike grace, Barbot was known to have eschewed solo performances except as parts of charitable fundraisers, in spite of having been prepared for a professional career.[15] However, not all criticism of her musical work was equally gendered; other notices describe with praise such as "the highest musical authority in Charleston," and her exceptional work as a musical director led to some characterizations of her, representative of the shifting attitudes toward women in music in the postwar South, that were more masculine and empowered.[16] Willard also noted that Barbot's "peculiar gift is in training and directing large musical forces. She has for years given cantatas, oratorios and operas with the amateurs of the city."[17] The reference to Barbot's control over large musical forces, the bulk of which were men, is very different from language used to describe women musicians before the war. This new kind of professional career and language describing its outcomes can also be found in reviews of three women organists from Mobile.

MOBILE, ALABAMA: MARIAH KOWALEWSKI, JOSEPHINE PILLOCHODY, AND FANNIE SANDS

Mariah Henrietta Dillon Kowalewski was a leading figure in Mobile music between about 1850 until her death in 1897. Born between 1810 and 1813 in Dublin, Ireland, Kowalewski displayed musical talents when she was young and attended Logiere College in Dublin, a school for musicians.[18] She played the organ for church services in a Dublin church when she was twelve and performed in public at fifteen; her repertory included Beethoven, Haydn, Mozart, and Mendelssohn (with whom she was purportedly friends). Kowalewski was also a composer; her first works, a set of waltzes written when she was sixteen, were popular enough to have been arranged for ensemble performances in Dublin. At about this age she became the full-time organist at St. James's Church in Dublin.[19]

Kowalewski's success as a performing musician in Ireland was short-lived. She married Dr. Kajetan Peter Kowalewski sometime before she turned twenty; he abruptly left for the United States in 1835, and she followed in 1836 or 1837.[20] Along with Mariah Kowalewski's mother, the couple settled in Pensacola, Florida, in 1838. In 1843 Kowalewski and her mother began advertising a singing school there, using "Wilhelm's new Vocal System," and two years later, the family (Kowalewski, her mother, her husband, and their sons) moved to Mobile.[21] There, Kowalewski taught music to young women and became the organist at the Episcopal Christ Church Cathedral in or around 1846, a position she maintained until her death in 1897.

Like Barbot, who also undertook her teaching and church work out of financial need, Kowalewski accepted all of the opportunities she could find for remunerative work so that she could support herself when her husband abandoned her in 1850.[22] She obviously worked hard; her reputation as a teacher grew rapidly, to the point where (Miss) E. McCord of Mobile composed the "Hollywood Waltz" and dedicated it to "Madame Kowelenski" in 1852.[23] Male teachers composed thousands of these pieces for their female students, but only in a few circumstances did students dedicate works to women teachers.[24] The waltz typifies the music young women, such as McCord, might have been taught by an instructor, in this case most probably Kowalewski herself; the work and its dedication suggest a special attachment to or appreciation of Kowalewski. Teaching and church work meant that Kowalewski could maintain herself and her children during the war, all while building up social capital as a professional and highly regarded musician. This accumulation of respect allowed her to become even more of a leader in Mobile's musical community after the war.

Kowalewski had long belonged to the Mobile Musical Association, a "music club" that included several leading musicians, including George Lingen (local medical doctor and cellist), Peter Gass (local "professor of music" and composer), Louise Parker (Mrs. Daniel) Geary; and Fannie (Mrs. James) Sands, who became Kowalewski's friend and musical collaborator.[25] The Mobile Musical Association encompassed a variety of social classes, with members ranging from amateurs to professional musicians. It was founded and initially led by the Schlesinger brothers, Sigmund and Jacob, and Joseph Bloch, a local music publisher and leader of a popular dance band in Mobile.[26] Although just a member of the group prior to the war, Kowalewski took over the operations of the club to acclaim in the 1870s, when women music directors were still often rare or overlooked. The March 1873 issue of the *Southern Musical Journal* reports that the Mobile Musical Association "gave their first concert under the management of that talented artist, Madame [Kowalewski]. It was a perfect success." A second concert was to be given a week later, and the writer notes that Kowalewski intended to revive the "Summer Night Concerts" with twenty-four musicians.[27] A later issue of the same journal reports: "The Musical Association is doing wonders under the skillful guidance of the talented Madame Kowaleski-Potz [sic]. Entertainments are enjoyable and well attended. She displays a great taste in introducing more instrumental music into the programme."[28] That a woman ran such an association, which was hitherto under the control of male musicians, speaks to

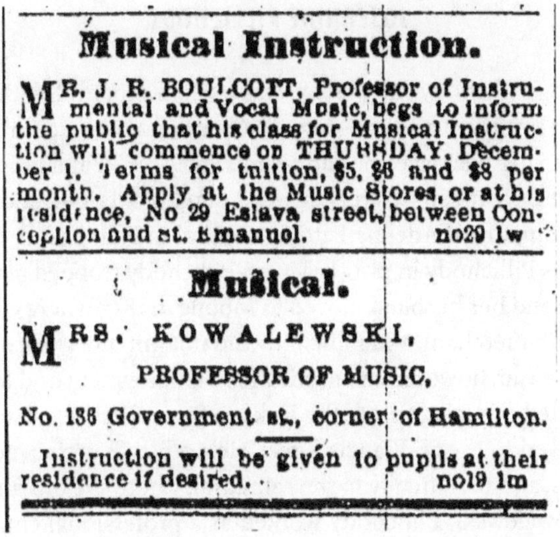

> **Musical Instruction.**
>
> MR. J. R. BOULCOTT, Professor of Instrumental and Vocal Music, begs to inform the public that his class for Musical Instruction will commence on THURSDAY, December 1. Terms for tuition, $5, $6 and $8 per month. Apply at the Music Stores, or at his residence, No 29 Eslava street, between Conception and St. Emanuel. no29 1w
>
> **Musical.**
>
> MRS. KOWALEWSKI,
>
> PROFESSOR OF MUSIC,
>
> No. 136 Government st., corner of Hamilton.
>
> Instruction will be given to pupils at their residence if desired. no19 1m

Fig. 1.1. Advertisement from the *Mobile Register*, December 7, 1870, 1.

the respect accorded Kowalewski in Mobile. Her involvement with instrumental music, too, stands out because women had been traditionally associated with piano, guitar, solo harp, or voice. These concerts, however, included men playing other instruments as well.

Between her position at Christ Church Cathedral, the devotion of her students, and her leadership role in reinvigorating the postwar Mobile Musical Association, Kowalewski clearly had significant stature in the musical community. As a sign acknowledging her own self-worth, she named herself "Professor of Music" in an 1870 advertisement in the *Mobile Register* (see Fig. 1.1).

This was a bold move on her part, because women music teachers did not use and were not conferred that title, which was traditionally reserved for men.[29] And the title was not taken without good reason; Kowalewski became an institution in Mobile's music scene, organizing and leading large-scale performances on a regular basis. She organized and led a performance of Mozart's *Requiem* in 1878; in 1879 she and Adelaide de V. Chaudron both accompanied a sacred concert at Government Street Presbyterian Church. The performers included Sigmund Schlesinger, Josephine Pillichody, Ruth Dargan (Mrs. Charles) Huger, and Ellen "Nellie" Tarlton (Mrs. D. P.) Bestor. It is clear that even though Schlesinger still lived in Mobile and was part of the musical establishment, Kowalewski was the individual in charge of much of Mobile's music scene.[30] When Kowalewski died in 1897, she was eulogized as "the architect of her own fortunes."[31] "Architect" implies considerable agency on the part of Mariah Kowalewski—substantially more than that associated with "music teacher" or "lady organist." Yet she was not alone in gaining such status in the postwar South, or even in Mobile: Kowalewski was joined in her professional success by Josephine Hutet Pillichody and Fannie Sands.

JOSEPHINE PILLICHODY

Josephine Hutet Pillichody (1834–1905) was born in Albany, New York. It is likely that Pillichody's musical career began with her being trained for public performances: prior to her marriage, she had a remarkable career as a prodigy. Her piano teacher, Ernest Boulanger, was reportedly a pupil of Chopin, and at age twelve, Pillichody accompanied Adelina Patti in a recital in New York.[32] With her marriage to Charles Pillichody in 1856, however, Pillichody stopped playing in public for a time. She and her husband moved to Mobile in 1857, where Charles became a wealthy cotton merchant, and Pillichody did not initially work outside of their home. After the war, however, she needed paid employment and took a position as a remunerated organist, first at the Jackson Street Presbyterian Church, after which she moved to the St. Francis Street Methodist Church, where she played for seven years, and then finally to the cathedral, where she remained for twelve years. Like Kowalewski, Pillichody worked as a professional church musician, rather than as a volunteer musician for her own church.

In addition to her church work, Pillichody also joined Kowalewski as an important leader in the secular musical community in Mobile, an arena formerly dominated by men such as the Schlesinger brothers and Bloch. A letter to the editor dated March 15, 1873, in the *Southern Music Journal* states that Pillichody and Kowalewski are among the most influential musicians in Mobile: "There is one lady artist here, who is known in the musical circles of friends as the 'American lady Pianist'—Madame Pillachody [sic].... Her particular forte is in the higher walks of music, where she shines as a true artist." These "higher walks of music" refer to large-scale works by Haydn and Mozart. Pillichody's fame equaled Kowalewski's: she is the only composer mentioned by name in *The WPA Guide to Alabama: The Camellia State*, which claims that she wrote "the first recorded compositions" in Alabama.[33] While this claim is made in error, Pillichody's inclusion in the *Guide* indicates her status in the state's musical community.

Kowalewski and Pillichody began performing together in the 1870s, and were often joined by Stephanie Lucy "Fannie" Durand Sands (1827–1878), one of the amateurs in the Kowalewski-led Mobile Musical Association. Sands, like Pillichody, was married to a wealthy merchant whose fortunes had tumbled after the war. Sands sometimes assisted Kowalewski at the organ in the cathedral on a volunteer basis, and the two women became friends. While she had not performed publicly before the war, Sands's musical activities blossomed during the Reconstruction period.

Kowalewski, Pillichody, and Sands are documented as performing together for the first time on June 15, 1874, and the extant review of the concert offers insight into the changing approach to describing and analyzing women's public performances. The *Southern Musical Journal* covered the event, a "Sacred Concert," and the reviewer credited Sands with "getting up" the concert with orchestral accompaniment. While Pillochody is described in traditional terms that emphasize her femininity, Sands is not. Of Pillochody, the journal article states, "Madame Pillachody, ever ready to aid and assist in her lady-like and artistic manner, anything to bring out good music, presided at the piano, interspersing such delicate and elaborate runs, as were necessary to make a piece complete, with a feathery touch that the keenest imagination could not tell where the *material* ended, and the *immaterial* began" [italics mine]. This illustrates the language typically reserved for women musicians, being "lady-like and artistic," "delicate" with a "feathery touch." Pillichody also played the organ at the concert, and her "'Heavens are telling' . . . was rendered more perfectly than ever before in this city."[34]

The language used to describe Sands's performance, on the other hand, charts a remarkable shift away from the gendered, feminine terms used for the rare women who performed in public before the war and to language emphasizing the women's strength and capability. "Madame Sands," wrote the reviewer, "presided at the organ, and under her skillful management it seemed to be an immense thing of life, which, when animated by its mighty lungs, sounded out its combinations with an unmistakable firmness and accuracy, forming a foundation upon which the others could build up the most elaborate accompaniment." The writer continues: "Madame Sands should be proud of her success. Her case is but another one of those who once reveled in wealth, ease and luxury but are now forced to toil for home and comfort. Music was her delight; her devotion to her church caused her when rich and independent, to volunteer her services as organist at the Cathedral; her mansion was the gathering place for the best of music talent. She lost her husband; like thousands of others, she lost her property, and was reduced to her own personal efforts for her support. She did not stop to cry about it—if she did, no one knew it. She had a fond mother to care for; like a true, courageous woman, she dashes away the bitter disappointed hopes, she takes up music as a profession, and this is her debut. May her spirit encourage others to do likewise. God bless you, Lady Sands!"[35] The most striking aspect of the newspaper review is how the author positions Sands's predicament, and, notably, that "she takes up music as a profession." This public fashioning of women's performance as acceptable follows other changes in how the press described women after the war and signals a new understanding of what women musicians could do if given the opportunity. Furthermore, the writer recommends that other women follow Fannie Sands into the world of remunerated organists—not merely a sweet, pretty thing playing waltzes in the parlor. Obviously, Sands's colleagues agreed: when Sands died in 1878, Kowalewski accompanied a commemorative performance of the Mozart *Requiem* given in Sands's honor as former organist at the cathedral, signifying not only the friendship between Kowalewski and Sands, but also Kowalewski's public recognition of Sands's musical career.[36]

CONCLUSIONS

As a wider public embraced alternative options for white women in the period following the Civil War, most importantly accepting their need for remunerated work and even encouraging them to "take up" careers, organists moved from the realm of the private, everyday musical vernacular to professional and publicly acknowledged self-supporting members of society. As I demonstrate here, this shift in how Southern women saw themselves can only be interrogated through the realization that more women than previously thought participated as professionals in musical activities before 1860 and contributed significantly to their local musical cultures not only as church musicians but also as leading figures in organizing and leading large-scale productions, an area long considered to be the purview of men. For every Mariah Kowalewski or Herminie Barbot, there are surely many other Southern women whose music-making moved from that of the vernacular gentility model of private playing to that of the competent woman working with both men and women of their musical communities. The cases presented here serve as examples of such musicians whose stories have yet to be told and whose careers, when known, will contribute to our understanding of women's musical lives in the American South in the nineteenth century.

NOTES

1. Candace Bailey, *Music and the Southern Belle: From Accomplished Lady to Confederate Composer* (Carbondale: Southern Illinois University Press, 2010).

2. In *Unbinding Gentility: Women Making Music in the Nineteenth-Century South* (Champaign: University of Illinois Press, 2021), I chart the paths of several women who worked as musicians, almost none of whom have been recognized in the scholarly literature to date.

3. Such women's stories occur throughout Bailey, *Unbinding Gentility*.

4. Richard Lyman Bushman, *The Refinement of America: Persons, Houses, Cities* (New York: Vintage Press, 1983), xiii and 207–37; see also Karen Halttunen, *Confidence Men and Painted Women: A Study of Middle-class Culture in America, 1830–1870* (New Haven, CT: Yale University Press, 1982).

5. Consider, for example, the following review of a concert given by Siminski in Raleigh, North Carolina: "The Raleigh papers contain not an item of local intelligence, but the Editors are in raptures over Madame Siminski, who is playing on the flute, for the delectation of the people of the city of oaks.—The rascals talk as if they would all willingly be flutes if the Madame would only press them to her lips like she does the one she plays on." *Daily Journal* (Wilmington, NC), March 23, 1854, 2. A writer in the *Richmond Whig* was more generous, noting her expressive tone, dynamic range, and "brilliant execution" of difficult passages. *Richmond Whig*, January 27, 1854, 2.

6. I am grateful to John Druesedow for sharing his research on Jones and on the organs at St. Matthew's, Hillsborough, *History of the Parish Church of St. Helena*, 170–71; George D.

Fisher, *History and Reminiscences of the Monumental Church, Richmond, Va.: From 1814 to 1878* (Richmond: Whittet & Shepperson, 1880), 187–88n, quoted in Albert Stoutamire, *Music of the Old South: Colony to Confederacy* (Rutherford NJ: Fairleigh Dickinson University Press, 1972), 128; and Bailey, *Music and the Southern Belle*, 39. Elizabeth Robertson Sully was the sister-in-law of the painter Thomas Sully.

7. Barbot Family Papers, South Carolina Historical Society, 1005.02.03, Box 11/069a. When Adelina Patti performed in Charleston, Victor Petit accompanied her.

8. Barbot Family Papers, SCHS. Thalberg later gave several concerts in Charleston in January and February 1858. John Hindman, "Concert life in ante-bellum Charleston" (PhD diss., University of North Carolina at Chapel Hill, 1972), 188–89.

9. Kelly Obernuefemann, "Crossing Invisible Lines: Social Interaction between the Free Women of Antebellum Charleston, South Carolina across Class and Race Lines" (PhD diss., George Washington University, 2001), 63. Barbot's biographical details are given in Bailey, *Music and the Southern Belle*, 111. See also Frances Elizabeth Willard and Mary Ashton Rice Livermore, *American Women: Fifteen Hundred Biographies with Over 1,400 Portraits; A Comprehensive Encyclopedia of the Lives and Achievements of American Women during the Nineteenth Century*, vol. 1 (New York and Chicago: Mast, Crowell & Kirkpatrick, 1897), 53.

10. George Walton Williams, *St. Michael's, Charleston, 1751–1951* (Charleston: University of South Carolina Press, 1951), 327.

11. *Charleston Daily News*, December 26, 1868.

12. *Charleston Daily News*, March 26, 1873.

13. *Charleston Daily News*, December 26, 1868, and December 27, 1872.

14. Willard, *American Women: Fifteen Hundred Biographies*, 53; obituary, Barbot Family Papers, SCHS.

15. Obituary, Barbot Family Papers, SCHS.

16. *Watchman and Southron*, October 17, 1900.

17. Willard, *American Women: Fifteen Hundred Biographies*, 53.

18. This almost certainly has to be connected with Johann Bernhard Logier, who arrived in Dublin in 1809. A composer, teacher, and publisher, Logier was one of the inventors of the chiroplast, a device that held the hands in "correct" positions for piano practice.

19. She reportedly transposed a Te Deum at sight while at St. James's, earning a reputation based on this ability. Obituary, *Mobile Register*, October 21, 1897. See also Kate Ayers Robert, "Madame Kowaleski," manuscript dated November 18, 1935, in Mobile Public Library, vertical file holder, "Mobile Musicians," Mobile Archives Office, Alabama.

20. Dublin, Ireland, Probate Record and Marriage License Index, 1270–1858, 280. It is unclear whether Kowalewski had been invited to join her husband in the United States or followed of her own accord.

21. *Pensacola Gazette*, May 6, 1843, 3.

22. Mariah Kovaliski divorced Razetan Kovaliski in January 1850. *Alabama Legislative Acts, 1849–50* (Montgomery, AL: Brittan & De Wolf, 1850), 101. In South Carolina, divorce was not an option at this time, and in many Southern states divorce still required an act of legislature.

23. E. McCord, "Hollywood Waltz" (Mobile, AL: W. D. Snyder, ca. 1852). Available at http://www.loc.gov/resource/sm1852.180060.0/?sp=1.

24. William Capers, age twelve, dedicated the "Buchanan Polka" to his teacher, Ann Sloman in Charleston in the late 1850s; and several students in New Orleans dedicated pieces to their piano teacher, Madame Jeanne Boyer.

25. Edward D. Brown, "A History of Theatrical Activities at the Mobile Theatre: Mobile, Alabama, from 1860–1875" (MA thesis, Michigan State College, 1952), 112.

26. Sigmund composed and published music for the Congregation Shaarei Shomayim (est. 1844) in Mobile. See "Jewish Voices in the New World," virtual exhibit from the Milken Archive of Jewish Music, www.milkenarchive.org/articles/virtual-exhibits/view/jewish-voices-new-world-sacred-music; Abraham Zebi Idelsohn, *Jewish Music: Its Historical Development* (New York: Henry Holt, 1929), 325. See also Robert N. Rosen, *The Jewish Confederates* (Charleston, University of South Carolina Press, 2000), 255–56.

27. Correspondence, *Southern Musical Journal* 2, no. 6 (1873): 6.

28. *Southern Musical Journal* 2, no. 7 (1873): 6. Kowalewski briefly used the name of her second husband, Nicholas G. Portz (sometimes Poetz), from 1859–63, when Portz died.

29. Only one other Southern woman was called "Professor" in the mid-nineteenth century, and it is a special case. Augusta Hagen took the title of Professor at the Greensborough Female College for one year until a male musician arrived to fill the position. Since Augusta was the daughter of the composer F. F. Hagen, this circumstance is less remarkable than that of Mariah Kowalewski.

30. *Evening Register* [Mobile], February 11, 1879.

31. Obituary, *Mobile Register*, October 21, 1897.

32. Kate Ayers Robert, "Madame Josephine Hutet Pillichody," MS article, Mobile archives; quoted in Brown, "History of Theatrical Activities," 113.

33. Federal Writers' Project, "Music," *The WPA Guide to Alabama: The Camellia State* (New York: Trinity University Press, 2013), [np].

34. *Southern Musical Journal* 3, no. 10 (1874): 10.

35. *Southern Musical Journal* 3, no. 10 (1874): 10.

36. Brown, "History of Theatrical Activities," 112.

BIBLIOGRAPHY

Charleston Daily News
Daily Journal (Wilmington, NC)
Evening Register (Mobile)
Mobile Register
Pensacola Gazette
Richmond Whig
Southern Musical Journal
Watchman and Southron (Sumter County, SC)

"Alabama Legislative Acts, 1849–1850 [Part 1 of 2]: Alabama Legislative Acts, Journals, and Constitutions." Accessed November 30, 2017. http://digital.archives.alabama.gov/cdm/ref/collection/legislature/id/19233.

Bailey, Candace. *Music and the Southern Belle: From Accomplished Lady to Confederate Composer*. Carbondale: Southern Illinois University Press, 2010.

Bailey, Candace. *Unbinding Gentility: Women Making Music in the Nineteenth-Century South*. Music in American Life. Urbana: University of Illinois Press, 2021.

Brown, Edward Devereaux. "A History of Theatrical Activities at the Mobile Theatre: Mobile, Alabama, from 1860–1875." MA thesis, Michigan State College, 1952.

Bushman, Richard Lyman. *The Refinement of America: Persons, Houses, Cities*. New York: Vintage, 1993.

Federal Writers' Project. *The WPA Guide to Alabama: The Camellia State*. New York: Trinity University Press, 2013.

Fisher, George D. *History and Reminiscences of the Monumental Church, Richmond, Va.: From 1814 to 1878*. Richmond, VA: Whittet & Shepperson, 1880.

Halttunen, Karen. *Confidence Men and Painted Women: A Study of Middle-Class Culture in America, 1830–1870*. New Haven, CT: Yale University Press, 1982.

Hartley, Florence. *The Ladies' Book of Etiquette: And Manual of Politeness: A Complete Hand Book for the Use of the Lady in Polite Society: Containing Full Directions for Correct Manners, Dress, Deportment, and Conversation . . . and Also Useful Receipts for the Complexion, Hair, and with Hints and Directions for the Care of the Wardrobe*. Boston: G. W. Cottrell, 1860.

Hindmann, John Joseph. "Concert Life in Ante-Bellum Charleston." PhD diss., University of North Carolina, 1972.

The History of the Parish Church of St. Helena, Beaufort, South Carolina: Church of England, 1712–1789, Protestant Episcopal, 1789–1990. Beaufort, SC: History Committee, 1990.

Howe, Sondra Wieland. *Women Music Educators in the United States: A History*. Lanham, MD: Scarecrow Press, 2014.

Idelsohn, Abraham Zebi. *Jewish Music: Its Historical Development*. Mineola, NY: Dover, 1992.

Lebsock, Suzanne. *The Free Women of Petersburg: Status and Culture in a Southern Town, 1784–1860*. New York: Norton, 1984.

Milken Archive of Jewish Music. "Jewish Voices in the New World." Accessed July 13, 2017. http://www.milkenarchive.org/articles/virtual-exhibits/view/jewish-voices-new-world-sacred-music.

Norris, Ethel Maureen. "Music in the Black and White Communities in Petersburg, Virginia, 1865–1900." PhD diss., Ohio State University, 1994.

Obernuefemann, Kelly. "Crossing Invisible Lines: Social Interaction Between the Free Women of Antebellum Charleston, South Carolina Across Class and Race Lines." Accessed July 13, 2017. https://www.researchgate.net/publication/35498502_Crossing_invisible_lines_social_interaction_between_the_free_women_of_antebellum_Charleston_South_Carolina_across_class_and_race_lines.

Robert, Kate Ayers. "Madame Josephine Hutet Pillichody," n.d. Mobile Archives Office, Mobile Public Library, Mobile, AL.

Robert, Kate Ayers. "Madame Kowaleski." November 18, 1935. Mobile Archives Office, Mobile Public Library, Mobile, AL.

Rosen, Robert N. *The Jewish Confederates*. Columbia: University of South Carolina Press, 2000.

Stoutamire, Albert. *Music of the Old South: Colony to Confederacy*. Rutherford, NJ: Fairleigh Dickinson University Press, 1972.

Willard, Frances Elizabeth, and Mary Ashton Rice Livermore. *American Women: Fifteen Hundred Biographies with Over 1,400 Portraits; a Comprehensive Encyclopedia of the Lives and Achievements of American Women During the Nineteenth Century*. New York and Chicago: Mast, Crowell & Kirkpatrick, 1897.

Williams, George Walton. *St. Michael's, Charleston, 1751–1951*. Columbia: University of South Carolina Press, 1951.

Chapter 2

Agnes Woodward's Whistling School and White Women's Musical Labor in the United States

—Maribeth Clark

> Whistling girls and crowing hens
> Were, as you know,
> Beneath the ban no longer than
> Ten years ago.
>
> But now they both get ample chance
> To show their skill,
> And any day can draw big pay
> In vaudeville.
>
> —*Los Angeles Herald*, June 12, 1910

White women who whistle in the United States have always done so against a silencing proverb: "Whistling girls and crowing hens / always come to some bad end."[1] In opposition to this prohibition; however, they began whistling professionally by the 1880s. At the beginning of the twentieth century, whistling had become an accepted form of white women's artistic expression in many circles. As one result of this increased acceptance, middle-class white women began teaching the technique alongside voice, piano, and elocution. The best known of these teachers in her day was Agnes Woodward (1872–1938), who founded the California School of Artistic Whistling in 1909 in Los Angeles. Woodward integrated bird imitation into her whistling technique, creating a vocabulary of ornamentation to adorn whistled tunes, be they of popular or classical provenance. Pianists often accompanied these whistlers, as is customary when singers perform. North American whistlers from a variety of backgrounds had imitated birds in their whistling before Woodward and her school were well known, but in *Whistling as an Art* (1925), Woodward formalized an approach in her method, while constructing and supporting networks of trained whistlers.[2] Her most accomplished students became proponents of her school as well as professional performers, and communities of Woodward-method whistlers emerged in pockets across the United States.[3]

Although many middle-class white women taught music, teaching whistling was an uncommon vocation for anyone when Agnes Woodward began her school. The idea of whistling as an art, which developed the marketplace for whistling lessons, began several decades earlier, when Mrs. Alice J. Shaw became a celebrity in 1887 and, through her career, raised the profile of women whistlers as amateurs and professionals.[4] Before this time many musicians—Black and white men in particular—whistled professionally, but few if any attracted the attention that led to celebrity specifically for the act of whistling.[5] Shaw pushed for recognition of whistling as an art rather than just an entertainment or a distraction. Her career and the many accounts of her successes in US newspapers that drove her celebrity fueled the expectation that women could earn a healthy income from whistling professionally.[6] Woodward's career was possible in part because of Alice J. Shaw's success. Her celebrity encouraged large numbers of women to whistle in the age of the New Woman, when women embraced new forms of self-expression in pursuit of health and wellness, the right to work, to vote, and to produce meaningful art outside of the home.[7]

As captured in her method book, *Whistling as an Art*, Woodward's technique combined the techniques of musical whistlers like Alice J. Shaw with the act of bird imitation. She instructed students in the creation of a well-supported tone as in singing with embellishments called "bird figures," her phrase to describe the vocabulary she codified. These imitative figures became a distinguishing feature of her technique—a selling point, or even what we today might call a "brand." Although a standardized vocabulary related to bird song defined her work, her method also emphasized the strength, accomplishment and financial independence she desired for her whistling students.[8] The ability to imitate birds contributed to the more important goals of whistling as an aesthetic, entertaining, educative, and lucrative activity, a point of view that Woodward outlined in the front matter of her method:

> WHISTLING AS AN ART ranks high in comparison with other musical arts. It is not a fad. It is refined, and when properly rendered, artistic and beautiful. It furnishes a happy medium for musical expression to those who are unable to sing or execute musically in other lines.

WHISTLING AS A BENEFIT TO HEALTH is unsurpassed. It strengthens, by the constant practice of deep breathing, the lungs, the throat and diaphragm.

WHISTLING AS AN ACCOMPLISHMENT is always attractive and much in demand. The rendition of bird-songs is always interesting and pleasing.

WHISTLING AS AN EDUCATIONAL FACTOR develops the power of observation and imitation, and leads to the study of bird life and bird habits.

WHISTLING AS A VOCATION furnishes to the competent and finished solo whistler a remunerative and satisfactory livelihood in concert, in Chautauqua and Lyceum work, in vaudeville, moving picture houses, and other places of entertainment, as well as in special solo work in church services. As a stable and reliable income to the intelligent and capable *instructor*, it is most lucrative.[9]

In the prose that follows, I explore Woodward's contributions to women's lives as not only a teacher but as a mentor who encouraged her students to find ways to use their skills to improve their lives. To that end, I discuss Woodward's unique method, her story of developing the method, and the careers of four of her students: Fay Epperson, Margaret McKee, Frances Hazelton, and Margaret Darlington. These women's whistling pursuits demonstrate how whistling expanded possibilities for women, and how Woodward's work supported opportunities for her students.

WOODWARD'S TECHNIQUE AND REPERTORY

Woodward rooted her multifaceted musical entrepreneurship in the creation of the bird whistling technique. She developed symbols placed over the melodies in sheet music to indicate to the performer the appropriate musical actions (see Fig. 2.1 and 2.2). Although sometimes providing a birdlike obbligato over the melody, performers more often integrated these "bird figures" into the tune. Woodward's process grew from the available types of articulation and ornaments known to classical musicians, such as staccato, trill, mordent, turn, and accent, to name a few. She added to these concepts her bird figures, most of which involved uttering strings of vocables—"hedala" or "cherokee," for example—while puckering the lips and blowing.[10] This combination of unvoiced speech and whistling provided the foundation for making bird sounds. The simplest of Woodward's figures, the chirp and reverse chirp, sound like scotch snaps or grace notes. They require a sharply articulated liquid glissando effect, moving up or down in pitch from above or below the written note, respectively. From these relatively simple ornaments, the vocabulary became more complicated in order to encompass Woodward's world of North American bird sounds. As one journalist describes the process in reviewing her method,

Fig. 2.1. The first page of Agnes Woodward's arrangement of Septimus Winner, "Listen to the Mockingbird," features chirps marked "c" and reverse chirps "Rc," in addition to more traditional ornamentation. From Agnes Woodward, *Whistling as an Art*, 2nd ed. (New York: Carl Fischer, 1938), 117.

Fig. 2.2. Mockingbird imitations inserted into Septimus Winner, "Listen to the Mockingbird," function much like a cadenza before the final four bars of the piano. From Woodward, *Whistling as an Art*, 120.

Appropriate names which she has coined to illustrate these bird figures are many and varied. A few are here given: Trills, yodels, chirps, reverses, hewies, whips, cries, whit-chas, hedalas, cudalees, lup-ees, thrup-ees, quittas, quitchaquias, etc. Regular musical embellishments are also used, such as mordents, turns, etc., and in addition many bird notes and figures are used, produced entirely by whistling certain words, for example: "Chicago" (the California Valley quail), "Bob White" (the Eastern and Middle West quail), "Cherokee," "Teakettle," "Theatre," "Who-are-you," etc. (notes of the mocking bird).[11]

A Woodward whistler applied this technique to a broad range of songs, character pieces, and other short musical genres, as demonstrated by the content of the "partial list of songs and instrumental selections" used in the school. These titles include parlor songs (Charles Wakefield Cadman, "At Dawning"; Carrie Jacobs-Bond, "A Perfect Day" and "Just a Wearyin' for You"; Cecile Chaminade, "Summer"), many songs that allude to birds, flowers, or spring (Haydn Wood, "Bird of Love Divine"; Edward Schneider, "Bird Raptures"; Robert Morrison Stults, "The Birds and the Brook"; Clare Kummer, "The Bluebird"; Amy Beach, "The Year's at the Spring"), popular operatic excerpts (Offenbach, "Barcarolle" from *Tales of Hoffman*; Puccini, "Musetta's Waltz Song" from *La Boheme* and "One Fine Day" from *Madame Butterfly*; Verdi, "La donna e mobile" and "Quartet" from *Rigoletto*), songs using dialect reminiscent of minstrelsy (Caro Roma [Carrie Northey], "Can't Yo' Heah Me Callin', Caroline?" and James A. Bland, "Carry Me Back to Old Virginny") as well as short instrumental pieces by composers like Robert Schumann, Franz Liszt, Frederic Chopin, and Rudolph Friml, to name just a few.[12] The list suggests that Woodward valued variety and brevity—none of these pieces last more than four minutes in performance, and most are much shorter. Considered together, they challenge notions of high and low, or elevate the whole repertory through Woodward's equation of art and whistling.

WOODWARD'S PATH TO WHISTLING

Woodward's career and support of others was rooted in professionalism that emanated in part from her training as a classical musician and a teacher. She began her career performing and teaching not as a whistler but as a singer. After graduating from high school in Tecumseh, Michigan, in 1891, she entered the Detroit Conservatory, and studied voice with the Canadian-born tenor Harold Jarvis and European-trained soprano Ida Norton. When she completed her studies at the conservatory, she taught harmony and sight singing at the Thomas Normal School in Detroit.[13] She left Detroit for Chillicothe, Ohio, during the 1895–96 school year to teach music in the public schools for a salary of $650, about $17,000 by today's standards.[14] In that role, Woodward attended social gatherings, such as evenings of playing progressive euchre, and performed regularly at receptions and professional functions in the community. A soprano, she sang on programs for club meetings and church-sponsored social occasions.[15] In addition to solo performances, she organized others, leading the high-school chorus in a program that lasted over an hour and a half, and attempted to organize a community-based choral society.[16]

While in Chillicothe, Woodward whistled publicly at least once on March 26, 1896, her first appearance on a program after having recovered from the measles.[17] The performance took place at a social held for the Church Aid Society at the home of fellow singer Mrs. F. M. DeWeese. Woodward performed two pieces, one sung and one whistled, the whistling described in the *Chillicothe Gazette* "as clear as a bird."[18] Although Woodward sang at several events after this premiere as a whistler, she did not whistle in public again in Chillicothe; or, if she did, it escaped the attention of the press.

Despite being well liked and successful during her year in Chillicothe, her contract was not renewed. The committee hired instead Grace Smith, a local woman and pianist who had returned to Chillicothe after attending the conservatory in Detroit, presumably the same one as Woodward. The *Chillicothe Gazette* framed the decision with some regret, acknowledging that Woodward had served the community well and had made many friends who would be disappointed by the committee's actions despite Smith's qualifications. Nevertheless, Smith accepted the job with a salary of $500 for the 1896–97 year, a cost reduction of $150 for the community.[19] Over the next few years Woodward lived in Detroit, where, before relocating to California, she composed songs, taught privately, and developed her skills as a whistler.[20]

Woodward's family experienced a terrible loss in October 1896 when Agnes's father, the surgeon Charles Meredyth Woodward, died of typhoid in Tecumseh.[21] Over the years after his death the survivors came to live together in a household of single women. When the unmarried thirty-year-old Agnes moved to Los Angeles from Detroit in 1902, her widowed mother and two of her mother's never-married sisters joined her. The extended family remained together for the rest of their lives as a household. According to census records, Woodward's mother, Martha L. Woodward, had her own income; her aunt Lizzy MacGlashan, on the other hand, was in need of support. Agnes and her aunt Ella MacGlashan worked outside the home, Woodward serving as a secretary and bookkeeper for the YWCA, in addition to performing as a whistler and teaching private whistling lessons.[22] Ella MacGlashan, a pianist and organist, played at churches and found opportunities to teach, continuing the activities she had pursued in Detroit.[23]

During these early years in Los Angeles, Woodward established herself as a whistler who occasionally sang. She appeared on programs for women's clubs and evening musicales, and in 1904 developed a vaudeville act with A. Rae Condit and Hazel Bryson.[24] A review in the *Los Angeles Times* described them as "three people who put their heads together and decided to do something startling."[25] Each reportedly sang delightfully (Bryson a soprano, Woodward an alto, and Condit a tenor) and interspersed whistled bird trills and staccatos in their song, accompanied at the piano by Maude Lowe. Although their varied program of singing, dancing, whistling, and recitation was generally well received, their whistling was deemed the best part of their act when they performed at Ocean Park Casino, a gambling establishment on the coast just south of Santa Monica that included a vaudeville stage.[26]

As with many such acts, the whistling trio was short-lived. Both Bryson and Condit had established themselves as performers in Los Angeles before Woodward's arrival, and continued with their independent careers after the trio dissolved the next year. The press rarely mentions Woodward performing in public after her first years in Los Angeles and the founding of her school. Although she joined her then sixteen-year-old student Margaret McKee on a trip to perform at Chautauqua, New York, in 1914, followed by at least one recital for a women's club as they made their way home, for the most part Woodward focused her energy on teaching privately and developing and directing a school of whistling.[27]

Woodward started the California School of Artistic Whistling with the support of her aunt Ella MacGlashan and Edna Zyl Modie, another teacher of artistic whistling, who only stayed with the school for a couple of years.[28] Although the name of Woodward's school emphasized whistling, in the school's early years she employed a group of teachers so that its students could also study expression (elocution), violin, voice, and piano. Jessie Stafford served as Woodward's assistant whistling instructor and taught mostly small children. Anna Fisher taught voice, and Woodward's aunt taught piano. Clara Iverson taught expression and physical culture (elocution), and Harold Walberg served as violin teacher and business manager. Over time, as the whistling component of the program attracted interest, the school focused more specifically on whistling at the expense of its original diversity.

In an interview in 1921, Woodward explained why she stopped singing and became a whistler, claiming that she ruined her voice for professional work by practicing an ill-advised method. When she arrived in California, a "discouraged, despondent girl," she was inspired to make music again by the native birds because she found the "bird notes" similar to the human whistle.

> "Well, if I can't sing, I can whistle," said Agnes Woodward. To the foothills of the high Sierras she went daily, music-paper and note-book in one hand, a sandwich in the other. She trailed the song birds, imitating their cries so perfectly that they came to bush and tree in answer to her call. Then she jotted down their notes, reproduced

and adapted them to musical selections, choosing appropriate names to illustrate the bird figures.[29]

Her description of experience in the "foothills of the high Sierras" may be apocryphal, a myth constructed to resonate with the work of naturalists such as John Muir as much as to represent her own experience. Her narrative suggests a time of almost spiritual isolation, a period of commune with nature ending with the acquisition of bird language. Less romantically, it reflects the value Woodward placed on hard work and persistence, as she put pencil to paper and recorded this avian vocabulary.

A good deal of the material in the method suggests influences from outside of California. It contains local birds represented next to a broad array of species well known across the United States. Woodward took a number of bird songs with permission from F. Schuyler Mathews, *Field Book of Wild Birds and their Music*.[30] The most commonly mentioned bird in her text is the "California Mockingbird," a local version of the Northern mockingbird, whose habitat spans North America. Mockingbirds are the perfect birds for whistlers to imitate, in that they themselves, as the name suggests, imitate other birds. Also mentioned are the red bird (cardinal), [western] meadowlark, bob white, California quail, California song sparrow, canary, robin, and the canyon wren, a bird Woodward heard on the trails to Mt. Wilson and Mt. Lowe east of Los Angeles. Although the canyon wren and the California quail are unique to the West, a number of the birds mentioned can be found on the eastern side of the North American continent. While the narrative of song collection places Woodward at home in California, the bird sounds themselves and their use as melodic ornaments construct a pan–North American vocabulary, uniting the wild and domestic, the east and the west. While Woodward's method encouraged attentiveness to birds and precision in imitation, it also tended toward what could be heard as generic representations of bird sounds in music.

WOODWARD'S RECITALS AS SOUND AND SPECTACLE

Part of the school's success came from its location in Los Angeles, a warm-weather mecca for tourists seeking entertainment and relief from the social isolation of agricultural life and the extremes of Midwestern weather. Woodward arrived in Los Angeles during a period of rapid urban growth, when opportunities multiplied for classically trained musicians to work in a number of professional contexts.[31] More than that, however, the school itself and its performances became a spectacle, a point of interest worthy of a line home on a postcard or a paragraph in the newspaper. Woodward held recitals open to the public that featured her students as soloists and in small ensembles, sometimes dressed in fanciful costumes. For the flower-themed concert in January 1913, student performers wore a host of flowered costumes, from dresses decorated with daffodils and roses to outfits transforming the whistlers into sunflowers.[32] The following January, the subheading for a review of the concert in the *Los Angeles Times* sums up the pageantry accompanying the whistling as follows: "Cleverly Executed Costumes of Fireflies, Moths, Dragon-fly and Mosquitoes, Combined With Electrical Effects, Add Great Novelty to Annual Whistling Concert.[33]

Woodward prepared her students for public performance from their first lessons, having a studio recital once a month and two evening recitals open to the public in a large auditorium every year, events that had a reputation for being entertaining musical events. Her students spanned in age from small children to mature adults, as did the members of the audience.[34] An author with the pseudonym "Aunt Jemimy," supposedly a tourist from Nebraska, captured some sense of the popularity of the Bird Recital on January 16, 1912:

> The plainly finished hall was one very pleasant to be in, but not large enough for Bird Recitals like this, for the people kept pouring in and pouring in, young mothers with babies, little boys and girls, young men and maidens, old men and ladies, in fact, persons of all ages, 'til the hall was pack, jam full. Couldn't possibly help noticing those two ladies dressed in the height of fashion going up and down the aisle, one of them with a costly plume waving to and fro, and saying to the other: "Well, if we can't get a seat together, we'll have to be separated."[35]

The theme of birds inspired the props for the theater as well as the program. Local businesses supplied potted palms and songbirds in birdcages to decorate the stage, the hall decorated with "a wealth of flowers."[36] Although whistling solos and small ensembles dominated the program, performances by elocutionists, a violin soloist, solo pianists, and instrumental ensembles provided variety. Leah McKee, a student of elocution teacher Clara Iverson, performed a poem by James Whitcomb Riley, "Old Bob White," with spoken refrains of "Old—Bob—White!" that were answered with a bobwhite whistle from her sister, Margaret McKee. Not all pieces or performances on the program included whistling: Dorothy Walker, another elocution student, performed an excerpt from a short story by Myra Kelly about children's thwarted desire to experience the swan boats in Central Park.[37] The violinist performed the only non-bird piece, the well-known minuet from Gluck's *Orfeo ed Euridice*. While the novelty of whistling drew the crowd, variety remained an important aspect of the overall shape of the recital.

Woodward's programs featured ensembles of whistlers as well as soloists. The bird whistling chorus provided the introduction to recitals like the one that Aunt Jemimy attended (see Fig. 2.3). In its early years it included a few men among

Fig. 2.3. The whistling chorus performs in 1928, conducted by Agnes Woodward. Photograph by Harold A. Parker. Reproduced courtesy of the Huntington Digital Library. Unique digital identifier: 174096. https://hdl.huntington.org/digital/collection/p15150coll2/id/2707.

the women, but photographs from the 1920s capture a group of women, as most descriptions of the bird chorus depict. In a letter to a student, Woodward described her whistling chorus's expectation of a concert on the USS *Maryland*:[38] "The girls are quite thrilled about this as it means a trip in a smaller boat out to the war vessel, and 'scads' of attentive 'jack-tars' to look after this bevy of beauty!"[39] The performance proved to be spectacular. As Woodward wrote in describing the event, "We had a great time on board the Maryland. Sailors and officers were stacked 'high' on towers, turrets, in life boats, etc., and when we closed the program I had them sing with us 'The Long, Long Trail'; and with those 1,000 voices it was thrilling!"[40]

In addition to leading the bird chorus and teaching privately, Woodward supported the careers of her most capable students. She began by grooming them for public performances, and then promoting them to appear in the Lyceum or Chautauqua circuits. These three- to seven-day educational events were held in small towns across the United States beginning in the 1870s and ending in the 1930s, with musicians and entertainers providing variety to the programs of lectures.[41] Most of the advertisements for Woodward's school are brief, resembling business cards that state the school's name, Woodward's name, and an address and phone number for more information; however, the most informative are much like small articles promoting the business, such as in the following passage praising the school's accomplished students, and listing those who have found work:

> The California School of Artistic Whistling of Los Angeles, of which Agnes Woodward is director, is sending whistlers out into Chautauqua and concert work. Mary Louise Hand, sixteen years of age, is the youngest one to tour, and she will travel under Ellison-White management for two months thru the West. Zillah Ernestine Withrow is with the Chautauqua Managers Association, Rosalynde Brunner is with the International Lyceum Bureau, and Felice Jung is touring with the "Cup of Gold" extravaganza.[42]

In December 1916, a full-page spread displayed photographs and brief biographies for six whistlers "who are open for 1917 engagements," including Margaret Gray McKee, "The Queen of Whistlers"; Mary Louise Hand, "The Pacific Coast Nightingale"; Shirley Irvine; Gertrude Willey; Nina Kellogg; and Felice Jung.[43] An advertisement several months later (March 1917) refers back to this spread from December, again emphasizing Woodward's role as the manager of the whistlers, but also depicting the size and diversity of her studio, in which she teaches up to sixty students, including some men: "Comely young maidens with rosebud lips are not the only students. Nay—there is a railroad engineer, a postal clerk, a merchant and a man totally blind among the group of men aspiring to be whistle artists."[44]

These advertisements demonstrate the transactional nature of Woodward's whistling business, the full dimensions of which are difficult to trace. Did students pay her to be featured in these advertisements, or did their successful activities provide a quid pro quo, with their photos and brief biographies supporting the growth of the school? A select number of women benefited from her promotion while, simultaneously, Woodward and her school benefited from publicity related to their professional successes. The majority of her students, including a few men, may have had different ambitions that made whistling a pastime rather than a vocation. Or, perhaps, whistlers not featured in such advertisements had fewer resources to commit to Woodward's management of them, or less promise as performers. Regardless of why or how, the promotional materials suggest an interdependence between instructor and instructed, the success stories of Woodward's students supporting her reputation and sustaining the whistling school.

Woodward responded to changes in the entertainment industry, and, despite the Depression, opportunities for her students continued to emerge. As a brief article from 1930 titled "Whistling Has New Field in Sound Films" stated, "the popularity of whistling, and especially 'bird imitations,' has grown to a marked degree since the talkies came into vogue, and if the song of a nightingale or of a mocking bird is desired, the whistler most proficient in this mimicry is selected."[45] As in other informational pieces about what had been renamed the Agnes Woodward School of Whistling, the article lists the professional accomplishments of Woodward's students, many of whom engaged with film in ways other than providing sound effects. Whistler Esther Campbell had just returned from a transcontinental tour with Fanchon and Marco, a sister-brother production company team that produced live prologues, which were brief variety shows that took place before the beginning of a film.[46] Ruby O'Hara appeared as a soloist with a Movietone chorus, and a rare dark-skinned woman, Diette Gross, a whistler whose exotic appearance was emphasized, would soon appear in a Movietone short subject film in an Indian act called "Fallen Leaf." These examples combined live and recorded versions of vaudeville with the new experience of cinema.[47]

The stories of the four Woodward-trained whistlers that follow illustrate a range of ways that Woodward's students entered into traditional spaces for women musicians, but pushed on the boundaries of those spaces to cultivate new opportunities.

FAY EPPERSON (1894–1984) AS TEACHER AND PERFORMER

Fay Epperson's career resembled Woodward's in many ways. Epperson began performing by combining child impersonation with whistling as part of Chautauqua entertainments, later developing a studio as a whistling teacher in Chicago, introducing the bird method to a new community.[48]

As a whistler she performed what might be termed popular classics—a repertory of light, short, lyric instrumental pieces such as Grieg, "To Spring"; Kreisler, "Caprice Viennoise" and "Tambourin Chinois"; and Liszt, "Dream of Love," to name a few of the best known.[49] As one audience member described her whistling at a meeting of the Oak Park Sorosis, a women's club that met in that western suburb of Chicago, "there is no doubt that Miss Epperson has mastered this type of music which she has elevated to an art."[50] She was also an imitator of birds, having mastered a list that one would expect of a Woodward student, including the robin, redbird, mourning dove, bluebird, meadowlark, California Linnet, loon, mockingbird, nightingale, bobwhite, and canary.[51] Although the child impersonation provided variety to her act, at least one observer commented on a preference for the whistling: "Although Miss Epperson is adept at this type of reading, one almost wished that she kept only to her whistling, at which she excels and delights."[52] Combining whistling with elocution, however, enhanced the flexibility of her programming. She joined other artists or performed with just an accompanist, which allowed for variety through reading and impersonation, whistling solos accompanied at the piano, solo piano pieces, and bird calls.[53]

Epperson's work on the Chautauqua circuit began in 1919, when she signed her first contract with the Ellison-White Bureau, one of a number of offices that organized educational activities and concerts for multi-day events associated with Chautauqua and Lyceum programs in small, rural towns in the United States.[54] The contract required performances over three months in a number of states, and the travel could be intense. During the summer of 1920, Epperson performed with the Stearns-Gregg Company, a trio including Vere Sternes, violinist; Ethel Sternes, cellist; and Lorna Gregg, pianist. Epperson's child impersonation and whistling, categorized as "entertainment," followed the concert of the trio. The group's performances took place twice—afternoon and evening—on the fifth of a five-day schedule of diverse events.

Starting around 1922, Epperson added the stability of teaching and performing in Chicago, her home base from around 1920 into the 1940s, to performances on the Chautauqua circuit. The first years were difficult. In 1927 she reflected on becoming established in a new city as a whistler, an "artist in a new field." Initially, she received the "cold shoulder" from established musicians because whistling had yet to find acceptance as a professional pursuit in Chicago.[55] In contrast to Epperson, Woodward never experienced this resistance in Los Angeles, where the musical establishment was newer and more flexible when she arrived decades earlier. Over time, however, Epperson created a space for whistling, as her numerous performances for women's clubs demonstrate. In 1927, her whistling trio entertained at events like the Beverly Hills Woman's Club Annual Luncheon and the Arche Club's celebration of Bird Day.[56] They also performed at the Premier Theater of Valparaiso, Indiana, for the Woman's Club, and the Catholic Woman's Club of Kenosha, Wisconsin, just to name a few.[57] In the years following 1927, she and her students continued Chautauqua work. They closed the Chautauqua in July 1930 in Dixon, Illinois, and were highlighted as performers at a Libertyville Chautauqua that took place in May 1935.[58] The Fay Epperson Whistling Trio performed at the meeting of the International Lyceum Association on the south shore of Lake Erie in Lakeside, Ohio, in 1936 and 1941.[59] Around 1942 she relocated to Racine, Wisconsin. On February 7 of that year, the Fay Epperson Whistling Trio performed in the children's theater series sponsored by the Woman's Club. By 1947, when the first *Who's Who in Wisconsin* appeared in print, Epperson had retired to California.[60]

All told, Fay Epperson's activities served as an extension of Woodward's work. She found spaces to perform through the sponsorship of Chautauqua and Woman's Clubs, employing her students in these performances throughout her career. Through these activities she spread Woodward's method with little change in repertory or adjustment in the basic message of health and wellness, connection with the natural world, artistic whistling, and making a living.

MARGARET MCKEE (1898–1961) ON RADIO AND BROADWAY

Margaret McKee became the best-known Woodward student in the United States during the 1920s and 1930s. A native of Los Angeles, McKee began studying with Woodward as a child and was one of her most accomplished students. Margaret and her sister, elocutionist Leah McKee, performed regularly together and as soloists on Woodward's school recitals from 1911 and 1912. In 1916 the sisters still performed together on the Chautauqua and Lyceum circuits, and as a vaudeville act.[61] Margaret made the national news performing as a whistler for services at the Temple Baptist Church of Los Angeles, causing more conservative Christians to complain that Baptists attracted parishioners through vaudeville entertainments.[62] She whistled with the Los Angeles symphony as a soloist, and with dance bands on the radio, and appeared on outdoor stages like the Hollywood Bowl.[63]

Interviews with the young McKee reveal the student's perspective toward the Woodward method of bird whistling. Her observations as a fourteen-year-old student in 1912 describe the detail-orientedness and repeatability required of Woodward's approach, as opposed to the license allowed the improviser. When asked why she whistled, she responded, "I like improvising . . . I just imagine what kind of song I would like to make if I were a bird, and then I whistle it. The trouble with that kind of song is that one cannot always remember it so that it may be whistled again. But improvising is only for one's own pleasure. In whistling in public it is safest to follow the rule."[64] In a later interview as part of publicity for *Annie Dear*, a 1924 Broadway show in which she had a whistling number, she explained how she began whistling, and how the skill could be taught:

> When I first wanted to take up this form of musical expression, I had no real natural ability for it. Someone told me, however, that I could go to a regular school and take systematic instructions; and I did so. Before long, I discovered that I could learn the art just as I could learn the violin or piano. Then I found, also, that there were many rich rewards attached to whistling. The position of the lips, assumed when whistling, for instance, is said to beautify the face. It somehow improves the curves of the lips, while the breathing exercises the facial muscles and improves the contour. After I learned routine whistling and the placing of tones in a straight melody, I applied myself to improving my repertoire and learning the song notes of birds. I have traveled extensively abroad and have learned not only the interesting notes of the skylark and the nightingale, but also those of the rare bullfinch. Every time that I have a vacation I spend it in virginal forests and listen attentively to bird calls and songs. Then, too, I strive in so far as possible to make whistling resemble the foremost art of the operatic soprano. Frequently, I interpolate into a whistling number all the cadenzas and trills that one finds in an operatic coloratura aria.[65]

The 1920s marked the beginning of an international career for McKee. She signed a contract with the Orpheum in 1920 "under the terms of which she . . . cover[ed] the western territory and then whistled her way on East to New York."[66] The move to New York allowed her to make recordings and perform regularly in a number of theaters not only in New York City but also in London.

McKee's New York and London performances capitalized on the novelty of the beautiful woman who whistled like a bird. Called the Hippodrome's "bird girl," she appeared regularly there between 1920 and 1924, featured in one act whistling in a suspended cage lowered to the stage, where she stepped out. She also appeared at the Hippodrome in a Toyland scene, and in a feature called "a Canary Opera."[67] In addition, she appeared with Miss Owen's Marionettes in the Schubert Theater in 1921 and in Irving Berlin's *Music Box Review* in 1922. During this same time, she appeared in variety shows in London, performing, for instance, in August 1921 at the New Oxford Theatre in *The League of Notions*.[68]

Beginning in the late 1920s, McKee performed regularly for a radio audience. By 1927 McKee, called "Micky" by impresario Samuel "Roxy" Rothafel, had joined "Roxy and His Gang." There too she was as much a novelty as a virtuoso, known for her ability to whistle four simultaneous notes as for her musicianship modeled in part on birdsong.[69] After achieving national recognition on the radio, she performed with commercial orchestras, appearing on the Lucky Strike Orchestra program.[70] In June 1931 "Today on the Radio" lists McKee, appearing nightly with Nestlé's Orchestra, as one of the "outstanding events on the radio" of that time.[71]

In the late 1930s McKee returned to Southern California, having coincidentally married a man with the last name Woodward, and spent the last decades of her life doing work on a regional rather than national or international scale. She returned to her musical roots in California, and to activities like whistling in church, giving talks about her career, and whistling for local women's clubs.[72]

FRANCES HAZELTON (1902–1991) BUILDS CONFIDENCE

Agnes Woodward had correspondence students in addition to those who took lessons at the studio in Blanchard Hall. One such student was Frances Hazelton, a resident of Bellows Falls, Vermont, who began her work with Woodward in 1922 and continued her studies until her marriage in 1926. The letters between Woodward and Hazelton covered a number of topics related to the teaching of whistling and starting a career, including Woodward's health, Hazelton's progress, and professional goals for women whistlers, such as recording and whistling on the radio.[73] Although much of the prose is dedicated to accounting (how much Hazelton had paid or owed for lessons, whistle-prepared sheet music, and postage), the letters show the development of a warm relationship between Woodward and Hazelton, and Hazelton's work toward becoming a professional, if but for a short time. The relationship between teacher and student developed through two periods of face-to-face training as well as the exchange of numerous letters. During January 1923, Hazelton spent several weeks in Los Angeles studying with Woodward, accompanied by her mother and father. She met again with Woodward over six weeks in New York in 1925, when Woodward stayed at the McAlpin Hotel and supervised the preparation of *Whistling as an Art* for publication.[74]

From the beginning of her training, Hazelton pursued opportunities to perform. Upon returning to Bellows Falls from her time in Los Angeles she regularly whistled for church organizations and women's clubs, such as the Unitarian Conference in Walpole, Vermont, and meetings of the Daughters of the American Revolution (DAR). When Hazelton took lessons in New York, Woodward encouraged her to audition to perform as part of radio broadcasts. Soon after, Hazelton auditioned with the Alber-Wickes Platform Service, which organized acts for the Orpheum, Lyceum, and Chautauqua circuits as well as scheduling performers for the radio. Hazelton traveled to Boston to audition for the manager. In a form letter from Boston dated January 19, 1925, Hazelton learned that she was assigned a twelve-minute slot for a hearing at the Cambridge YWCA on February 4, 1925. Further, she was required to wear evening dress and provide her own accompanist, and advised to return to the office the next week to hear the manager's assessment of her audition.[75] Hazelton expressed her excitement about the audition in a letter to her fiancé, William Junior Bryant. "I am supposed to appear for twelve minutes! It sounds so funny when they get it down to minutes, doesn't it? So that means I go to Boston next Monday anyway, I guess."[76]

Hazelton's experiences provide a perspective on radio programming's growth out of live performance in its early years. Although Hazelton was required to wear evening attire, she described the isolation of the radio performance for WBZ Springfield in another letter to her fiancé after the event: "It's great fun broadcasting because there's nobody looking at you! Just my accompanist and me alone in the funny little room. Of course we had signals. But the queerest thing is the way it sounds to yourself. The room is so closely sealed that your tones sound dead and weak and cut off somehow."[77]

The positive responses to Hazelton's performance demonstrated the newness of radio as a medium. Many of her closest relatives and friends had no access. Either they did not own a radio yet, or they could not pick up the signals from Springfield or Boston, where the radio stations were located. Those who did hear her, such as her aunt Nan in Boston and Phil Delphos, a college student in the "Phi Gams" fraternity house in Worcester, were in Massachusetts. These listeners congratulated her warmly in personal letters, her aunt comparing her pride in Hazelton to her feelings when her son had his first piano recital.[78] Delphos joked about the bird whistling: "We are hearing the results of the bird seed—sounds wonderful!"[79]

Although her mother in Bellow's Falls could not tune in WNAC, a far-flung, anonymous radio audience praised her with "applause cards," as the post cards and letters that listeners wrote were called.[80] These responses, again, demonstrate the newness of the radio experience, and showed that the broadcast was heard as far east as Nova Scotia, far west as eastern Iowa, far north as Ottawa, Ontario, and as far south as West Virginia. Many other listeners heard her in New York, Maine, Michigan, Pennsylvania, and Ohio. A number of these listeners, especially those some distance away, marveled at their ability to tune in a station from the Northeast, the radio being a new experience for them. Hazelton preserved these cards, mementos of her experience, to the end of her life.

Hazelton revealed in her correspondence how important whistling was to her developing identity as a modern woman. The privileged daughter of a medical doctor, Hazelton reflected on the personal benefits she experienced as a whistler, but articulated no aspirations to a career.[81] From before the beginning of her whistling studies she corresponded with her fiancé as a prospective wife, as someone who would ultimately spend her life with him as he contributed to the family manufacturing business. For the time between 1923 and 1925, however, before her father and then her mother died unexpectedly, and before she married, whistling filled an important place in her life as a reason to travel, to work with focus toward a goal, to build her self-confidence and enjoy independence. As she wrote to her fiancé while she prepared for her WBZ appearance in Springfield on February 16, "I have enjoyed so much my 'business' this past week. It brings me some of that much-needed confidence in myself. Maybe you never suspected it, but I've always lacked that very much! And then it's such fun to come and go in the city as I like—(I have a latchkey!) and to smoke comfortably now and then when I really want it."[82] Having experienced such independence, she chose to relinquish it.

MARION DARLINGTON, WOODWARD WHISTLERS, AND THE VOICES OF DISNEY WILDLIFE

Perhaps the Woodward-trained whistler most heard across the globe still today is Marion Darlington, who provided the whistled voices for early Disney shorts such as the Silly Symphonies and feature-length films such as *Snow White and the Seven Dwarfs* (1937), *Bambi* (1942), *Cinderella* (1950), and *Sleeping Beauty* (1959).[83] Darlington provided the songs of birds and other musical and not-so-musical sound effects—she was said to have the "prettiest off-stage scream in the business."[84] Although numerous Woodward students worked in these early films, Darlington alone received a line in the credits because, although numerous other whistlers provided background sounds, "all distinguishable songs were Marion's."

According to journalist Nell Randolph, Darlington often whistled duets and trios with herself, taking the parts of two or more characters at one time. After her introduction to sound effects work through Disney, Darlington worked with almost every major studio in Hollywood, with a long list of movies to her credit.

Like Woodward, Darlington had a story for why she whistled. As a child she would not practice piano, but she loved whistling, so her mother found her a teacher to study whistling instead. Rather than follow whistlers like Epperson and McKee in their work on the Chautauqua circuit, Darlington moved directly from whistling for women's club entertainments to whistling on the radio. Her radio performance with Raymond Paige and his Sierra Symphonists in 1929 led to her discovery by "big moving picture companies," which led to further demand for her whistling on the radio and in film.[85]

Disney's employment of whistlers other than Darlington was more episodic, the work of Arvada Meyers, a throat or ventriloquistic whistler (she made the sounds through her vocal cords without puckering her mouth), serving as one example. Disney talent scouts "discovered" her while she taught a nature bird whistling class at a local park. In *Snow White and the Seven Dwarfs* she served as the lead voice of seven "bird singers." Discussing the experience of working for Disney many years later in 1971, she reported that she earned nine dollars a week for about six weeks, equivalent to about $150/week today. The short length of time and modesty of the sum suggests that whistling for Disney in and of itself was not a career, but one of a number of activities for the working musician.[86] Another Woodward student, Marie Jeannerette, worked as a whistler in films when not serving as a legal secretary, again suggesting that while it was possible to make money whistling for Disney, those who required an income maintained other positions.[87] Even Darlington, who worked regularly beginning in the 1930s for a variety of movie studios, moved between performance and teaching. In the 1950s she taught whistling to groups of tourists in Long Beach, California, and sent them home with scores marked in the style that Agnes Woodward had developed.

Woodward's whistling school continued after her death at sixty-six in 1938, when Helen Ward Jeffs, who had been an instructor in Woodward's school since 1925, took over operations.[88] The school still existed in 1946, when a brief article about Woodward's technique appeared in *Coronet*, celebrating the success of Marion Darlington.[89]

In 1917, when Woodward's school had been in existence for almost a decade, she commented on the discouragement she received from friends and family when she first shared ideas about founding such a school.[90] No doubt these associates found it difficult to imagine the success of an institution committed to teaching people to whistle like birds. Yet Woodward's business acumen, her commitment to her students, and the variety of venues in which a whistler could find employment contributed to her long-term livelihood, a success attributable to consistent, disciplined, almost uninterrupted work.

Woodward's musical entrepreneurship provided structure and support for students, mostly young women, to develop musical skills that led to independence. In the earliest years of the school, as one might expect, these women filled roles in Chautauqua and vaudeville work, community-based recitals, and teaching. As new opportunities arose, Woodward's students pursued them. They performed as part of radio shows. They appeared in film shorts and provided sound effects for film. They traveled across the United States and sometimes across the Atlantic Ocean to perform. Their flexible approach to sound and music accommodated a broad range of ambitions, from the desire to make something of oneself before marriage to having an international career in film or on stage. Although all but forgotten today, whistling as work enriched many women's lives in the first half of the twentieth century.

NOTES

1. The whistling-girl proverb has inspired a number of responses over the years, a select few of which I cite here. For support of women whistlers, see Charles Dudley Warner, "A Whistling Woman" ["Editor's Drawer"], *Harper's Magazine* 84 (January 1892): 322–23. For an analysis of the idea of whistling as masculine, see Havelock Ellis, *Studies in the Psychology of Sex: Sexual Inversion*, vol. II, 3rd ed. (1901; Philadelphia: F. A. Davis, 1921), 8. The topic of the crowing hen also preoccupied past specialists in poultry. See Gail Hamilton, "Scientific Farming," *Atlantic Monthly* 16, no. 94 (1865); Thomas R. Forbes, "The Crowing Hen: Early Observations on Spontaneous Sex Reversal in Birds," *Yale Journal of Biology and Medicine* 19, no. 6 (1947): 955–70.

2. Agnes Woodward, *Whistling as an Art* (New York: Carl Fischer, 1925). An expanded second edition appeared in 1938, the year of Woodward's death.

3. For his account of Agnes Woodward, based in part on engagement with Woodward-trained whistlers who were still alive when his article was published, see Daniel H. Resneck, "Whistling Women," *American Heritage* 33, no. 1 (August/September 1982), https://www.americanheritage.com/whistling-women.

4. Resneck, "Whistling Women."

5. Tim Brooks discusses the early recordings of African American whistler George Washington Johnson, and the white men who built on Johnson's successes, such as Joseph Belmont and S. H. Dudley, in *Lost Sounds: Blacks and the Birth of the Recording Industry 1890–1919* (Urbana and Chicago: University of Illinois Press, 2005), 58–63.

6. Numerous newspaper articles document Alice J. Shaw's fame and her inspirational effect on women as whistlers in the United States beginning in 1887. See, for example, "Mrs. Shaw, the Whistler. Plenty of New York Women Are Trying to Whistle like Her. But She Remains without a Peer and is Constantly Improving—A Minister's Tribute to Mrs. Shaw—The Shaw Children," *New York Sun*, January 1, 1888.

7. Carroll Smith-Rosenberg discusses the development of the New Woman in *Disorderly Conduct: Visions of Gender in Victorian America* (New York: Alfred A. Knopf, 1985).

8. Jacob Smith and Craig Eley have suggested that whistlers who imitated birds functioned like a type of recording technology. The whistler served as a reliable means for capturing and reproducing elusive high-frequency sounds before technological refinements allowed for the recording of true birds outside. See Jacob Smith, *Eco-Sonic Media* (Berkeley: University of California Press, 2015), 60–61; Craig Eley, "Sound Recording, Nature Imitation, and Performance Whistling," *Velvet Light Trap* 74 (Fall 2014), http://www.utexaspressjournals.org/doi/10.7560/VLT7402.

9. Woodward, *Whistling as an Art*, xi.

10. Although other whistling techniques existed, such as finger whistling and throat whistling, Woodward's students were pucker whistlers.

11. "Whistlers Study Birds and their Music," *Washington* [DC] *Times*, November 14, 1918.

12. Woodward, *Whistling as an Art*, 110.

13. Details of Woodward's biography reproduced here appear in *Who's Who in the Pacific Southwest: A Compilation of Authentic Biographical Sketches of Citizens of Southern California and Arizona* (Los Angeles: Times-Mirror Printing & Binding House, 1913), 403; John Steven McGroarty, *Los Angeles: From the Mountains to the Sea*, vol. III (Chicago and New York: American Historical Society, 1921), 539–40.

14. The *Chillicothe Gazette* reported Woodward's hiring and salary on July 26, 1895. It mentioned her again on September 6, 1895, when the school board granted her a three-year certificate to teach music. http://chillicothegazette.newspapers.com/. Modern equivalents of past salaries in this essay are based on the calculator at measuringworth.com.

15. The *Chillicothe Gazette* documents Woodward's activities in Chillicothe on a regular basis from September 1895 to June 1896, the period she resided there. On November 8, 1895, Woodward's name appeared in a list of five vocalists who performed at the St. Catharine's Guild's meeting at St. Paul's Episcopal Church. On December 6, 1895, the newspaper documented Woodward's attendance at a reception held at the Rectory of St. Paul's. On December 20, 1895, it reported that Woodward's mother had been staying with her for three weeks, and that she and her mother would travel to Detroit and remain there for two weeks. On January 4, 1896, the paper reported Woodward's imminent return from Detroit to resume teaching music. A brief article titled "It Will Be Organized" followed on January 16, 1896, discussing the need for twenty-five singers to form a choral society at the Third Presbyterian Church, which Woodward planned to lead. On January 22, 1896, an article reporting on a gathering to play progressive euchre noted that Woodward won a violet bookmark for her second-place score. She again was mentioned as one of several singers to perform at the quarterly meeting of St. Catharine's Guild at St. Paul's church on February 5 and 7, 1896, singing De Koven, "Past and Future," and "the pretty little ballad, 'You.'" She was one of a number of guests who performed at a small party of friends on May 15, 1896. On June 5, 1896, as part of a reception sponsored by the Ladies' Auxiliary of St. Paul's, she was praised for a solo performance of "'Goodbye Sweet Day' in her usual perfect style."

16. When the *Chillicothe Gazette* reported on plans for the gathering of the Ross County Teachers Association (Chillicothe is the county seat), it mentioned the plan for Woodward's performance of a soprano solo and leadership of a twelve-member chorus of high school "young ladies," who would perform in a break between lectures. On May 30, 1896, the newspaper reported on a concert organized by Woodward: "The scholars show the effect of the careful training they are receiving from Miss Woodward, and a more pleasing concert was never given at the high school."

17. On Friday, February 14, 1896, the *Chillicothe Gazette* reported that Woodward, "instructor of music in the public schools," had measles and would take at least a week to recuperate.

18. "A Very Pleasant Success," *Chillicothe Gazette*, May 27, 1896.

19. "Prof. Faye Lands an Easy Winner," *Chillicothe Gazette*, June 26, 1896.

20. After Woodward left Chillicothe, newspapers provided only spotty indications of her activities until she moved to Los Angeles. On January 17, 1901, the *Chillicothe Gazette* reported that Miss Anna Socin performed Woodward's song "Supposin'," describing it as "a dainty ballad by Helen Maud Walthman set to extremely pretty music [by Woodward]." Woodward whistled at a party for the YMCA reported in the *Detroit Free Press*, June 5, 1901.

21. *Chillicothe Gazette*, October 31, 1896.

22. The *Los Angeles City Directory* for 1904 indicates that Woodward served as the YWCA bookkeeper. In 1905 it lists her as the YWCA business secretary (1583). "Vocal tchr [teacher]" follows her name in the volume from 1906 (1912), which becomes "music [teacher]" in 1907, (1619), 1908 (1569), and 1909 (1490). In 1910 she first appears listed as the director of the California School of Artistic Whistling (1612). Digitized Los Angeles city directories can be found at the Los Angeles Public Library, https://rescarta.lapl.org/ResCarta-Web/jsp/RcWebBrowse.jsp.

23. MacGlashan is listed as a teacher in the *Los Angeles City Directory* 1905 (949), and in later volumes as a teacher at Woodward's school. On December 12, 1909, the *Los Angeles Times* reports that she would serve as accompanist at Woodward's new school. On June 9, 1911, the *Los Angeles Times* reflects on her particular strength in teaching young children piano. Despite this involvement in the school, her obituary in the *Los Angeles Times* on March 15, 1935, describes her as a church organist, having served at St. Paul's Cathedral and Plymouth Congregational and Unitarian Churches. No mention is made of her work as an accompanist or as a piano teacher with the whistling school.

Woodward had other family in the Los Angeles area as well. In addition to this aunt, her mother, and her sister, Woodward's niece, actor and screenwriter Bess Meredyth, also resided in Southern California, but had little association with the musical members of the family. John Meredyth Lucas, Bess Meredyth's son, provides a telling anecdote about the relationship between Woodward and Meredyth in *Eighty Odd Years in Hollywood* (Jefferson, NC, and London: McFarland, 2004), 18. His embarrassed mother sank in her chair, hoping not to be noticed, while attending an event at which Woodward's American Bird Whistling Chorus provided entertainment.

24. On September 21, 1904, the *Los Angeles Times* reported on details of the vaudeville act, and the orchestral accompaniment provided the whistling trio in performance.

25. "Whistling Girls Expect a Good End," *Los Angeles Times*, August 5, 1904.

26. "Whistling Girls Expect a Good End," *Los Angeles Times*, August 5, 1904.

27. Woodward and McKee performed in Oak Park, Illinois (in the Chicago suburbs), after having appeared in Chautauqua, New York, and other East Coast locations. See "Famous California Whistlers," *Oak Leaves* (Oak Park, IL), October 17, 1914.

28. Edna Zyl Modie (1886–1981) is not mentioned in Los Angeles newspapers in association with the school after 1911. She briefly mentions her career as a professional whistler in her memoir, an unpublished manuscript, Huntington Library, Los Angeles. HM 73986–73989.

29. Elizabeth Deuel, "Interesting Westerners," *Sunset Magazine* (March 1921), 47. *Who's Who in the Pacific Southwest: A Compilation of Authentic Biographical Sketches of Citizens of Southern California and Arizona* (Los Angeles: Times-Mirror Printing and Binding House, 1913), 402.

30. F. Schuyler Mathews, *Field Book of Wild Birds and their Music*, 2nd ed. (New York and London: G. P. Putnam's Sons, 1921). Woodward sent a sheet of music manuscript paper to her correspondence student Frances Hazelton with a number of bird songs copied with permission from Mathew's *Field Book*, found in the Papers of William Junior Bryant and the Bryant Family, Rauner Special Collections, Dartmouth College, ML-88, box 5, folder 37.

31. Catherine Parsons Smith discusses the musical landscape of Los Angeles from 1880 to 1930 in *Making Music in Los Angeles: Transforming the Popular* (Berkeley: University of California Press, 2007), 1–11.

32. Hector Alliot, "Warblers. The Novel Art of Whistling. Flower Recital Program by Whistling Maidens. Roses, Daffodils, and Pansies Interpret their Lives in Whistle," *Los Angeles Times*, January 29, 1913.

33. Hector Alliot, "Human Insects Hum, Whistle: Elaborate Setting of Woodland Garden Scenes," *Los Angeles Times*, March 6, 1914.

34. Alliot's reviews from January 29, 1913, and March 6, 1914, for the *Los Angeles Times* provide details of the performers' names and relative ages as well as details of the program and descriptions of costumes and the setting.

35. Uncle Jim and Aunt Jemimy's last name is omitted from the travelogue of their time in Los Angeles. Although catalogued as a work of fiction, the events described as occurring in the recital correspond with a program and newspaper accounts from the 1912 recital. See Aunt Jemimy, *Uncle Jim and Aunt Jemimy in Southern California* (Lincoln, NE: Woodruff Press, 1912), 33–36, https://hdl.handle.net/2027/hvd.hn1zsg.

36. The enterprising Woodward found business sponsors to supply the potted plants, which came from Howard & Smith, nurserymen; and birds in cages from Grider's Birdland, both credited in the program, which can be found in Kenyon, Stanley, and Crellin Family Papers, Special Collections and Archives, University of California Irvine Libraries, MS.R.049, Personal Papers, 1883–1964, Box 1, Folder 6.

37. Myra Kelly, "Land of Heart's Desire," in *Little Citizens: The Humours of School Life* (New York: McClure, Phillips, 1904), 239–78; *McClure's Magazine* 23, no. 7 (July 1904): 240–52.

38. The images are available through University of Southern California's digital collection: group portrait of America's Bird Whistling Chorus, at the Hollenbeck Home, July 9, 1926, http://digitallibrary.usc.edu/cdm/ref/collection/p15799coll65/id/25285; October 1, 1926; and at the Raymond Hotel in Pasadena, March 19, 1928: http://digitallibrary.usc.edu/cdm/ref/collection/p15799coll65/id/25284; http://digitallibrary.usc.edu/cdm/ref/collection/p15799coll65/id/25282.

39. Agnes Woodward to Frances Hazelton, May 12, 1924, Papers of William Junior Bryant, ML-88, box 5, folder 37.

40. Agnes Woodward to Frances Hazelton, June 10, 1924, Papers of William Junior Bryant, ML-88, box 5, folder 37.

41. For a discussion of the important role that the Chautauqua and Lyceum systems played in small towns of the United States, see Paige Lush, *Music in the Chautauqua Movement* (Jefferson, NC, and London: McFarland, 2013), 9–25. Marian Wilson Kimber also explores the Chautauqua and Lyceum circuits as providing important spaces for elocutionists as they developed as artists and professional performers. See Wilson Kimber, *The Elocutionists: Women, Music, and the Spoken Word* (Urbana, Chicago, and Springfield: University of Illinois Press, 2017).

42. *Lyceum Magazine* (July 1916), 24.

43. *Lyceum Magazine* (December 1916), 19.

44. "Teaching Many to Whistle," *Lyceum Magazine* (March 1917), 44.

45. "Whistling Has New Field in Sound Films," *Los Angeles Times*, August 31, 1930.

46. For more on Fanchon and Marco, see Phil Wagner, "'An America Not Quite Mechanized': Fanchon and Marco, Inc. Perform Modernity," *Film History* 23, no. 3 (2011): 251–67, doi:10.2979/filmhistory.23.3.251.

47. "Whistling Has New Field in Sound Films," *Los Angeles Times*, August 31, 1930. African American women whistlers are unusual, and I have not been able to find this film.

Diette's surname is spelled as Gross, Grass, and Cross in the various newspaper articles that mention her.

48. "Whistling Has New Field in Sound Films."

49. "Whistling Has New Field in Sound Films."

50. "Sorosis Guest Day: Fay Epperson, Whistler, and Mildred Waugh, Pianist, Entertain Members and Friends at Colonial Club," *Oak Leaves* (Oak Park, IL), March 12, 1927.

51. "Sorosis Guest Day."

52. "Sorosis Guest Day."

53. *Lyceum Magazine*, 32, no. 1 (June 1922): 48.

54. For a discussion of Chautauqua framed from the standpoint of elocutionists, see Marian Wilson Kimber, *The Elocutionists* (Urbana: University of Illinois Press, 2017), 150–72.

55. "Sorosis Guest Day."

56. "Beverly Hills Club Plans Annual Luncheon April 6," *Suburbanite Economist* (Chicago), March 22, 1927; "Arche Club to Hear Lecture on Birds," *Suburbanite Economist*, January 20, 1928.

57. "Whistling Trio Appears at First Meeting of Club," *Kenosha News* (Kenosha, Wisconsin), September 14, 1927.

58. "Chautauqua to Close with Fay Epperson Trio," *Dixon Evening Telegraph* (Dixon, Illinois), July 18, 1930; "Coming this Friday Night, Fay Epperson Whistling Ensemble," *Libertyville News* (Libertyville, Illinois), May 9, 1935.

59. *Sandusky Register* (Sandusky, Ohio), August 27, 1936 and August 20, 1941.

60. *Who's Who in Wisconsin: A Biographical Dictionary of Leading Men and Women of the Commonwealth* (Chicago: Larken, Roosevelt & Larken, 1947), 57.

61. A program from the Ventura Chautauqua of 1916 documents their performance. See Traveling Culture; Circuit Chautauqua in the Twentieth Century, University of Iowa Special Collections, Digital Collection, http://digital.lib.uiowa.edu/cdm/ref/collection/tc/id/33259.

62. "A Strenuous Sunday," *New York Tribune Review*, March 31, 1918.

63. "Thousands attend Fete in Hollywood," *Los Angeles Times*, June 12, 1919.

64. "Songs of the Birds Inspire These Girls," *Los Angeles Times*, January 21, 1912.

65. "Whistler Imitates Art of Coloratura," *Daily Register Gazette* (Rockford, IL), January 12, 1925.

66. Grace Kingsley, "Flashes. Signs with Circuit. Margaret McKee Again to Have Whistling Act," *Los Angeles Times*, August 7, 1920.

67. "Features at Hippodrome," *Brooklyn Daily Eagle*, December 26, 1920; "She Whistles," *Brooklyn Daily Eagle*, January 9, 1921; "Hippodrome's Bird Girl," *New-York Tribune*, February 6, 1921.

68. "The League of Notions [sic]," *Sunday Times*, August 28, 1921

69. Her collaboration with folk singer Rosalind Fuller and marionettes is described in the *New-York Tribune*, December 18, 1921; McKee's inclusion in Irving Berlin's *Music Box Review* is announced in the *New-York Tribune*, October 15, 1922; *New York Times*, February 10, 1924. For accounts of McKee as part of Roxy's Gang, see "Canary Joins Radio Whistler in a Duet," *Boston Herald*, December 18, 1927, and "Merry-Go-Round of the Air," *New York Times*, July 28, 1935.

70. Margaret "Micky" McKee performed two recent fox trots: "Deep Night (1929)" and "Old Man Sunshine (1928)," August 10, 1929, Radio Continuity, Lucky Strike, 1928–29. American Tobacco Records, https://www.industrydocumentslibrary.ucsf.edu/tobacco/docs/gpvx0000, 237 (ATX01 0262041).

71. *New York Times*, June 12, 1931.

72. Advertisements for church services and accounts of club meetings, weddings, and other community-based performances document this shift in her career. On September 21, 1935, an advertisement in the *Brooklyn Times Union* for a service at the Baptist Temple featured

Margaret McKee, who "makes last appearance before moving to California." A similar notice for the Glendale Baptist Church appeared in the *Los Angeles Times* on April 4, 1836, and mentioned Margaret McKee, "well-known whistler," documenting her continued participation in the Baptist church as a musician. A notice in the *Daily News* (Los Angeles) on May 6, 1936, mentioned her performance at a meeting of the Los Angeles Breakfast Club, which was heard as part of a KFWB broadcast. She also received notice the same day in the *Los Angeles Evening Citizen News* for performing at a gathering of Hollywood High School Alumni, which she attended, and on June 23, 1936, for entertaining at a wedding. The *Riverside Daily Press* on December 31, 1936, and January 2, 1937, reported her impending performance for the Riverside Woman's Club, where she entertained the gathering with stories of her international career as well as her whistling. These are just a few of the many mentions of her activities in Southern California after leaving New York.

73. These letters between Frances Hazelton and a number of friends and family members, including her whistling teacher Agnes Woodward, are held by Dartmouth College, Rauner Special Collections Library, which houses the papers of William Junior Bryant, whom Frances Hazelton married. See ML 88: William Junior Bryant papers, Series: 1, 1822–1997, Box: 9, 1917–1998, folders 1, 3, and 4.

74. Frances Hazelton to William Junior Bryant, November 17, 1924.

75. Monica H. Grey to Frances Hazelton, January 19, 1925.

76. Frances Hazelton to William Junior Bryant, January 24, 1925.

77. Frances Hazelton to William Junior Bryant, February 10, 1925.

78. Aunt Nan to Frances Hazelton, February 1925.

79. Frances Hazelton to William Junior Bryant, February 17, 1925.

80. A number of these "applause cards" for Frances Hazelton, postcards that listeners sent in care of the radio station to performers they heard on the radio, are held at Rauner Special Collections, ML 88: William Junior Bryant papers, Series: 1, Box: 5, folder 37.

81. A brief biography of her father, William French Hazelton (1860–1925), appeared in Albert Nelson Marquis, *Who's Who in New England* (Chicago: A. N. Marquis, 1916), 529. It provides Fran's date of birth, the date her parents married, and outlines her family's roots in Salem, Massachusetts, which date from 1637. It details her father's education at a number of Vermont preparatory schools, his preparation to become doctor and assume a career as a surgeon, as well as his activities and service to the community as a Republican, Episcopalian, Mason, and trustee of Vermont Academy, among other details.

82. Frances Hazelton to William Junior Bryant, February 10, 1925.

83. According to the *Williams News* (Williams, AZ), July 8, 1954, Marion Darlington was "Walt Disney's official whistler in the Disney productions"; she is the only whistler credited in *Snow White*. Her work as a transcriber of birdsong appears in the second edition of *Whistling as an Art* (1938), where a transcription of the western meadowlark, a tune she had "used in a movie cartoon," is attributed to her (73). Numerous brief feature articles in the years following the earliest Disney films' releases document the existence of a number of whistlers who contributed to the soundtracks. Journalist Muriel Dinsmore described the whistling career of Woodward-trained whistler Arvada Meyers McBride, which included work with Disney, in, "She Sings like a Bird," *Times Standard* (Eureka, CA), April 25, 1971. Marie Jeanerette, also a Woodward student, was mentioned as a Disney whistler by the *Brownsville Herald* (Brownsville, TX), June 29, 1939. Jeanerette's status as a Woodward bird whistler is further confirmed by her inclusion in the photograph of the Whistling Bird Chorus performing at Raymond Hall and reproduced as part of this essay. She stands in the back row. http://digitallibrary.usc.edu/digital/collection/p15799coll65/id/25282/rec/1. Ernest Nichols and Esther Campbell

Ragland were also credited with contributing whistling to the soundtrack of *Snow White*. For Nichols, see the *Sandusky Register* (Sandusky, OH), July 15, 1953. For Ragland, see her obituary, *Richmond Times-Dispatch* (Richmond, VA), July 9, 1939. In addition, Sheer White is mentioned as "one of Walt Disney's whistlers in '*Snow White and the Seven Dwarfs*'" in the *Albuquerque Journal* (Albuquerque, NM), on July 15, 1951.

84. Nell Randolph, "Princess of Pucker," *Long Beach Telegram: Southland Magazine* (Long Beach, CA), September 19, 1948.

85. Darlington's appearance with Raymond Paige's orchestra is described in "Merry Makers to Present Program of Fun and Noise," *Santa Ana* (CA) *Register*, December 22, 1929. See also Laura Rawson, "Talented Whistler Captivates Audience at Caroline Swope School; Whistled 'Snow White,'" *Santa Cruz* (CA) *Sentinel*, August 10, 1939.

86. Muriel Dinsmore, "She Sings Like a Bird," *Times Standard* (Eureka, CA), April 25, 1971.

87. Esther Campbell might have had a robust career in film had she not died two years after the release of *Snow White* at the age of twenty-seven from appendicitis. *Hutchinson News* (Hutchinson, KS), July 13, 1939.

88. Helen Ward Jeffs's name appears on Woodward's letterhead as an assistant in 1925, and as an associate in 1927 in Woodward's cards and letters to Frances Hazelton, Papers of William Junior Bryant, ML-88, box 5, folder 37. Woodward's obituary appeared in the *Los Angeles Times*, June 21, 1938, describing her as a whistling instructor and director of the Agnes Woodward School of Whistling.

89. Grace Poston, "School for Whistlers," *Coronet* (February 1946): 131–32.

90. "Whistling, a Modern Art, and What a Los Angeles Woman Has Done for It," *Out West Magazine* 45, no. 3 (April 1917): 119.

BIBLIOGRAPHY

Archives

Papers of William Junior Bryant and the Bryant Family, Rauner Special Collections, Dartmouth College, ML-88, box 5, folder 37.

Kenyon, Stanley, and Crellin Family Papers, Special Collections and Archives, University of California Irvine Libraries, MS.R.049, Personal Papers, 1883–1964, Box 1, Folder 6.

Traveling Culture; Circuit Chautauqua in the Twentieth Century, University of Iowa Special Collections, Digital Collection, http://digital.lib.uiowa.edu/cdm/ref/collection/tc/id/33259.

Print Sources

Albuquerque Journal (Albuquerque, NM), July 15, 1951.

Alliot, Hector. "Warblers. The Novel Art of Whistling. Flower Recital Program by Whistling Maidens. Roses, Daffodils, and Pansies Interpret their Lives in Whistle." *Los Angeles Times*, January 29, 1913.

Alliot, Hector. "Human Insects Hum, Whistle: Elaborate Setting of Woodland Garden Scenes." *Los Angeles Times*, March 6, 1914.

"Arche Club to Hear Lecture on Birds." *Suburbanite Economist*, January 20, 1928.

"Aunt Jemimy." *Uncle Jim and Aunt Jemimy in Southern California*. Lincoln, NE: Woodruff Press, 1912. https://hdl.handle.net/2027/hvd.hn1zsg.

Belmont Joseph, and S. H. Dudley. *Lost Sounds: Blacks and the Birth of the Recording Industry 1890–1919*. Urbana and Chicago: University of Illinois Press, 2005.
"Beverly Hills Club Plans Annual Luncheon April 6." *Suburbanite Economist* (Chicago), March 22, 1927.
Brownsville Herald (Brownsville, TX), June 29, 1939.
"Canary Joins Radio Whistler in a Duet." *Boston Herald*, December 18, 1927.
"Chautauqua to Close with Fay Epperson Trio." *Dixon Evening Telegraph* (Dixon, IL), July 18, 1930.
Chillicothe Gazette (Chillicothe, OH), July 26, 1895; September 6, 1895; November 8, 1895; December 6 and 20, 1895; January 4, 16, and 22, 1896; February 5, 7, and 14, 1896; May 15 and 30, 1896; June 5, 1896; October 31, 1896; January 17, 1901.
"Coming this Friday Night, Fay Epperson Whistling Ensemble." *Libertyville News* (Libertyville, IL), May 9, 1935.
Detroit Free Press, June 5, 1901.
Deuel, Elizabeth. "Interesting Westerners." *Sunset Magazine* (March 1921).
Dinsmore, Muriel. "She Sings Like a Bird." *Times Standard* (Eureka, CA), April 25, 1971.
Eley, Craig. "Sound Recording, Nature Imitation, and Performance Whistling." *Velvet Light Trap* 74 (Fall 2014).
"Esther Campbell Ragland." Obituary, *Richmond Times-Dispatch* (Richmond, VA), July 9, 1939; see also *Hutchinson News* (Hutchinson, KS), July 13, 1939.
"Features at Hippodrome." *Brooklyn Daily Eagle*, December 26, 1920.
"Hippodrome's Bird Girl." *New-York Tribune*, February 6, 1921.
Kelly, Myra. "Land of Heart's Desire." In *Little Citizens: The Humours of School Life*. New York: McClure, Phillips, 1904; and *McClure's Magazine* 23, no. 7 (July 1904).
Kingsley, Grace. "Flashes. Signs with Circuit. Margaret McKee Again to Have Whistling Act." *Los Angeles Times*, August 7, 1920.
"The League of Notions." *Sunday Times*, August 28, 1921.
Los Angeles City Directory. Entries for MacGlashan: 1905: 949.
Los Angeles City Directory. Entries for Woodward: 1905: 1583; 1906: 1912; 1907: 1619; 1908: 1569; 1909: 1490; 1910: 1612.
Los Angeles Times, September 21, 1904; December 12, 1909; June 9, 1911; March 15, 1935.
Lucas, John Meredyth. *Eighty Odd Years in Hollywood*. Jefferson, NC, and London: McFarland, 2004.
Lush, Paige. *Music in the Chautauqua Movement*. Jefferson, NC, and London: McFarland, 2013.
Lyceum Magazine, July 1916; December 1916; June 1922.
Marquis, Albert Nelson. *Who's Who in New England*. Chicago: A. N. Marquis, 1916.
Mathews, F. Schuyler. *Field Book of Wild Birds and Their Music*, 2nd ed. New York and London: G. P. Putnam's Sons, 1921.
McGroarty, John Steven. *Los Angeles: From the Mountains to the Sea*, vol. III. Chicago and New York: American Historical Society, 1921.
McKee, Margaret ("Micky"). "Deep Night (1929)" and "Old Man Sunshine (1928)." August 10, 1929, Radio Continuity, Lucky Strike, 1928–29. American Tobacco Records.
McKee, Margaret. Advertisements. *Brooklyn Times Union*, September 21, 1935; *Los Angeles Times*, April 4, 1936; *Daily News* (Los Angeles), May 6, 1936.
"Merry-Go-Round of the Air." *New York Times*, July 28, 1935.
"Merry Makers to Present Program of Fun and Noise." *Santa Ana* (CA) *Register*, December 22, 1929.
"Mrs. Shaw, the Whistler. Plenty of New York Women Are Trying to Whistle like Her. But She Remains without a Peer and is Constantly Improving—A Minister's Tribute to Mrs. Shaw—The Shaw Children." New York *Sun*, January 1, 1888.

New York Times, February 10, 1924; June 12, 1931.
New-York Tribune, October 15, 1922.
Oak Leaves (Oak Park, IL), October 17, 1914.
Poston, Grace. "School for Whistlers." *Coronet* (February 1946).
"Prof. Faye Lands an Easy Winner." *Chillicothe* (OH) *Gazette*, June 26, 1896.
Randolph, Nell. "Princess of Pucker." *Long Beach* (CA) *Telegram: Southland Magazine*, September 19, 1948.
Rawson, Laura, "Talented Whistler Captivates Audience at Caroline Swope School; Whistled 'Snow White.'" *Santa Cruz* (CA) *Sentinel*, August 10, 1939.
Resneck, Daniel H. "Whistling Women." *American Heritage* 33, no. 1 (August/September 1982). https://www.americanheritage.com/whistling-women
Sandusky Register (Sandusky, OH), August 27, 1936; August 20, 1941; July 15, 1953.
"She Whistles." *Brooklyn Daily Eagle*, January 9, 1921.
Smith, Catherine Parsons. *Making Music in Los Angeles: Transforming the Popular*. Berkeley: University of California Press, 2007.
Smith, Jacob. *Eco-Sonic Media*. Berkeley: University of California Press, 2015.
Smith-Rosenberg, Carroll. *Disorderly Conduct: Visions of Gender in Victorian America*. New York: Alfred A. Knopf, 1985.
"Songs of the Birds Inspire These Girls." *Los Angeles Times*, January 21, 1912.
"Sorosis Guest Day: Fay Epperson, Whistler, and Mildred Waugh, Pianist, Entertain Members and Friends at Colonial Club." *Oak Leaves* (Oak Park, IL), March 12, 1927.
"A Strenuous Sunday." *New York Tribune Review*, March 31, 1918.
"Teaching Many to Whistle." *Lyceum Magazine* (March 1917).
"Thousands Attend Fete in Hollywood." *Los Angeles Times*, June 12, 1919.
Ventura Chautauqua, 1916. Traveling Culture; Circuit Chautauqua in the Twentieth Century, University of Iowa Special Collections, Digital Collection, http://digital.lib.uiowa.edu/cdm/ref/collection/tc/id/33259.
"A Very Pleasant Success." *Chillicothe* (OH) *Gazette*, May 27, 1896.
"Whistler Imitates Art of Coloratura." *Daily Register Gazette* (Rockford, IL), January 12, 1925
"Whistlers Study Birds and Their Music." *Washington* (DC) *Times*, November 14, 1918.
"Whistling, a Modern Art, and What a Los Angeles Woman Has Done for It." *Out West Magazine* 45, no. 3 (April 1917).
"Whistling Girls Expect a Good End." *Los Angeles Times*, August 5, 1904.
"Whistling Has New Field in Sound Films." *Los Angeles Times*, August 31, 1930.
"Whistling Trio Appears at First Meeting of Club." *Kenosha* (WI) *News*, September 14, 1927.
Who's Who in the Pacific Southwest: A Compilation of Authentic Biographical Sketches of Citizens of Southern California and Arizona. Los Angeles: Times-Mirror Printing & Binding House, 1913.
Who's Who in Wisconsin: A Biographical Dictionary of Leading Men and Women of the Commonwealth. Chicago: Larken, Roosevelt & Larken, 1947.
Williams News (Williams, AZ), July 8, 1954.
Wilson Kimber, Marian. *The Elocutionists: Women, Music, and the Spoken Word*. Urbana, Chicago, and Springfield: University of Illinois Press, 2017.
Woodward, Agnes. *Whistling as an Art*. New York: Carl Fischer, 1925, 1938.

Additional Reading

Ellis, Havelock. *Sexual Inversion*. Philadelphia: F. A. Davis, 1921, 8.
Forbes, Thomas R. "The Crowing Hen: Early Observations on Spontaneous Sex Reversal in Birds." *Yale Journal of Biology and Medicine* 19, no. 6 (1947): 955–70.

Hamilton, Gail. "Scientific Farming." *Atlantic Monthly* 16, no. 94 (1865).
On Margaret "Micky" McKee: *Los Angeles Evening Citizen News*, May 6, 1936; *Riverside Daily Press*, June 23, 1936.
Warner, Charles Dudley. "A Whistling Woman" (in "Editor's Drawer" column). *Harper's Magazine* 84 (January 1892): 322–23.

Chapter 3

Women's Compiled Scores in Early Film Music

—Kendra Preston Leonard

In my previous work, I have written about the careers of female accompanists and music directors in the early cinema. That research reveals that women from across the United States were highly successful and effective composers, arrangers, and recording artists.[1] In this essay I address an area of cinematic musical development where the importance of women's contributions has gone un(der)noticed: the compiled score, a film score created for early film primarily from pre-existing pieces, in both its written and recorded varieties.[2] I examine written and recorded compiled scores created by Hazel Burnett, Alice Smythe Burton Jay, and Carrie Hetherington. All three were music directors at some of the largest motion picture houses in the United States between 1908 and 1927, but despite their contributions to cinema music, they are today unknown. Jay and Hetherington were also entrepreneurs whose desire for better musical accompaniment for motion pictures eventually led them from compiling written scores to developing the technology and processes necessary for creating recorded compilations for automated instruments for use in the early cinema.

It is important to recognize the overall participation of women in early cinema music. Although no census of cinema accompanists was ever taken, reports from trade and industry publications suggest that while male musicians were in the majority in the earliest days of cinema accompaniment, women, both White and of color, soon outnumbered them.[3] Women almost certainly comprised the majority of cinema accompanists after the spring of 1917, when the United States joined the war effort and many all-male cinema orchestras were dissolved so that their members could join the military.

Even before the war, women were crucial to cinema music making. The job of cinema accompanist was a respectable one for women, and its salary compared positively with secretarial work, teaching, and nursing.[4] The presence of a female accompanist indicated that a cinema was intent on being an artistic and moral institution, especially as the film industry worked to establish itself as a legitimate business producing respectable and creative works.[5] These accomplished pianists encompassed those who made the cinema their career as well as musicians who went on to work in other arenas, like Florence Price, who accompanied films before she became recognized as a symphonic composer; and blues great Victoria Spivey, who played in the cinema when she was a teenager.[6] After 1918, when all-men's cinema orchestras were disbanded so that their members could serve in the military, the sounds of the cinema—the music that evolved into modern soundtracks—were thus chosen, developed, created, curated, and circulated primarily by women, although a handful of men continued to play or conduct in large cinemas and remained in control of the rather monopolistic business of creating the cue sheets.[7] Composers for early sound films like Max Steiner would likely have heard women's accompaniments far more frequently than those that adhered exactly—or even closely—to men's scores or suggestions for music when they experienced cinema music as young people. Women in the audience may well have witnessed the work of female accompanists and felt empowered to pursue similar careers.

RACE AND WOMEN MUSICIANS IN THE EARLY CINEMA

In this essay, I discuss the contributions of three White women to music for the early cinema, and it is important to understand why I have not included any Black women. As I have written in my study of women as accompanists and spirit mediums, a primary reason is the institutional racism present in the historiographies of the United States. Just as the hierarchies of historiography have traditionally privileged historical records documenting men's work and lives over women's, they privilege the work and lives of White women over those of women of color. Despite the efforts of archives to preserve the documents of Black, Asian, Latinx, Native American, and other communities of color, the fact remains that primary source materials in the cultural history of the United States are overwhelmingly those of White people. Thus, while scholars have digital and physical access to both large and small White newspapers from all over the country, for example, we have only limited access to even the most important Black newspapers. Census records, often an excellent source of information about occupational training and employment, include more detailed and correct information on White residents of the United States than those of color, and other government sources have only very limited materials documenting the lives of people of color.[8] The National Archives only began to collate information on its holdings regarding Black Americans in 1947, and that effort has been woefully underfunded.[9] The multiple diasporas of people of color, such as the Great Migration, which took place between 1916 and 1970, caused the displacement and loss of many records and histories.

Despite this lack of extant sources, I have managed to find some information about Black women musicians in cinemas, mostly on the East Coast and in Chicago. However, because there were no industry-specific publications about or for the Black cinema, many of the references I've found are isolated mentions of individuals. Olive Ormes, writes the *New York Age* in 1909, is the up-and-coming "musical directress" of the Princess Theater in Cleveland, Ohio, where she "is filling the position with great credit," having studied classical music and worked at several other theaters including an Edison cinema.[10] At the Manilla Theater in Indianapolis, "music is furnished by Mrs. Allura [sic] Mack who sings and plays the piano."[11] At the Booker Washington Theatre in Washington, DC, the cinema orchestra is comprised of five musicians including pianist Ruth Heath.[12]

Cultural and political differences also contributed to discouraging women of color—Black women in particular—from becoming professional cinema musicians. The philosophy of "racial uplift" was omnipresent in Black communities during the time period considered here, and as Kevin K. Gaines has written, this ideology meant that simply matching the artistic successes of Whites was not enough for Americans of color to be considered equals: they had to be better.[13] As Amy Absher writes, "classically trained musicians resisted [vernacular musics] in both the South and Chicago by demanding a place in higher education and by bringing African American folk traditions to their classical compositions."[14] Lawrence Schenbeck has detailed how uplift was articulated in the perceived conflict between art music and vernacular music:

> Within the cultural sphere, black elites often resorted to an aesthetic based on European models as a vehicle for cultural vindication. Their response to white America's pervasive minstrelsy-based constructions of blackness was to champion African American art that, while safely grounded in forms and styles derived from Shakespeare or Dvořák, was morally positive and politically inoffensive and represented the Race in heroic, idealized terms.[15]

Playing for the pictures was a reputable and desirable job for white women, but uplift philosophy instructed Black musicians—both men and women—to aim for more traditionally elite careers in their musical ambitions. Because of the much higher value Black communities invested in uplift placed on concert performance, Black American musicians did not generally view playing in the cinema as a profession of status for women. A report in the *Crisis* from January 1911 decried the conditions that forced a woman who was a recent graduate from the Chicago Conservatory of Music to take a job playing "in a low concert hall in one of the worst sections of the city, from 8 in the evening till 4 in the morning," for just $18 a week when other female musicians of color were touring in Europe and making recordings.[16] In comparison, a church organist could reasonably expect to make $500 a year for playing services only, and up to $1200 a year if they also taught music at the church or directed the choir.[17] The *Chicago Defender*, a leading Black newspaper, also stressed the greater significance of concert appearances and performances of classical music over those of cinema musicians or those performing in vernacular traditions. It was not until the very end of the era in 1927—when sound technologies were already regularly appearing in the cinema—that the *Defender*'s music critic began discussing musical accompaniment for film as an acceptable form of employment in music for men and a legitimate topic of discussion for readers interested in the arts.[18]

The fact that Black women do not seem to have worked as cinema musicians as frequently as did White women could also stem from the fact that in much of the country, cinemas were far more White-owned and -operated theaters than those owned and/or operated by Blacks. As Esther Morgan-Ellis writes, "These white-managed cinemas hired white musicians and, while many allowed Black audiences, they kept audiences segregated by relegating people of color to the balcony."[19] Black vaudeville houses began showing films in the 1910s, where the house musicians, usually all-male bands, accompanied them. In addition, Black cinemas were often the targets of community and competitor discrimination and more extreme forms of mistreatment. In 1914 the *Crisis* wrote that despite the outstanding new theaters being built for Black audiences in Black communities, they were not always safe places. "A crowd of two hundred white men wrecked a moving picture house for colored people in Jackson, Miss.," reported the journal. "They ran the ticket seller out of the office, cut the wires, disconnected the moving picture apparatus and locked the doors." Events like this were not uncommon, and as a result, cinema employment became viewed as potentially too dangerous for women of color.

Contemporary newspapers generally indicate that Black cinemas employed individual men as pianists or organists and men and boys' bands to accompany films. These bands, many of them developed out of the male confraternities that were active in Black communities in the late nineteenth and early twentieth centuries, consisted of players from a wide range of musical training and aptitude. These confraternity bands—which might be a brass band with vocal soloists one day and an ensemble of singers with a pianist the next, depending on the event—performed for weddings, funerals, cotillions, parades, charity fundraisers, and in theaters. Although many of the musicians in the confraternity bands and the groups that came out of them remained amateurs, those with talent and drive became professionals. These gigging musicians performed throughout the Midwest in ensembles of three to eight players, providing music for Black cinemas, sometimes alternating parts of a screening with professional male pianists or organists.[20]

THE COMPILED SCORE

As Richard Abel, Rick Altman, Julie Hubbert, Martin Marks, and other scholars of early film sound have documented, there were no standardized practices among musicians for supplying music for films.[21] Music for accompanying films initially came from vaudeville music libraries, popular song, pre-existing art music, and original compositions, only some of which were committed to paper, piano rolls, or shellac. In the 1910s, publications of music expressly for film accompaniment began to proliferate, offering what is known as genre music or mood music for actions, events, and emotions commonly found in film scenarios. Using published collections of genre music called photoplay albums, cinema pianists, organists, or ensemble directors could patch together a handful of pieces to create a compiled score of pieces that in some way matched or supported the action on screen. For example, works for "hurry" or "gallop" were quick in tempo, mimicked the sound of hoofbeats or heartbeats, and employed short note values and a quick tempo, all of which suggested the associated speed of motion given in the title.

The compiled score was the most popular type of musical accompaniment for film. Martin Marks writes that the compiled score blossomed in the United States between 1910 and 1914 and especially following the success of Joseph Carl Breil's full-length compiled score for D. W. Griffith's 1915 picture *The Birth of a Nation*, with studios regularly producing compiled scores for their pictures, but it was far from the first and seems to be heralded as unique only because of the film's notorious reputation.[22] Most of the full-length film scores produced by studios during the late teens and early twenties were compiled scores with a few original sections; only the most prestigious films with the largest budgets received fully original scores for their presentation in cinemas. The presence of a compiled score for a film suggests that the film's makers expected it to be popular. In some cases, however, compiled scores were created after a film, suggesting that the longer a film was shown on a regular basis in a cinema, the more cinema managers believed it to be deserving of an individual score.

Cinema musicians also created compiled scores for recordings used to accompany films. During the early film era, there were also numerous mechanical methods of producing sound for film accompaniment including piano rolls, wax cylinders, and shellac discs. Inventors developed several versions of player pianos with added percussion and other elements for use in the theater. Companies like the Victor Talking Machine Company, Warner Brothers, the Mastertouch Piano Roll Company, and others sought to provide music, sound effects, and/

or speech for films in addition to their recordings of well-known musicians like Gustav Mahler and Teresa Carreño. Such recordings came in multiple formats, of which two were the most successful: those designed so that each disc or piano roll was meant to accompany a single reel of film, and those designed to be quickly swapped out between scenes.[23] Hetherington promoted this kind of scoring through the use of the Fotoplayer, invented by Hetherington in 1910 or 1911 and enormously popular with cinemas after becoming available in 1912 for its technology that allowed operators to switch between piano rolls seamlessly, creating a continuous accompaniment. These recordings had to be carefully made using music arranged and performed by an expert film accompanist. For example, Phonotone issued a set of records for the 1928 film *Four Sons*. The recordings included forty pieces that were used for sixty-seven cues. Each individual piece was recorded onto a separate disc for playing with the screening of the film. Excerpts ranged in duration from fifteen seconds to three and a half minutes and were timed precisely by the recording artist. At the cinema, an employee (sometimes the regular accompanist, sometimes an usher) worked from a list of cues and durations, quickly swapping records on and off multiple turntables to match the music with the film. This process created a compiled score from the recordings.

Far more male composers are represented in the published repertoire for early film, including photoplay albums, full scores, and cue sheets. The vast majority of published music was by a group of mostly European-trained White men, including William Axt, Erno Rapée, and J. S. Zamecnik. The editors of photoplay albums included only a few pieces by women in their collections, and cue sheet creators rarely recommended works by women in cue sheets. Only five women composers appear in Rapée's enormous *Motion Picture Moods*, and of the approximately 5,000 individual cues listed in the cue sheets that belonged to accompanists Adele V. Sullivan and Claire Hamack, only five are by women.[24] Music for the early cinema was also highly ephemeral, and of that which remains extant, the vast majority is by male composers. However, there is considerable evidence of music by women for the cinema: contemporary periodicals document women's compiled scores, as do archival collections including the Silent Film Music Collection at the University of Colorado Boulder and the Josephine Burnett Collection at the Harry Ransom Center. Collections like Sullivan's demonstrate that women were active in compiling scores. Sullivan unbound all of her photoplay albums so that she could rearrange the order of pieces for specific films.[25] While Sullivan did not leave behind enough cues in order for scholars to attach pieces to film titles, it is clear that she used martial music and chase music from three *Academic Edition Albums of Photo-Play Music* edited by G. Martaine (1914), and the 1915 B. F. Wood Music Co. *Collection of Characteristics Selections for the Motion Pictures*. Music and materials having belonged to other accompanists also show evidence of women compiling scores for film, both for their own and for other cinemas. The collections of Inez Garrison, the accompanist at the Garden Theater in Marion, Kansas; Pauline Alpert, an Eastman School of Music graduate who was called the "Whirlwind Pianist" for her technical facility and who not only played for multiple New York City theaters but also recorded piano rolls for automated accompaniment machines, like Jay and Hetherington; and Charlotte Stafford, a Rochester, New York, accompanist, all indicate that these women compiled scores for film.

Ironically, the gendered musical education popular in the late nineteenth and early twentieth centuries uniquely positioned women for creating cinema accompaniment: women whose upbringing during this period had included traditional piano lessons had generally been taught song and opera repertoire and short descriptive or characteristic pieces that worked well in cinematic accompaniment, and particularly well in compiled scores. Compiled scores often required several dozen brief pieces intended to depict very specific scenes, emotions, or actions, and the vast repertoire of such pieces by composers like Felix Mendelssohn, Arthur Sullivan, and Carrie Jacobs-Bond fit the bill. Such pianists also often already owned a large selection of recent or contemporary popular songs, as music publishers marketed these for playing at home by women. These women came from a variety of ethnic, socioeconomic, and educational backgrounds to take up positions as cinema musicians and were not, in general, members of the elite, male-mentored group of female art music composers and performers of the period, exemplified by Amy Beach and Maude Powell, although women from the upper economic echelon and those with advanced musical training also worked in the cinema.

Industry insiders credited outstanding accompanist-composers with the success of many theaters and for providing artistic excellence in the burgeoning medium.[26] Many cinema managers found that a thoughtful, competent female pianist would draw in bigger and (socially) "better" audiences than many male organists or ensembles who were more interested in displaying their technical skills and less interested in the art of playing to the picture.[27] Reporting on the success of the Madrid Theater in New York City, *Motion Picture News* noted that the "musical program of the Madrid is entrusted to Miss Lillian Greenberg, who is a graduate of a Leipsic [sic] conservatory of music. She has made the incidental music accompanying pictures a matter of neighborhood comment."[28] In an issue of *Motion Picture Magazine* from March 1914, Stanley Todd, a regular commentator on music for the cinema, described women as more emotional and passionate players, making them appropriate accompanists for film. Film, he claimed, needed performers with three essential skills found primarily in female accompanists: technical skill, a sensibility about romantic and dramatic repertoire, and a willingness to put the success of a picture before personal ego. Reporting from Denver, he noted:

> Theatres are large, the entrances dazzlingly brilliant, and like as not you will find a wonderful pipe-organ, ready in an instant to change its song of sadness to paeans of joy. It is in Denver, too, where a mere slip of a girl presides at the console of one of these great instruments, and each night plays, with her heart and soul, to the finest of screen projections.... In this way, music lends its valuable aid in interpreting the gamut of emotions, which only the picture can bring into play with that subtle power that has been one of its secrets of success.[29]

Female accompanists, including celebrated cinema organist Edith Lang, the lead author of a textbook on cinema accompaniment, agreed with Todd.[30] Thus, the history of women in early film music is a case in which theater managers valued women performers for what were widely thought to be the superior accompaniments women could create for films. When cinema musicians like Lang, Burnett, Jay, or Hetherington made suggestions about scoring and issued recordings for accompaniment, their male colleagues often paid attention, hoping to glean insight into how to improve their own film accompaniment. Journals and magazines like *Melody* and *American Organist* frequently included reviews of and features about women accompanists and their approaches, reviewing their work in the cinema on the same terms and using the same language they applied to reviews of male performers.

I examine the compiled scores of Hazel Burnett, Alice Smythe Jay, and Carrie Hetherington here because of the three women's large spheres of influence. Each of these women compiled scores for cinemas in major metropolitan areas; these cinemas seated at least 750 people and had at least three screenings a day. Burnett's scores were frequently reviewed by large regional and national publications, and Jay and Hetherington directed cinema ensembles and were frequent correspondents with national journals on the topic of photoplaying. This is not to devalue the importance of women playing in smaller communities, as they too influenced what audiences came to hear as the sound of the cinema, but rather to make use of the larger bodies of material relating to the work of Burnett, Jay, and Hetherington.

Hazel Burnett performed daily at Texas's largest motion picture palaces, including San Antonio's Aztec and Queen Theaters and the Majestic Theater in Austin, throughout the 1910s and 1920s.[31] In addition to creating her own cue sheets and editing published sets of cues, Burnett created compiled scores from both the theater libraries and from her own personal library of thousands of short, characteristic pieces, many of which were clipped from *The Etude* and *Melody* magazines.[32] Burnett's compiled scores in particular reflect on repertoire specifically designed for women: several of the music anthologies in Hazel Burnett's music library came with *ossia* parts "for small hands" or are blatantly marketed for women through the use of cover art, title, and/or other factors. Burnett wrote the titles of accompaniment-appropriate pieces on the covers of the photoplay albums that contained the pieces, often including the page number for quick access in playing a compiled score. She also interleaved pieces of sheet music and pieces cut from magazines between pages of her photoplay albums and taped together musical selections cut from *Melody* and *The Etude* to create original modular scores, such as she did for the 1920 melodrama *Humoresque*. Burnett appears in some cases to have included pieces that would have local resonances into her compiled scores; her Texan audiences would have heard songs by Texan composers and pieces about Texas and the Southwest in Burnett's accompaniments.[33] And like Lang, Burnett apparently took an interest in promoting works by women, frequently scoring films with pieces written by Black English composer Amanda Aldridge (under the pseudonym Montague Ring); Carrie Jacobs Bond; Esther Gronow; Mae Davis; and many others.

Burnett's archival materials include notes and music for several compiled scores, including *Humoresque*, which I discuss at length elsewhere, and the 1922 feature film *My Old Kentucky Home*.[34] At seven reels, *My Old Kentucky Home* ran about seventy minutes.[35] For this score, Burnett used music from several issues of *The Etude* published between October 1920 and August 1921, a few pieces of sheet music, and songs by Stephen Foster. She opened the film with "Plaisantrie" [sic] by film composer Irenée Bergé and used Chapman Tyler's "Afternoon at the Villa" when the hero arrives at his mother's home. In keeping with the practice of assigning leitmotivs to characters, Burnett assigned "Merry Hunting Party" by Emil Söchting to the character of Calamity Jane and accompanied workouts at the horse track with "Saltarello" by Richard Goerdeler.[36] At the end of the film, Burnett led the audience in a sing-along of the title song. The film was widely advertised as a picture for the entire family: it did well and ran for several months in large cinemas such as the ones in which Burnett played.[37] At the Majestic in Austin, Burnett's compiled score for *My Old Kentucky Home* could have been heard by as many as 3,810 people a day during the height of the film's popularity.[38]

In addition to clippings, Burnett also used published collections of characteristic or descriptive pieces in her compiled scores. For the 1925 film *Old Home Week*, she drew most of the music from Cedric Wilmot Lemont's *Dream Pictures*, a collection of character pieces for intermediate-level pianists published in 1916. Lemont had published a number of short pieces in *The Etude*, which may be how Burnett came to know his music; he was the composer of about seventy works in total, most for solo piano and highly descriptive. "On the Bayou," "Cinderella: a fairy tale for piano," and "Children at Play" were among his popular titles. Burnett accompanied *Old Home Week*, which is now lost, with Lemont's "At Eventide" as an introduction as the camera focuses in on a wreath on a door, a dance titled "The Nautch Girl" for several conflicts, and a "Valse Intermezzo" to depict a "Grouch" and "Bitter Taste." Because all of the pieces in *Dream Pictures* were related by the composer in theme and style, using them as the basis for a compiled score resulted in the kind of holistic film score that was valued at the time.

Burnett's compiled scores indicate that she drew from a variety of genres, using music from the Western art tradition, what we might call "light classical" today, and vernacular song. Most of the pieces she used were widely available either through sheet music vendors or publications marketed for home performance. Although the theaters at which she worked had large music libraries, Burnett used those holdings less frequently than her personal collection of pieces and the clippings from the magazines. This suggests that Burnett required a selection of works she either already knew or could learn quickly for accompanying, and that she was always seeking new music to use in the cinema. The pieces from *The Etude* and *Melody*, intended for wide use (*Melody* advertised itself as "for the Photoplay Musician and the Musical Home"), were ideal for her needs. The multiple handwritten notes and cue numbers on individual pieces indicates that Burnett maintained some kind of system or had excellent recall for what pieces she had used for what kinds of scenes; it is clear that she reused both sheet music and clippings in compiled scores for various films. The one source Burnett does not seem to have used for her accompaniments is opera, which was also eschewed by Jay because of its pre-existing associations.

Alice Smythe Burton Jay, a highly regarded cinema organist, conductor, composer, and inventor, spent most of her accompanying career on the West Coast and in Hawai'i with occasional tours to other parts of the United States. She was a strong proponent for using compiled scores that included complete sections of pieces either fully realized for keyboard or for ensemble. While she did not "intend to give [the cue sheet] a black eye," in advocating for holistic scores, Jay wrote that cue sheets often stuck together pieces that may have been fine for scenes shown separately, but when played in sequence created jarring changes of key and even more abrupt changes of character within short timespans. "I do not think it necessary to change music every time a man runs up and down stairs," she wrote. Synchronizing music to the picture was "to adapt correct music to the scene," she declared, not match each and every action on screen with a musical gesture. The compiled score that used only a handful of pieces was more "sympathetic" to a film's nature than the cue sheet and even some complete scores.[39] Jay encouraged musicians to edit cue sheets heavily to better fit the film to be accompanied, replacing many of the printed suggestions with other works or to compile their own scores. In a 1915 letter to Ernst Luz's "Music and the Picture" column in *Motion Picture News*, titled "A Woman's Suggestion for Musical Scores," she held that scores should be compiled according to an understanding of the film acquired through a prescreening for the accompanist (which was not always common or practical for cinema managers to arrange), common sense, and a mix of works from various origins that themselves included a variety of tempi, keys, and "moods," as characters were known in cinema accompanying. It was essential, she wrote in the letter, that cinema musicians have a comprehensive knowledge of Western art music as well as current popular songs. She noted that her own sources were the Western European canon of art music, often as offered in piano or organ arrangement; vernacular songs that were well established in the common culture of her audiences, who would have been primarily White and middle to upper class; and new music, both that written for the screen and published as photoplay music and new popular songs.[40] She certainly knew the repertoire very well herself: her letters to various journals often identify other compilers' and composers' borrowings of preexisting material, which ranged from the concert hall to vaudeville hall to recent popular songs and sheet music.

Jay had very specific ideas about how a compiled score should be constructed. She critiqued the practice of using too many pieces in a single score, suggesting that performers should not be too quick to switch between multiple pieces, but rather to select a handful of pieces that could be adapted to a complete film; this was her own practice, and she often chose a single album of characteristic pieces that she used to outfit an entire film.[41] She also objected to the use of music from grand opera (although not popular operetta), which, she felt, brought "the words [of the libretto] to a person's mind, and seldom if ever fit the scene." Her one exception from this was her response to the studio-produced score composed by Hugo Riesenfeld and based on Georges Bizet's opera score, for Cecil B. DeMille's famous 1915 screen adaptation of Prosper Mérimée's novella *Carmen*. Eschewing Riesenfeld's score, Jay's program for the film used just Bizet's Overture, "Toreador Song," and "Cigarette Song" along with Elgar's "Liebes Gruss," a "Mazurka-Satanelle" by contemporary film composer Charles J. Roberts, "Solveig's Song" by Grieg, and her own "Improvisation-Agitato."[42] This score, one of the few by Jay that has extant documentation, is otherwise very much in keeping with her score-creation philosophies and is likely a fair representation of her work in that it draws minimally but crucially from a small selection of useful sources, includes music both old and new, and incorporates Jay's own compositional and improvisational skills.

Jay's method of selecting music for compiled scores is on display in her criticism of the studio-issued score by Edward J. Howe for the Mary Pickford–produced *Less Than the Dust* (1916). Although the score (now lost), which used Amy Woodforde-Finden's song "Less Than the Dust" from her orientalist suite *Four Indian Love Lyrics*, was described in *Motography* magazine as "appropriate in every detail to the mysticism and superstition of the far East and portrays beyond criticism of a small village of modern India," Jay and her sixteen orchestral players found it "misfitting."[43] Other contributors to the *Motion Picture News* also complained that the score as "impossible"; one asked for a cue sheet instead, indicating that perhaps not only was the music of the score poorly composed (or, as Jay's notes about plagiarism suggest, chosen) for the subject but may also not have fit the film's screening time. In response, Ernst Luz, the editor of the column, provided his own cue suggestions for the film. Like the score issued by the studio, it consisted of a plethora of different pieces—thirty-four individual titles, all of them linked through their exoticism. Jay's score, compiled according to her philosophy and in contrast with Luz's, drew from a suite from Rudolf Friml's operetta *Katinka*, whose pieces had long become synonymous for exoticism, a several other "Oriental pieces," and her own improvisations, which she notated for her orchestra. It was this compilation—not Howe's score or Luz's cue sheet—that audiences heard in conjunction with screenings of the film in Jay's California cinemas, where it apparently was well received.

Jay's belief in the superiority of the compiled score sourced from classical art music, the occasional new song, and improvisations modeled after those of nineteenth-century virtuoso pianists like Liszt and her frequent frustration with poor accompaniments led her to begin making cylinder recordings of her scores. Jay emphasized not only her production of rolls for individual films, but also shorter rolls that could be used for specific kinds of scenes and combined to create a compiled soundtrack of rolls.[44] As more theaters began to use automated instruments in the 1920s, Jay's recorded compilations and short rolls designed to be used in compilations would likely have been quite popular: the late 1910s saw the development of automated instruments with dual rolls so that users could easily change out recordings and more from one to another just as Jay predicted, in part thanks to her colleague and rival Carrie Hetherington.

Carrie Hetherington, who, like Jay was a celebrated film accompanist and cinema music director, spent the first part of her career in Los Angeles and the second part in Illinois.[45] She too advocated for compiled scores over cue sheets and, eventually, made and marketed recorded accompaniments. Hetherington's philosophy of playing for the pictures incorporated a belief that cinema musicians should be as well informed as possible, and that their responsibilities included rejecting poorly constructed cue sheets and studio-provided scores. As the music director at Miller's Theater in Los Angeles, Hetherington also placed some responsibility for the creation of good accompaniments with theater managers, stating that it was essential for cinemas to screen films for their accompanists ahead of public screenings so that the accompanists had time to create informed and intelligent compiled scores. The musician's role, she wrote, was "being there to break the silence and improve the picture with proper and correct music," and she urged cinema musicians to avoid "fancy" music that called attention to themselves rather than the film, arguing for scores created from classical and popular favorites rather than virtuoso showpieces.[46] It is possible that she too found male musicians inclined to play showy works to the detriment of the film, and hoped to put an end to the practice through her editorializing and advice.

She had little use for new generic works written for cinema accompaniment, finding them unnecessary:

> All the Cue Sheets I ever read, when it came to a part of the picture where heavy music is needed, it will read something like this: "Dramatic Tension No. 9," or "Mysterioso Dramatic No. 22." Will some one tell me why on earth some of these musicians don't use some of the old masters' works on the heavies?[47]

She excoriated studio and magazine score compilers for not being familiar with the vast repertoire available for use in accompanying. "The musical programs as are gotten out by the different companies, or are, as a rule, printed in different magazines, are 'impossible,'" she wrote in a letter published by Luz in his "Music and the Picture" column, echoing Jay's criticism. Hetherington continues:

> I am very particular as to the proper and correct selections being used to fit scenes, and all the explanation I can find for these poor miserable apologies for programs, is that the one who picks them has never played for pictures, but reads over the synopsis and if one scene is preceded by the title "Dawn," they place At Title . . . . . . Dawn . . . . . . use Dawn . . . . . . by Vamah. [The compiler] does not know if a midnight party is breaking up at dawn or if the lover is killing his sweetheart at dawn, or what the scene is, nor does he stop to think of the effect of the music[;] if Dawn appears on the music, that is enough.[48]

As opposed to Jay, Hetherington's compiled scores show that she didn't think preexisting significations were problematic in creating a score, and so her compiled scores use a mix of genres from the Western canon—often including opera—and popular songs. In her score for the 1915 Fox production *Princess Romanoff*, Hetherington demonstrates her method of score compilation, using contemporary compositions and popular songs alongside works by Bizet, Grieg, Massenet, Bellini, Beethoven, Mozart, and Gounod. At a time when film composers were only starting to recognize the value of using leitmotifs in their work, Hetherington's score is more holistic than many cue sheets of the period; its use of repeated themes from classical music for individual characters and settings, selective incorporation of more recent tunes that were evocative of the scenes they accompanied and familiar to the audience, and careful arrangement of transitions made it a model for accompanists compiling their own scores. She assigns Bizet's "Pastorale" as the primary theme for the movie overall and likewise appoints Anton Rubinstein's "Melody in F" as a leitmotif for the title character. She incorporates several pieces common to film accompaniment as background music and employs Mozart, Beethoven, and Gounod for suspenseful scenes. Her sources also include five contemporary songs with relevant lyrics, such as "Last Night Was the End of the World" (1912) and "Love Is a Weaver of Dreams" (1912).

Hetherington's compiled score for a second Fox film from 1915, the Theda Bara vehicle *Lady Audley's Secret*, displays a similar approach, using a mix of established and newer pieces, quoting liberally from opera, particularly *Semiramide*, and employing music she used in *Princess Romanoff*, most notably Massenet's *Phèdre* overture.[49] Miller's Theater (now demolished), where Hetherington was music director, seated approximately 800 and ran seven shows a day, all of them accompanied by her compiled scores.[50] But Hetherington remained frustrated with the quality of published scores and cue sheets. Although her published recommendations for compiled scores reached thousands of readers, she sought to improve both upon the quality of scores and her reach in film music. Hetherington began working closely with the American Photoplayer Company to develop a new kind of player piano called the American Fotoplayer that made it easier for cinemas to use recordings to accompany films.[51] At the same time, Hetherington produced and marketed compiled scores using rolls for the instrument, becoming the company's primary spokesperson and traveling the United States demonstrating the instrument. Hetherington was able to provide cinemas with hundreds of rolls with which music directors could compile scores that could be performed even in their absence.

Ultimately, the role of women in early film music was a crucial one, and their compiled scores were essential in creating long-lasting sounds and the structures of music in the cinema. Burnett, Jay, and Hetherington were only three of the many women who accompanied film and created materials for the accompaniment of film during the early film era, and hundreds if not thousands of people heard their compiled scores in cinemas across the United States. Although much of their music is lost today, we can nevertheless analyze what does exist in terms of aesthetics movements in cinema music. All three women had a deep and broad knowledge of the Western art music repertoire, and included works from the canon in their scores as a matter of course. As a whole, they insisted on the importance of developing this knowledge as essential to being able to create effective scores and to communicate with audiences. At the same time, they also recognized the value of descriptive, characteristic, and "light" music: music written in the traditional "classical" manner but intended not for the symphonic stage, but for the amateur home musician. They further regarded popular song as an equally valid genre for accompaniment, using recent hits as they saw fit. Studios often released new songs as movie tie-ins, and while Burnett, Jay, and Hetherington may also have used those as part of their accompaniments, they were very careful about identifying and applying the ideal music for each scene. They were constantly scouring the music magazines and new publications for new material they could use, and Burnett's archival materials show that she often set aside pieces for future use even when she didn't have a film to use them in immediately. Audiences who heard and accompanists who made use of compiled scores by Jay and Hetherington experienced a blend of musical genres and sources that can be located in scores to the present. Such scores thus helped solidify the practice of American film accompaniment drawing from multiple spheres of music. In addition, through their consistent approaches and frequent performances, Burnett, Jay, and Hetherington contributed to audience expectations for film music by codifying the relationship between film genres and types of music, by creating now-standard audio-visual significations, and developing standard musical approaches to specific topics, scenes, events, and characters. As prominent taste-makers in their communities, all three women—and countless others who worked in the same ways—influenced their audiences' understandings of film narrative and musical representation and set the direction for future film composers.

Furthermore, Burnett, Jay, and Hetherington were among those film accompanists who argued for and created highly cohesive scores using leitmotifs and specific musical signifiers for characters, events, and places in films. While this was hardly unusual in early film accompaniment, there remained considerable variation in actual practice and in published suggestions like cue sheets. In presenting consistently unified scores and presenting them to large audiences, the three women profiled here contributed to the development of the holistic music score for films. This approach to scoring presaged and influenced the highly thematic scores of the 1930s, such as those by Erich Wolfgang Korngold, Jerome Moross, Alfred Newman, and Max Steiner—any of whom might have heard one or even many scores by Burnett, Jay, or Hetherington as young cinemagoers thinking about music.

NOTES

1. Kendra Preston Leonard, "Women at the Pedals: Female Cinema Musicians during the Great War," in *Over Here, Over There: Transatlantic Conversations on the Music of World War I*, ed. William Brooks, Christina Bashford, and Gayle Magee (Urbana: University of Illinois Press, 2019), 149–73.

2. There is some controversy in musicology about the use of the term *silent film* and its lexicographical cousins. Some scholars object to the labeling of film during this period as "silent," because such film was almost never silent: it was most frequently accompanied by live music, but was at times also provided with external sound via the means of sound-on-disc, unscored sound effects, and other sonic technologies that preceded the invention and widespread use of sound-on-film technology. In this essay, I refer to this body of film as "early film" or "early cinema."

3. I capitalize Black and White in concordance with the Center for the Study of Social Policy's statement "Recognizing Race in Language: Why We Capitalize 'Black' and 'White,'" by

Ann Thúy Nguyễn and Maya Pendleton, posted March 23, 2020 at https://cssp.org/2020/03/recognizing-race-in-language-why-we-capitalize-black-and-White/.

4. Sidney Steinheimer, advertisement, *American Organist* 2, no. 5 (1919): 212. "Union Scale of Wages and Hours of Labor, Union Scale of Wages and Hours of Labor, May 15, 1921: Bulletin of the United States Bureau of Labor Statistics, No. 302 | FRASER | St. Louis Fed," accessed November 2, 2017, https://fraser.stlouisfed.org/scribd/?item_id=492986&filepath=/files/docs/publications/bls/bls_0302_1922.pdf&start_page=68; "Letter to the Editor," *American Organist* 3, no. 7 (1920): 263; "Trade Notes," *American Organist* 3, no. 9 (1920): 339.

5. Leonard, "Women at the Pedals."

6. Victoria Spivey, *The Blues Is Life* (LP, Folkways Records, 1976), https://folkways-media.si.edu/liner_notes/folkways/FW03541.pdf.

7. "Abandon Orchestras," *Film Daily*, August 28, 1918.

8. Henry S. Shryock and Jacob S. Siegel, *The Methods and Materials of Demography* (US Department of Commerce, Bureau of the Census, 1980), 262.

9. Walter B. Hill Jr., "Institutions of Memory and the Documentation of African Americans in Federal Records," National Archives, August 15, 2016, https://www.archives.gov/publications/prologue/1997/summer/institutions-of-memory.html.

10. Lester A. Walton, "Music and the Stage," *New York Age*, March 25, 1909, 6.

11. "The Manilla Theater," *Indianapolis Recorder*, May 24, 1913, 2.

12. "Dramatics and Athletics," *New York Age*, October 16, 1913, 6.

13. Kevin K. Gaines, *Uplifting the Race* (Chapel Hill: University of North Carolina Press, 2012), 6, https://uncpress.org/book/9780807845431/uplifting-the-race/.

14. Amy Absher, *The Black Musician and the White City: Race and Music in Chicago, 1900–1967* (Ann Arbor: University of Michigan Press, 2014), 11.

15. Lawrence Schenbeck, *Racial Uplift and American Music, 1878–1943* (Jackson: University Press of Mississippi, 2012), 6–7.

16. "Employment of Colored Women in Chicago from a Study Made by the Chicago School of Civics and Philanthropy," *Crisis* 1, no. 3 (1911): 24.

17. "Church and Parish," *Churchman* (October 30, 1909): 639.

18. Dave Peyton, "The Musical Bunch: How to Play Picture Music," *Chicago Defender* (National Edition) (1921–1967); Chicago, August 13, 1927, sec. *The Defender*'s Movie and Stage Department, 6.

19. Esther M. Morgan-Ellis, *Everybody Sing! Community Singing in the American Picture Palace* (Athens: University of Georgia Press, 2018), 8–9.

20. Kendra Preston Leonard, *Music for the Kingdom of Shadows: Cinema Accompaniment in the Age of Spiritualism* (Humanities Commons, 2019), https://doi.org/10.17613/HWVW-WG90.

21. Richard Abel and Rick Altman, ed., *The Sounds of Early Cinema* (Bloomington: Indiana University Press, 2001); Julie Hubbert, *Celluloid Symphonies Texts and Contexts in Film Music History* (Berkeley: University of California Press, 2011); Martin Miller Marks, *Music and the Silent Film: Contexts and Case Studies, 1895–1924* (New York: Oxford University Press, 1997).

22. Marks, 62.

23. These shellac soundtrack discs, of which the 1926 Vitaphone motion picture sound system was an early example, were the forerunners of the LP. The discs were 16-inch discs played at 33⅓ RPM to match the eleven-minute running time of a standard (1,000 foot) reel of film. They used the same "standard groove" size and single-use steel needles as the 78s that were produced at the same time for home use. Richard Osborne, *Vinyl: A History of the Analogue Record* (New York: Routledge, 2016), 90.

24. Works by Cecile Chaminade (1), Theodora Dutton (pseudonym for Blanche Ray Alden) (3), Alice Hawthorne (1), Lily Strickland (2), and N. Louise Wright (1), are included in *Motion Picture Moods*. Cues from the Sullivan and Hamack collections are in the Silent Film Music Collection, American Music Research Center at the University of Colorado-Boulder. The women represented are Cecile Chaminade (1), Patricia Collinge (2), María Grever (1), and Carmen Santos (1).

25. Silent Film Collection, American Music Research Center, University of Colorado-Boulder.

26. Leonard, "Women at the Pedals."

27. Pray, "Good and Bad M. P. Theaters," *Motion Picture Magazine*, July 1914, 102.

28. "His Three Rules," *Motion Picture News* 9, no. 12 (March 28, 1914), 27.

29. Stanley Todd, "Music and the Photoplay," *Motion Picture Magazine*, March 1914.

30. Jerry Lorenz, *The National Magazine: An Illustrated Monthly* (Bostonian Publishing, 1922), 64.

31. Josephine Burnett Collection, Harry Ransom Center, University of Texas at Austin.

32. Kendra Preston Leonard, "Cue Sheets, Musical Suggestions, and Performance Practices for Hollywood Films, 1908–1927," in *Music and Sound in Silent Film: From the Nickelodeon to the Artist*, ed. Ruth Barton and Simon Trezise (New York: Routledge, 2018), 45–60.

33. Josephine Burnett Collection, Harry Ransom Center, University of Texas-Austin.

34. Leonard, "Cue Sheets, Musical Suggestions, and Performance Practices for Hollywood Films, 1908–1927."

35. "*My Old Kentucky Home* Technical Specifications," IMDb, http://www.imdb.com/title/tt0013421/technical?ref_=tt_dt_spec. Accessed May 18, 2017.

36. A clip of Calamity Jane synched with "Merry Hunting" can be viewed at https://www.youtube.com/watch?v=OMhjfhPsQcQ.

37. "What the Picture Did for Me," *Exhibitors Herald*, December 1921–March 1923.

38. The Majestic Theater (now the Paramount), built in 1915, has a seating capacity of 1,270.

39. Alice Smythe [Burton] Jay, letter, "Music and the Picture," ed. Ernst Luz, *Motion Picture News* 15, no. 8 (February 24, 1917), 1278.

40. Alice S. Burton, "A Woman's Suggestion for Musical Scores" in "Music and the Picture," ed. Ernst Luz, *Motion Picture News* 12, no. 2 (July 17, 1915), 191.

41. Alice S. Burton Jay, letter, "Music and the Picture," *Motion Picture News* 15, no. 8 (February 24, 1917), 1278.

42. Alice Smythe Jay, letter, "Music and the Picture," ed. Ernst Luz, *Motion Picture News* 15, no. 11 (March 17, 1917), 1739.

43. "Artcraft Film to Open Coast Houses: Edward J. Howe has Completed Elaborate Score for Pickford Picture," *Motography* 16, no. 20 (November 11, 1916), 1082. Jay also found several instances of plagiarism in the score, which was marketed as wholly original other than the Woodforde-Finden piece, and not a compilation. Uncredited works included "Serenade" by Drdla and "Dance Parisian" by Lee S. Roberts.

44. Smythe Jay Music Company advertisement, *Motion Picture News* 13, no. 9 (March 4, 1916), 1365.

45. Clarence Sinn, "Musical Accessories to Motion Pictures," *Moving Picture World*, July 11, 1914, 534.

46. Carrie Hetherington, letter, "Music and the Picture," ed. Ernst Luz, *Motion Picture News* 14, no. 9 (November 11, 1916), 3049.

47. Carrie Hetherington, letter, "Music and the Picture," ed. Ernst Luz, *Motion Picture News* 14, no. 9 (November 11, 1916), 3049.

48. Carrie Hetherington, letter, "Music and the Picture," ed. Ernst Luz, *Motion Picture News* 14, no. 15 (October 14, 1916), 2426.

49. Carrie Hetherington, "Lady Audley's Secret," in "Music for the Picture," ed. Clarence E. Sinn, *Moving Picture World* 26, no. 3 (October 16, 1915), 495.

50. "Miller's Theater, Los Angeles," *Moving Picture World* 25, no. 2 (July 10, 1915), 263.

51. These names sometimes cause confusion. The American Photoplayer Company (sometimes written as "American Photo Player Company") manufactured the American Fotoplayer, using an alternate spelling to avoid consumer confusion with other automated instruments known generically as "photoplayers," or even human accompanists, who were also sometimes referred to as "photoplayers."

BIBLIOGRAPHY

"Abandon Orchestras." *Film Daily*, August 28, 1918.

Absher, Amy. *The Black Musician and the White City: Race and Music in Chicago, 1900–1967.* Ann Arbor: University of Michigan Press, 2014.

"Dramatics and Athletics." *New York Age*, October 16, 1913.

Gaines, Kevin K. *Uplifting the Race*. Chapel Hill: University of North Carolina Press, 2012. https://uncpress.org/book/9780807845431/uplifting-the-race/.

Hill, Walter B., Jr. "Institutions of Memory and the Documentation of African Americans in Federal Records." National Archives, August 15, 2016. https://www.archives.gov/publications/prologue/1997/summer/institutions-of-memory.html.

Leonard, Kendra Preston. *Music for the Kingdom of Shadows: Cinema Accompaniment in the Age of Spiritualism.* Humanities Commons, 2019. https://doi.org/10.17613/HWVW-WG90.

Leonard, Kendra Preston. "Cue Sheets, Musical Suggestions, and Performance Practices for Hollywood Films, 1908–1927." In *Music and Sound in Silent Film: From the Nickelodeon to the Artist*, edited by Ruth Barton and Simon Trezise. New York: Routledge, 2018.

Leonard, Kendra Preston. "Women at the Pedals: Female Cinema Musicians during the Great War." In *Over Here, Over There: Transatlantic Conversations on the Music of World War I*, edited by William Brooks, Christina Bashford, and Gayle Magee. Urbana: University of Illinois Press, 2018.

Lorenz, Jerry. *The National Magazine: An Illustrated Monthly*. Bostonian Publishing, 1922.

"The Manilla Theater." *Indianapolis Recorder*, May 24, 1913.

Morgan-Ellis, Esther M. *Everybody Sing! Community Singing in the American Picture Palace*. Athens: University of Georgia Press, 2018.

Peyton, Dave. "The Musical Bunch: How to Play Picture Music." *Chicago Defender (National Edition)*, August 13, 1927, sec. The Defender's Movie and Stage Department.

Schenbeck, Lawrence. *Racial Uplift and American Music, 1878–1943*. Jackson: University Press of Mississippi, 2012.

Shryock, Henry S., and Jacob S. Siegel. *The Methods and Materials of Demography*. US Department of Commerce, Bureau of the Census, 1980.

Sinn, Clarence. "Musical Accessories to Motion Pictures." *Moving Picture World*, July 11, 1914.

Spivey, Victoria. *The Blues Is Life*. LP, Folkways Records, 1976. https://folkways-media.si.edu/liner_notes/folkways/FW03541.pdf.

Todd, Stanley. "Music and the Photoplay." *Motion Picture Magazine*, March 1914.

"Union Scale of Wages and Hours of Labor, Union Scale of Wages and Hours of Labor, May 15, 1921: Bulletin of the United States Bureau of Labor Statistics, No. 302 | Fraser | St. Louis Fed." Accessed November 2, 2017. https://fraser.stlouisfed.org/scribd/?item_id=492986&filepath=/files/docs/publications/bls/bls_0302_1922.pdf&start_page=68.

Walton, Lester A. "Music and the Stage." *New York Age*, March 25, 1909.

Chapter 4

Listen to the "Poor Girl Story": (Re)Considering Southern Femininity in Early Old-Time Music

—April L. Prince

Rosa Lee Carson was born in Atlanta in 1909. She started buck-and-wing dancing alongside her famous Georgia fiddling father, Fiddlin' John Carson, when she was only seven years old. By fourteen she was proficient on the banjo and guitar, by 1925 she was accompanying her father on his records and making a few solo cuts of her own, and by the time she graduated high school she was a regular member of her father's recording and touring bands.[1] Carson's first solo entry in OKeh Records Old Time catalog was in June 1925, meaning that she was one of the earliest women to record country music. But she was not the first.[2] A year earlier, fifteen-year-old Roba Stanley made a few solo cuts for OKeh during a location recording in Atlanta.[3] Stanley was also the daughter of a famous Georgia fiddler, Robert Stanley, and like Carson, she frequently collaborated and recorded as part of her father's ensemble. Her foray into the commercial music world was brief but legendary.

Stanley recorded barely a year after Fiddlin' John's 1923 inaugural Old-Time record, and Carson remained an important fixture as an ensemble and solo recording artist up until the 1930s. While it is undeniable that these women were a radical, formative presence within the early history of country music, their musical contributions remain thoroughly unexplored. This chapter seeks to understand their position at the vanguard of commercial country music by situating a few of their songs within the larger contexts of the regional and cultural spaces they inhabited and represented. In particular, I investigate various facets of their performative identities by exploring their placement within the segregated soundscapes that defined Old-time music; their compliance with constructions of Southern white femininity; and their musical friction with the revisionist histories that have morally whitewashed women's roles in early country music. I then read "Little Frankie," "The Poor Girl Story," and "My Man's a Jolly Railroad Man" as songs that both uphold and abandon expectations regarding early white women's participation within Old-time music and the South.

Carson and Stanley emerged on the commercial recording scene precisely at a time in which competing ideologies of Southern music and identity were established through the powerful and enduring medium of recorded sound. As Karl Hagstrom Miller argues, the distinct marketing categories of Race and Old-time records were the result of a tenuous fusion of the commercial record industry's expansion into the Jim Crow South and the rising influence of folklore studies. Both paradigms—the recording industry and the power of folk authenticity—denied the many points of musical overlap that had long existed across the color line in the South and between Southern artists and popular music. Preserving and fragmenting distinct strands of vernacular culture, however, also meant establishing distinct strands of Southern identity along racial, gender, and class lines. Race records largely restricted their artists to the blues to reinforce certain kinds of Southern Black racial identity, while Old-time music traded in constructions of rural, white hillbilly identity across countless musical genres: blues, pop tunes, traditional ballads, minstrel songs, "coon songs," and religious numbers. White Southern artists would modify all kinds of mainstream popular tunes to fit their own sense of Southern identity.[4] This music was in part defined by its heterogeneity of musical source material, even as it sounded a kind of homogeneity.

Southern artists of the early twentieth century thus continued to engage with popular and folk songs that had long circulated throughout the South, while also sustaining the nation's continued fascination with the region. To be sure, the South of the early twentieth century was a site of contesting narratives—all of which were debated nationally throughout academic and popular discourses. Some scholars of the era sought to decry and reform the region's vast poverty in their brutal critiques of the barbaric, rural, and diseased "Problem South"; while others celebrated the progress, modernity, and industrialization of the "New South"; revisionist histories—springing up almost immediately after the Civil War—continued to re-form the region's past into a kind of romanticized nostalgia for the racial and social order of the Old South.[5] For Southern white women, these paradigms would offer social opportunities and barriers, many of which were negotiated through the lens of traditional gender roles. On the one hand, the sacred cultural icon of the white Southern lady—defined by her graciousness, purity, gentility, and piousness—"set the standard of behavior for generations of white southern women."[6] Her symbolism endured well into the twentieth century and cast a wide shadow across all kinds of class, racial, and musical lines. On the other hand, the rural and mountain woman—defined by her primitive isolation—lived in an imagined space where gender roles were not only from an earlier era, but also clearly defined. She accepted her lot in life and "contented herself with weaving, spinning, suckling babes, and singing."[7]

Both notions of white femininity emphasized powerful connections to the past, which women would sometimes use to their advantage. Elite Southern women used commemoration of the Lost Cause to form new, more powerful public roles as they embraced "the mantle of 'guardians of the past' to a degree without precedence in the region's history."[8] Instrumental in erecting Confederate monuments and memorials, these women also founded and populated patriotic and hereditary societies like the Daughters of the Confederacy.[9] Within the domestic sphere, the conflation of the past with the present was also an essential source of the Southern white woman's power.[10] Rural, mountain women, however, would come to embody and even idle in an isolated past, as reformers struggled to deal with the "Caucasian problem" within the Problem South.[11] Similar to the cultural strategies that reformed the history of the Southern plantation into a place of refined gentility, Appalachian poor whites were situated as the harbingers of "racial purity and old-fashioned gender roles . . . [ideals] that promised to remedy countless urban cares and confusions."[12] For those who expressed anxiety about the floundering state of modern masculinity, this gendered mythology would provide rationale to restore and sustain Southern virility.[13]

These versions of Southern femininity would reverberate throughout popular music, especially with the establishment of the musical color line. Segregated sound eventually reflected the segregationist ideology that purported connections between moralism and racial and gender identities.[14] Within a musical space that "[drew] moral distinctions based on race and [reinforced] gender stereotypes . . . commercial country music was politicized, and decency itself became the product."[15] These connections between race and gender, which depended on white women's moral virtue within the bounds of Southern womanhood, would continue to police and circumscribe the limited role women played in the genre. By the late 1930s or so, the country music woman would largely embrace and perpetuate the moral whitewashing of the segregated soundscape; she would learn to keep "her morals high, her skirts low, and her Christian virtue front and center."[16] Country music's newly established decency hinged on a constructed racial identity within music—one that celebrated white feminine morality and excised Black depravity.

The reformation of country music as a site of moral decency, however, denied the sexual content and interracial nature of early Old-time music.[17] As Rebecca Thomas notes, "the sexuality of . . . early country stars was undeniable, the scandals were often true, and the intangibles between Black and white southern men and women were legitimate."[18] Early catalogs were filled with all kinds of blues, for example, as record companies oversaw integrated field recording sessions with various groups—Black gospel quartets, blues singers, white string bands, and fiddles—trading musical ideas as they did turns on the microphone. Early recorded music reflected the cultural exchange at the heart of the interracial music of the South.[19] Given the ambiguity of Old-time repertoire—and the sheer difficulty in controlling the meanings of sounds—these racial and gendered musical boundaries were not only spurious but also unstable.[20]

Rosa Lee Carson and Roba Stanley thus worked within an ambiguous complex of cultural politics that reverberated throughout the South and early Old-time music. While these paradoxical categories of musical and Southern identity would influence women's participation in the genre, even more importantly, they have shaped how historians have subsequently made sense of their contributions. Rather than considering their music as examples of cultural interest or critique, scholars have largely dismissed these early songs as sites of uninteresting conformity or stereotype or because the identities within the music seem so unstable that it is seemingly impossible to make sense of it all.[21] Most potently, historians have long positioned early Old-time women performers as compliant with certain ideals of femininity within the ideology of segregated sound. Of course, many Old-time musicians upheld notions of Southern womanhood because the commercial market demanded it; yet within the inherently diverse Southern region, song subject matter, and soundscape that defined early country music, we can also hear how the relatively few female singers worked within these notions with nuance. In my view, the ambiguity around early Old-time music's eclectic and shifting musical boundaries gave Carson and Stanley a musical range that afforded them the freedom to sing some "strikingly feminist stuff, even by today's standards."[22] They could draw on all kinds of musical sources to express a dynamic, ambivalent, and even unstable kind of Southern womanhood that did not fit as firmly within the ideals of Southern femininity, segregated soundscapes, or country music decency.

(RE)CONSIDERING THEIR REPERTOIRE

As noted earlier, Carson and Stanley's repertoire is varied, even though their solo output is relatively small. Between 1925 and 1931 Carson recorded around sixteen tracks, four of which were unissued. She also played on many of her father's records and starred in about eighteen rural drama recordings. While Carson certainly cultivated her comedic hillbilly persona, "Moonshine Kate," in these musical skits, her solo output intersects with and destabilizes that character in intriguing ways. Set in the north Georgia mountains, Kate was a high-spirited daughter who kept moonshine pints and snuff in her bosom, cracked jokes about housework, and comically defended her moonshining father. Stanley, hailed as America's first country sweetheart, recorded only around ten sides that featured her as lead soloist. She was married within a year and left the industry.

As expected, their output included British and American ballads: Carson recorded songs like "The Dying Hobo," "Little Mary Phagan," and "Raggedy

Riley," and Stanley's best-selling effort was her version of the familiar "Devilish Mary." Carson also cut a Tin Pan Alley song, "The Lone Child" (more well known as "If I Only Had a Home Sweet Home"), and a few blues tunes such as "Are You Going to Leave the Old Home" (a version of "You're Going to Leave the Old Home, Jim"), "Texas Blues" (the Jimmie Rodgers standard "T for Texas"), and "The Last Dollar is Gone" (also called "Don't Let Your Deal Go Down"). Stanley's blues consisted of "All Night Long" and "Little Frankie" (an American classic ballad-turned-blues song often called "Frankie and Johnny"). Minstrel tunes and "coon songs" were staples of the fiddling contests that Carson and Stanley frequented, and Stanley recorded versions of "Mister Chicken" (an adaptation of "Chicken Don't Roost Too High"), "Nellie Gray," and "Whoa Mule," while Carson covered one of the staples of her father's repertoire, "Log Cabin Home."[23] Of particular note are their recordings of newly composed songs, such as Carson's versions of "The Poor Girl Story" and "My Man's a Jolly Railroad Man." Stanley's "A Single Life" stands out as a unique self-composition, which is often discussed as a curious, rule-breaking, and even feminist song.[24] They, like their fathers and other early Old-time artists, came ready to play anything and everything.

The ambiguity of their repertoire is front and center in their versions of songs that were, as Charles Wolfe puts it, "an odd mixture of the new and the old."[25] An empowering and flexible approach within the confines of early commercial recordings, many Old-time musicians recorded well-known tunes but changed them to fit their own sense of self. While I am most interested in songs that were newly written within the context of their recording careers, I would like to begin my analyses with a captivating example of this commercial strategy. In 1925 OKeh released Stanley's version of the classic "Little Frankie"—a well-known ballad-blues song recorded in the later 1920s by the likes of Mississippi John Hurt, Charley Patton, Jimmie Rodgers, and many others.[26] In attending to the changes Stanley made to the song's narration and musical stylings, I hope to peel back a few analytical layers that uphold and question the expectations of the Problem South and its oft-associated rural feminine identity.

The song tells the story of a deceptive lover and brutal vengeance; as she sings throughout in the refrain, "he's my man, but he's done me wrong." Stanley's version starts unusually, as Frankie wakes up to hear the dog barking and Alvin leaving. Hurt and Patton's songs start with a declaration that Frankie was a "good girl," while Rodgers emphasizes the love between the "sweethearts." Stanley's, however, focuses solely on her suspicion and intuition from the song's outset.

> Frankie woke up one morning,
> She heard old Rover bark,
> I bet you half a hundred,
> Poor Alvin's in the dark.

Frankie then heads to the bartender for a "glass of beer," and he confirms her hunch. "He hadn't been left an hour ago with a gal named Alice Fry." In calculated revenge, Frankie looks for Alvin "with a forty-one in hand," finds and shoots him "turned and [running]" three gruesome times, and ultimately kills him while declaring, "you're my man, but you're about to die." While the story of the song is relatively similar across most versions, Stanley's ending sings Frankie's acquittal. Hurt similarly sings the murder as justified, Patton's tells of Frankie hanged, and Rodgers sings of her sentence to the electric chair. In her version, Stanley goes farther; the final verse not only sees Frankie freed, but her murderous inclination encouraged.

> And when they tried little Frankie,
> They placed her on the stand,
> Says, "Frankie, you're a free woman,
> Go kill you another man."

While traditional ballads had long told morbid tales of broken promises, revenge, and death, Stanley's low, haunting voice, muted and driving guitar, poignant harmonica accompaniment, and constant switch to first person throughout results in a powerful rendering. Coming from a young woman of fifteen years old, it sounds almost surreal. The song gains in tempo and strength as Stanley tells the tale, showing the increased determination of Frankie—a fortitude for which she is ultimately rewarded.

This old story sung from the perspective of a young woman seems decidedly modern. Stanley embodies feminine independence and danger—a warning her commercial recording exacerbates. This song also possibly intersects with the various stereotypes of "manly gun-toting women and wild mountain girls" that were circulating in pop culture in the early decades of the twentieth century.[27] As Anthony Harkins outlines, this trend exposed the anxieties of women's increasing social power through the lens of mountain violence, feminine deviance, and sexual desire. The feminine aberrations in the scenarios were short-lived, however, as the leading men eventually conquered the mountain women and reasserted "civilized" social and gender order. But just as audience members left satisfied with the restoration of "proper" social order, they also left exhilarated by the possibilities of transgressing social and gender norms. In Stanley's song, her deviance is rewarded in the court of civilized law and order.[28] So, even if Frankie personifies a version of femininity that could serve as a warning to the damage that resulted when traditional social orders were upended, the warning in Stanley's version ends decisively with a kind of state-sanctioned feminine modernity. Brutal emasculation, however, is the cost. This cost seems to confirm and intensify the anxiety that was swirling around Southern white masculinity.

From the "pale, underdeveloped, feeble bodies" of the Problem South to the effeminate urbanite of the modern New South, Southern white masculinity was in crisis.[29] Given that Old-time music was often celebrated by its practitioners and listeners as a balm to bolster traditional notions of Southern masculinity, it is fascinating that Stanley's song does little to refute or pacify those anxieties.[30]

In exacerbating these tensions, audiences could hear Stanley as Frankie, or even put themselves in her position. While she sings with an almost lackadaisical candor that both supports and resists her conflation with the character in her song, an Old-time musician's uneasy connection to and even embodiment of the tales she sang about "was the result of the evolving relationship between the minstrel and the folkloric paradigms, between the notion that genuine music was an act and the insistence that it was not."[31] The Southern music market of the early twentieth century increasingly interpreted Southern artists as folk artists, which created an ever-fragile fusion between the singer, song subject matter, and listener. Under the folkloric paradigm, it is very possible that sometimes listeners heard Stanley and Carson as singing constructed personal truths, even as these truths abounded with all kinds of contradictions.[32]

These early Old-time and blues records are also unique in their desire to sound an almost personal interaction between the singer and the Southern listener. From extensive spoken dialogues as preludes, interludes, and postludes; to the exhaustive recordings of familiar folk songs; to the fascinating drama recordings that included substantial music—this repertoire included idiosyncratic, participatory musical elements that invited and encouraged listeners to become a part of the song. In John Minton's view, "performers and audiences understood each other not as disembodied strangers separated by an ostensibly impersonal medium, but as known or knowable persons whose common backgrounds gave them a very real stake in one another's personal experiences."[33]

In her unique personalization of this well-known tale, Stanley can be heard in all kinds of ways: from storyteller to protagonist to caricature.[34] Her version of the song embraces these various possibilities with ease, as she creates a kind dynamic feminine agency that listeners could engage with on their own terms. In singing this old song, Stanley could get away with a lot—this was a well-established, familiar tune, after all. Listeners would have been acquainted with its general narrative and themes and probably sang versions of their own at home. To change the song to fit oneself would be routine. In destabilizing traditional notions of gender by changing the stories and perspectives within consistent performing conventions and Problem South identities, Stanley safely challenged normative notions of Southern white femininity, while also satisfying the expectations of Northern and Southern listeners.

This kind of modern, potentially deviant femininity would suffuse Carson's later songs. In "The Poor Girl Story" and "My Man's a Jolly Railroad Man" she seems to deepen what Pamela Fox calls the "shifting intersections of whiteness and Blackness, femininity and masculinity, and low and "respectable" classes" at the core of Old-time music.[35] Both songs emphasize not only Carson's professional independence and viability within the genre, but also how she worked to stay relevant within country music's ever-shifting parameters and subject matters. The femininities that she expresses support her professionalism and her distinction from elite, middle-class, and even rural feminine identities.

Carson's independence within the New South is front and center in her 1930 OKeh cut of "The Poor Girl Story." Written by Carson J. Robison in 1929, he recorded the first version for Victor in September under the title "The Railroad Boomer."[36] While there were about fourteen recorded versions of this tune between 1929 and 1941, Carson was the only artist who altogether changed the title to fit her own perspective—a perspective that immediately underscored her social class and femininity. In her version, she celebrates her modernity and independence, even as she frames the song from the point of view of an old, weary traveler who sings a message of pity and warning:

> Come and gather all around me
> Listen to my tale of woe
> Got some good advice to give you
> Lots of things you oughta know.
>
> Take a tip from one who's traveled
> Never start to ramblin' around
> Your liable to get the wanderin' fever
> Never wanna settle down

Couched within these opening lines, Carson expertly mediates her expression to moderate the threat of independent womanhood. For that matter, the past she recollects in this song is decisively modern. Her "tale of woe" hinges on her musical professionalism and its empowering independence, and on one of the most potent symbols of modernity: the train. This song disconnects her femininity completely from Old South imagery and that of the "hillbilly" tradition. Instead, she embraces the paradoxical power of a modernized South that pervaded the blues and later Old-time repertory.

Throughout the song, she transforms the concept of a "railroad boomer" to fit her own feminine perspective. She wanders the continent traveling everywhere and longs to be buried next to the railroad. The train takes her far outside the South, as she journeys "from Maine to California" and "ends up in Mexico." While she clearly has a chance to marry, and "settle down for life" the "Georgia train" calls to her in a way she cannot deny. As her second verse outlines:

I met a little boy in Frisco
I asked him if he had a wife
Told him I was tired of roamin'
I wanna settle down for life

Then I heard the whistle blowin'
I knew it was the Georgia train
I left him standin' by the railroad
I'll never see that man again

Carson describes the man she does come upon in Frisco a diminutive "little boy," and she decides she should marry him. She quickly rejects conventional domesticity, however, because of her professional, musical travels, and the results—especially the way she sings them—seem nothing like regret. Her past is one of modernity, freedom, and movement; even though it has left her alone, she remains committed to her professional freedom.

Although she changes very little text from Robison's original, Carson dramatically transforms its performing conventions. She weaves a musical soundscape that contains a rustic feel but also showcases her musical ability in a frank, sincere way. The simplicity of the fiddle and guitar coupled with her high, clear voice shares characteristics with the rural blues, and yet her version contains none of the novelty of some hillbilly tunes (like the inclusion of trains whistling, chickens clucking, or hound dogs howling in the background). Her thin voice stretches for the higher notes, and at times she rushes to include all the necessary syllables as if her Southern drawl gets in her way a bit. Her straightforward, sparse instrumentals and other performative choices differ dramatically from Robison's Victor recording. His more polished version opens with train whistle effects, which intrude throughout the song. Robison's robust accompanying ensemble features a steel guitar, guitar, coronet, clarinets, and vocal harmony throughout by Frank Luther. His style emphasizes the hectic, populated, excitement of train travel as the life of a "boomer" or bum. Carson's take seems to accentuate this excitement differently; she declares her independence and freedom by celebrating her solitude. In the context of a rapidly modernizing world, she finds her own place.

The codes of white feminine morality are even more confounded in Carson's "My Man's a Jolly Railroad Man." Recorded in October 1931, her version is the only known recording of this song, whose origins are still somewhat mysterious.[37] Similar to "The Poor Girl Story," this song revels in an ambiguity related to romanticized, almost sacred modernity alongside secular, sexual freedom. These jarring juxtapositions speak to the paradoxes of Southern progress and problems in immediate ways, and yet center around a distinctive white feminine perspective. Chronicling her life with a "jolly railroad man," the song emphasizes the power of various kinds of technology that cuts through "hill and dale"; comforts with a longing for the nostalgic "home sweet home" "as soon as you start to mourn"; and calls attention to her "railroad man's" masculine virility through this powerful "engine" and "throttle stick," and even his ability to satisfy her with "his head out the cab."

> An engineer is what he is,
> For him I'll go the limit
> So try and beat him if you can
> His engine's never timid.
>
> His hand upon the throttle stick,
> His head out the cab.

In comparison with the two other songs, which show fractured or nonexistent relationships with impotent or diminutive men, this song celebrates his sexual expertise and her commitment. The chorus reiterates throughout, "If you want a better man, you'll have to go to heaven." This domesticity, however, occurs firmly within a new, modern South, as "telephone poles" dot the landscape and "look like teeth in a comb" because of the power and speed generated by the engine's "red hot dome." The song concludes with this paradox of modernity and nature as paradise:

> O'er hill and dale, we roll with speed
> By streams like White [Street] River.
> A pair of wings is all we need
> To take our fare to heaven.

The trend that had long suffused Old-time music—as a nostalgic romanticization of the rural to counter modern ills—has been completely reconfigured and detached from that imagery.

Carson's performative choices also speak to the changing soundscape of Old-time music, which had gone crazy for Jimmie Rodgers's yodel and his "singing brakeman" persona. The yodel has a long history within popular music and was a hallmark of interracial Southern music culture.[38] Rodgers made it one of his musical signatures when he burst on the scene in 1927, and his blue yodel was widely imitated throughout the genre. Carson embraces the popularity of this sound as she sings with a gentle, note-bending yodel and solo guitar. She also slows the tempo toward the end of each phrase. When coupled with her lilting moan and pronounced drawl, this technique gives the song a dramatic, performative edge. The train, an incredibly powerful symbol throughout blues and Old-time music, also encapsulated this diverse musical culture. With its unclear segregated "spatial" boundaries and consumer-centered trade, the Southern train in the late nineteenth and early twentieth centuries had become a site of constantly destabilized and restabilized racial and class identities in the early Jim Crow South.[39] The volatility of the railroad, and its symbolism, allowed all kinds of musical artists to use it to their own ends. Carson was no exception. In so doing, she both upends and expands the boundaries of her professional repertoire, while also exposing the fragility of segregated soundscapes.[40] And, like many other Old-time and blues men and women, her musicianship gave her a way out of poverty and oppression, with the train as a symbolic metaphor for freedom.[41]

Her desire to escape from and celebrate the modernity of the New South subtly challenges the connections that white femininity had long cultivated with the past. As discussed earlier, Southern white femininity across the region varied widely and yet often emphasized connections to the past. Carson's class ambiguity, however, positioned her on the outskirts of these trends. She was neither elite, middle class, or even completely rural. Carson was a child of the working poor who grew up in the Fulton Mill Village. These working-class white neighborhoods were home to a "poor, closely knit, clannish, and loyal" group made up of "all the mountain people who came to Atlanta to work in the mills in 1885 (when the Exposition Mill started) and all their descendants."[42] Her class perspective rises to the fore with songs that emphasize her disconnect from and nostalgia for a revisionist Southern past. In her railroad tunes, Carson romanticizes a modern past via a detailed description of her professional travels and through an explicit invocation of her poor, white girl identity. Her nostalgia is tied to the train and her musical mobility. By embracing modernity, Carson subtly infers her denial of both upper- and lower-class white mores—strictures that policed femininity through its connection to the past. A modern past becomes the space wherein she can renegotiate her own position within society, even as she pleads with us to "listen to a poor girl story, listen to the things [she says]." She concludes the song with a warning (one that she herself refuses to heed, however) as she "hears another train a-coming, and [she'll] soon be on [her] way."

While "Little Frankie," "The Poor Girl Story," and "My Man's a Jolly Railroad Man" intersect with and uphold certain expectations of the South and white Southern femininity, at times they also resist and subtly destabilize these ideals. Most importantly, these songs position Roba Stanley and Rosa Lee Carson as full-fledged professionals within the early Old-time music soundscape. Stanley transformed a popular folk song into a provocative commentary on feminine and masculine identities, while Carson embraced the various trends of the genre to situate herself more firmly as a professional. Stanley engaged with well-worn stereotypes of the Problem South and rural identity and yet also refuted them. By incorporating romanticized aspects of modernity, Carson expanded the parameters of "Moonshine Kate" and asserted her own unique class identity. As white women throughout the New South increased their social and domestic power through a connection to the Southern past, Carson created a nostalgia outside of those parameters. Both Carson and Stanley complicate ideas of independence, sexual desire, and Southern caricature while refusing to shy away from challenging Southern masculinity in its various guises. Their music provides an interesting window into the diverse history of the genre and women's long-fraught presence. While these identities are certainly unstable and ambiguous at times, they situate Stanley and Carson as core contributors to the early country-music sound as opposed to mere outliers. Indeed, the ambivalence of the South across these examples seems to confirm what Edward Ayers has long declared: "The very story of the South is a story of unresolvable identity, unsettled and restless, unsure and defensive. The South . . . was not a fixed, known, and unified place, but rather a place of constant movement, struggle, and negotiation."[43] Cultural products reveal both the restlessness of the region, and the power of musical expressions to mean many different things to many different people.

NOTES

1. See Charles Wolfe, "'And No Man Shall Control Me': The Strange Case of Roba Stanley, Country's First Woman Recording Star," in *The Women of Country Music: A Reader*, ed. Charles K. Wolfe and James E. Akenson (Lexington: University Press of Kentucky, 2003), 18–29.

2. Aside from Eva Davis and Samantha Bumgarner's 1924 Columbia recordings, Stanley and Carson cut some of the earliest records in April 1924 and June 1925.

3. For an overview of early Old-time location recordings, see Tony Russell, "Music on Location: 'Field Recording' before Bristol," *Popular Music* 26, no. 1 (2007): 23–31.

4. See Karl Hagstrom Miller, "Old Time Pop Songs," in *Segregating Sound: Inventing Folk and Pop Music in the Age of Jim Crow* (Durham, NC: Duke University Press, 2010), 227–40.

5. The Old South references the antebellum (often romanticized) pre–Civil War South. The New South refers to the post-Reconstruction South. The Problem South refers to the early twentieth-century discourse mythologizing the region as culturally backward, plagued by disease, and economically stifled. For an overview of these topics, see W. Fitzhugh Brundage, *The Southern Past: A Clash of Race and Memory* (Cambridge, MA: Belknap Press of Harvard University, 2005); James C. Cobb, *Away Down South: A History of Southern Identity* (Oxford: Oxford University Press, 2005); Don H. Doyle and Larry J. Griffin, ed., *The South as an American Problem* (Athens: University of Georgia Press, 1995); Leigh Anne Duck, *The Nation's Region: Southern Modernism, Segregation, and U.S. Nationalism* (Athens: University of Georgia Press, 2006); Tara McPherson, *Reconstructing Dixie: Race, Gender, and Nostalgia in the Imagined South* (Durham, NC: Duke University Press, 2003); and Natalie J. Ring, *The Problem South: Region, Empire, and the New Liberal State, 1880–1930* (Athens: University of Georgia Press, 2012).

6. Anastatia Sims, *The Power of Femininity in the New South: Women's Organizations and Politics in North Carolina, 1880–1930* (Columbia: University of South Carolina Press, 1997), 6.

7. Gavin James Campbell, *Music and the Making of a New South* (Chapel Hill: University of North Carolina Press, 2004), 116.

8. Brundage, *The Southern Past*, 15.

9. See Brundage, "A Duty Peculiarly Fitting to Women," in *The Southern Past*, 12–54.

10. Grace Elizabeth Hale outlines the connection between the households of the Old and New South thusly: "Profound differences existed between the relatively self-sufficient agrarianism of the Old South and the more urban and consumer-oriented domesticity of the new. White southern men and women of the rising middle class, however, insisted on conflating the plantation household and the post-Reconstruction white home in order to ground their own cultural authority within the power—which by the late nineteenth century had grown to mythical proportions—of the plantation-based planter class." Grace Elizabeth Hale, *Making Whiteness: The Culture of Segregation in the South, 1890–1940* (New York: Vintage Books, 1998), 87.

11. Generally speaking, the *Caucasian problem* refers to "the mass of uneducated, diseased poor whites that seemed to have been left behind during the wave of industrial progress sweeping the region." Natalie J. Ring, *The Problem South*, 138. For a more expansive discussion, see Ring, "The Evolution of the Caucasian Problem," in *The Problem South*, 138–47.

12. Campbell, *Music and the Making of a New South*, 116. See also Bill Malone, *Singing Cowboys and Musical Mountaineers* (Athens: University of Georgia Press, 2003), 76.

13. As Campbell notes, "For those restless about the state of modern masculinity, the contrast between highland and urban men could hardly have been more telling. City men lay waste their powers in a daily round of getting and spending. Their luxurious surroundings sapped them of their independence, resourcefulness, and virility." Campbell, *Music and the Making of a New South*, 112–13.

14. Sims argues that "The lady was more than a role model for southern women; she also served as a potent political symbol. At the turn of the century, white supremacists invoked her name to justify segregation, disfranchisement, and lynching." Sims, *The Power of Femininity in the New South*, 2.

15. Rebecca Thomas, "The Cow That's Ugly Has the Sweetest Milk," in *The Women of Country Music: A Reader*, ed. Charles K. Wolfe and James E. Akenson (Lexington: University Press of Kentucky, 2003), 132. See also Richard A. Peterson, *Creating Country Music: Fabricating Authenticity* (Chicago: University of Chicago Press, 1997); Pamela Fox, *Natural Acts: Gender, Race, and Rusticity in Country Music* (Ann Arbor: University of Michigan Press, 2009); Wayne W. Daniel, *Pickin' on Peachtree: A History of Country Music in Atlanta, Georgia* (Urbana: University of Illinois Press, 1990).

16. Thomas, "The Cow That's Ugly," 142.

17. For some examples, listen to Jimmie Davis's 1935 "Jelly Roll Blues," Jimmie Rodgers's 1930 "Blue Yodel No. 8," Uncle Dave Macon's 1924 "Keep My Skillet Good and Greasy," and Fiddlin' John Carson's 1924 "Papa's Billy Goat."

18. Thomas, "The Cow That's Ugly," 144.

19. Miller, *Segregating Sound*, 233. As Miller notes, however, white musicians had greater freedom to record blues, while African American artists were rarely able to record white styles. See also Anthony Harkins, *Hillbilly: A Cultural History of an American Icon* (Oxford: Oxford University Press, 2004), 75.

20. As Eric Nunn eloquently puts it, "sounds constantly leak through the racial barriers such institutions place around and between them." Eric Nunn, *Sounding the Color Line: Music and Race in the Southern Imagination* (Athens: University of Georgia Press, 2015), 5.

21. Carson and Stanley appear in many histories of early country music, and yet their biographies and musical contributions have become relatively staid. Their careers are often

oversimplified within the early Old-time music trade, and their repertoire is discussed very generally. For example, Jeffrey Lange argues that "female country music performers projected an image that adhered more to prevailing stereotypes than estimable representations. Country music songs performed by male and female performers in the 1920s and 1930s accentuated the preconception of women as virtuous homebodies providing a refuge from the corrupting influences of a secular society. The infamous tribute to mother reflected this projection of women more than anything else, as did songs that placed females' roles squarely within the boundaries of southern womanhood." Jeffrey J. Lange, *Smile When You Call Me a Hillbilly: Country Music's Struggle for Respectability 1939–1954* (Athens: University of Georgia Press, 2004), 13.

22. Mary A. Bufwack and Robert K. Oermann, *Finding Her Voice: The Saga of Women in Country Music* (New York: Crown, 1993), 68.

23. I have been unable to find a recording of this song, as it was unissued. It could be a version of "The Little Old Cabin in the Lane" or "The Little Old Log Cabin in the Lane." These songs tell a story of an old slave looking back on his enslavement with nostalgic longing. This song might also be a version of "In My Old Cabin Home," which hears an old minstrel performer reflecting on the end of his career and returning home. Interestingly for my arguments here, this song is perhaps one of the only across their catalogs that describes a longing for a romanticized, pre-industrial South through the eyes of an old slave or minstrel. More pointedly, it is one of the only songs that contains a kind of imaginative space where the "Southern lady" or "Southern belle" character of white femininity reigned. Of course, these songs had long been at the core of the minstrel show and flourished throughout early twentieth-century recordings. Songs like "Arkansas Blues" and "Down Home Blues" are explicit remnants of this trend and were recorded by the likes of Mamie Smith, Mary Stafford, and Ethel Waters in 1921. See Gene Wiggins, *Fiddlin' Georgia Crazy: Fiddlin' John Carson, His Real World, and the World of His Songs* (Urbana: University of Illinois Press, 1987), 220–24. See also Miller, "Race Records and Old-Time Music," in *Segregating Sound*, 187–214.

24. See Wolfe, "'And No Man Shall Control Me,'" 18–29.

25. Wolfe, "'And No Man Shall Control Me,'" 20.

26. Roba Stanley and Bill Patterson, "Little Frankie" (OKeh 40436, January 9, 1925). https://www.youtube.com/watch?v=Z2JVvSWC7R4.

27. Harkins, *Hillbilly*, 59.

28. Harkins, *Hillbilly*, 59.

29. In the context of the Problem South, "descriptions of diseased bodies in the South consistently emphasized the themes of degradation and emasculation. . . . Americans viewed a virile masculine body not only as the key to economic productivity but also as a prerequisite for success in politics and imperialist ventures. The call to take up the 'strenuous life,' best embodied in President Theodore Roosevelt's Rough Riders, linked nationalism, racial imperialism, and manhood. National unity required a virile American manhood ready for military ventures abroad and a vigorous life at home." Ring, *The Problem South*, 78–79.

30. See Campbell, "The Georgia Old-Time Fiddling Contest," in *Music and the Making of a New South*, 100–142.

31. Miller, *Segregating Sound*, 216. Of course, this connection had long been a standard on the minstrel stage as performers put on and took off all kinds of masks. The folkloric paradigm, however, reshaped ideas of authenticity. Under this new ideal, there were no masks and artists were more immediately intertwined with the folk they sang about in their songs.

32. See Simon Frith, "Genre Rules," in *Performing Rites: On the Value of Popular Music* (Cambridge, MA: Harvard University Press, 1996), 75–95.

33. John Minton, *78 Blues: Folksongs and Phonographs in the American South* (Jackson: University Press of Mississippi, 2008), 35.

34. As Minton writes, "a folk tradition usually embodies an entire range of performance, stretching from mere reports, through differing degrees of total involvement, to self-reflective irony or self-conscious parody." John Minton, *78 Blues*, 36.

35. Pamela Fox, *Natural Acts: Gender, Race, and Rusticity in Country Music* (Ann Arbor: University of Michigan Press, 2009), 6.

36. Rosa Lee Carson, "The Poor Girl Story" (OKeh 45547, December 9, 1930). https://www.youtube.com/watch?v=pPq0NM-5UGA.

37. Rosa Lee Carson, "My Man's a Jolly Railroad Man" (OKeh 45555, October 30, 1931). https://www.youtube.com/watch?v=oCh-Gg7QiNA.

38. It is important to note that while many African American musicians also sang Jimmie Rodgers's songs, they were unable to release their own recorded versions of his blue yodel. Indeed, the yodel had a long history within popular music on the minstrel and the vaudeville stages. Early African American blues had also featured this technique. For a more detailed discussion of the history of the yodel, its presence throughout American popular music, and its interracial history, see Miller, *Segregating Sound*, 238–39.

39. See Hale, "Training the Ground of Difference," in *Making Whiteness*, 125–38.

40. As with many white women performers before and after her, Carson's transgressive femininity intersected with the sounds and imagery of blues culture and the perceived deviancy of Blackness. Cultural appropriation is never benign. This discussion is somewhat outside the immediate scope of this paper, even as it lurks in the background.

41. For Carson, her musicianship gave her an escape from the factories. As with many other blues and Old-time musicians, to become a professional was to assert independence and escape conditions that were untenable. Wiggins outlines, "Before John left the Exposition Mill in 1911, there were Clarence, Mary, Maggie, Horace, Grady, Mamie, Lou, Clyde, and Rosa Lee. The four oldest had worked in the mill, and Grady and Mamie eventually worked in Fulton Bag and Cotton Mill. Clyde, Rosa Lee, and a still later child, John L., were to escape working in the cotton mills. Horace had started working at Exposition at age 9." Cotton mill hours were six to six, and John Carson's children worked as floor sweepers and doffers. See Wiggins, *Fiddlin' Georgia Crazy*, 22. For a discussion of additional context regarding cotton mill conditions and the mills' place in the national imagination, see Ring, "White Slavery in the Southern Mills," in *The Problem South*, 147–52.

42. Wiggins, *Fiddlin' Georgia Crazy*, xiv.

43. Edward Ayers, *What Caused the Civil War? Reflections on the South and Southern History* (New York: W. W. Norton, 2005), 62–63.

BIBLIOGRAPHY

Ayers, Edward. *What Caused the Civil War? Reflections on the South and Southern History.* New York: W. W. Norton, 2005.

Brundage, W. Fitzhugh. *The Southern Past: A Clash of Race and Memory.* Cambridge, MA: Belknap Press of Harvard University, 2005.

Bufwack, Mary A., and Robert K. Oermann. *Finding Her Voice: The Saga of Women in Country Music.* New York: Crown, 1993.

Campbell, Gavin James. *Music and the Making of a New South.* Chapel Hill: University of North Carolina Press, 2004.

Carson, Rosa Lee. "My Man's a Jolly Railroad Man." OKeh 45555, October 30, 1931. https://www.youtube.com/watch?v=oCh-Gg7QiNA.

Carson, Rosa Lee. "The Poor Girl Story." OKeh 45547, December 9, 1930. https://www.youtube.com/watch?v=pPqoNM-5UGA.

Cobb, James C. *Away Down South: A History of Southern Identity*. Oxford: Oxford University Press, 2005.

Daniel, Wayne W. *Pickin' on Peachtree: A History of Country Music in Atlanta, Georgia*. Urbana: University of Illinois Press, 1990.

Doyle, Don H., and Larry J. Griffin, ed. *The South as an American Problem*. Athens: University of Georgia Press, 1995.

Duck, Leigh Anne. *The Nation's Region: Southern Modernism, Segregation, and U.S. Nationalism*. Athens: University of Georgia Press, 2006.

Fox, Pamela. *Natural Acts: Gender, Race, and Rusticity in Country Music*. Ann Arbor: University of Michigan Press, 2009.

Frith, Simon. *Performing Rites: On the Value of Popular Music*. Cambridge: Harvard University Press, 1996.

Hale, Grace Elizabeth. *Making Whiteness: The Culture of Segregation in the South, 1890–1940*. New York: Vintage Books, 1998.

Harkins, Anthony. *Hillbilly: A Cultural History of an American Icon*. Oxford: Oxford University Press, 2004.

Lange, Jeffrey J. *Smile When You Call Me a Hillbilly: Country Music's Struggle for Respectability, 1939–1954*. Athens: University of Georgia Press, 2004.

Malone, Bill. *Singing Cowboys and Musical Mountaineers*. Athens: University of Georgia Press, 2003.

McPherson, Tara. *Reconstructing Dixie: Race, Gender, and Nostalgia in the Imagined South*. Durham, NC: Duke University Press, 2003.

Miller, Karl Hagstrom. *Segregating Sound: Inventing Folk and Pop Music in the Age of Jim Crow*. Durham, NC: Duke University Press, 2010.

Minton, John. *78 Blues: Folksongs and Phonographs in the American South*. Jackson: University Press of Mississippi, 2008.

Nunn, Eric. *Sounding the Color Line: Music and Race in the Southern Imagination*. Athens: University of Georgia Press, 2015.

Peterson, Richard A. *Creating Country Music: Fabricating Authenticity*. Chicago: University of Chicago Press, 1997.

Ring, Natalie J. *The Problem South: Region, Empire, and the New Liberal State, 1880–1930*. Athens: University of Georgia Press, 2012.

Russell, Tony. "Music on Location: 'Field Recording' before Bristol." *Popular Music* 26, no. 1 (2007): 23–31.

Sims, Anastatia. *The Power of Femininity in the New South: Women's Organizations and Politics in North Carolina, 1880–1930*. Columbia: University of South Carolina Press, 1997.

Stanley, Roba, and Bill Patterson. "Little Frankie." OKeh 40436, January 9, 1925. https://www.youtube.com/watch?v=Z2JVvSWC7R4.

Thomas, Rebecca. "The Cow That's Ugly Has the Sweetest Milk." In *The Women of Country Music: A Reader*, edited by Charles K. Wolfe and James E. Akenson, 131–47. Lexington: University Press of Kentucky, 2003.

Wiggins, Gene. *Fiddlin' Georgia Crazy: Fiddlin' John Carson, His Real World, and the World of His Songs*. Urbana: University of Illinois Press, 1987.

Wolfe, Charles. "'And No Man Shall Control Me': The Strange Case of Roba Stanley, Country's First Woman Recording Star." In *The Women of Country Music: A Reader*, edited by Charles K. Wolfe and James E. Akenson, 18–29. Lexington: University Press of Kentucky, 2003.

Chapter 5

Housewives' Choice?: Vera Lynn as Lady DJ in the 1950s and 1960s

—Christina Baade

The DJ sits in semi-profile before the windows of the sound booth, holding a record and looking purposefully past a BBC microphone into the middle distance. Smiling, with her hair coiffed, makeup perfect, and pearl necklace, she is the image of white feminine poise, respectability, and professionalism.

The music fans and industry professionals who read *Melody Maker*, which printed the photograph on page 4 of its January 12, 1957, issue, would have recognized the subject—the singer Vera Lynn, who came to fame as the Forces Sweetheart during World War II and had just signed a major contract with the British Broadcasting Corporation—but they may have been surprised by her pose. The photograph showed Lynn in a moment of transformation: "Vera Lynn turned disc-jockey on Thursday for a thirteen-week series on the Light Programme. She is seen here at Broadcasting House choosing the next record for her opening programme."[1]

This image of Lynn as DJ is unexpected not simply because she was known as a singer but also because, during the "golden age of the disc jockey," which lasted from the 1950s to the 1970s, the role was gendered as masculine.[2] As Alice Bennett writes, "The initial role of the disc jockey was purely functional. His (as it invariably was a man) job was to cue the records and ensure the smooth continuity of the show."[3] By the late 1950s, DJs emerged as distinctive personalities in their own right: B. Lee Cooper observed that these "[h]eroes of free flight music broadcasting varied dramatically.... Salesmen, song hucksters, egomaniacs, wild men, wordsmith wizards, and boppin' boys grabbed microphones and linked with their listeners."[4] Films like *American Graffiti* (1973), set in 1962 California, and

Fig. 05.1 Vera Lynn as disc jockey, "choosing the next record for her opening programme" (Melody Maker, January 12, 1957, 5).

Pirate Radio (2009), set on a ship off the coast of Britain in 1966, have helped sustain this romanticized image of DJs as transgressive, slang-talking, white men who played popular music (often by Black American artists) for their teenaged audiences. Meanwhile, the scholarly literature has focused on the role of DJs like Alan Freed and John Peel as important tastemakers, entrepreneurs, and gatekeepers in the development of rock 'n' roll and rock.[5] This focus has obscured the work of DJs in other genres and periods and contributed to the erasure of women in the field.⁶ Arguably, it also overlooks the thread that connects the work of all DJs: the construction of intimate publics through music and speech.

Although DJs' autonomy, communicative style, and genre associations differ significantly across time and context, they all share the task of sustaining the sense that radio "is a 'live,' predominantly *personal* medium"; their speech between recordings fulfills the "need for the human presence, the companionship" for their audience.⁷ DJs navigate what Jason Loviglio has called an "intimate public," in which the mass medium of radio enters the home and listeners' "feelings about its intimacy become heightened."⁸ But DJs (both men and women), whose job it is to play commercial recordings, also navigate another sort of intimate public—as theorized by Lauren Berlant in her work on mid-century women's culture (e.g., Hollywood melodramas)—that is organized around commoditized entertainment and a sense of emotional connection built upon normative femininity and sentimental love.⁹

Recovering the story of Lynn's DJ work touches on three gaps in popular music histories of Britain during the 1950s and early 1960s: the role of women DJs on the BBC; the significance of Lynn and other mature women performers who specialized in mainstream popular music; and the ways in which their work and reception were shaped by ideologies of domesticity and shifting notions of national belonging. Indeed, Lynn's DJ broadcasts represented a significant part of her exclusive contract with BBC television and radio, which ran from 1957 to 1959. She aired over fifty times on the BBC's Light Programme as a DJ in two series, *Records at Six* and *Vera's Evening Record Album*. Lynn also returned in 1963 to serve for a week as DJ for the iconic Light Programme request show *Housewives' Choice*.

Recovering Lynn's DJ work is complicated by the fact that the documentation is limited: there are no scripts or recordings, and the press coverage is paltry. However, the BBC Programmes as Broadcast logs detail every record played in the programs. By analyzing the playlists, which reveal a range of musical and cultural affinities—across lines of genre, nationality, race, and gender—and engaging in thick description of the context in which Lynn did her DJ work, during a period when popular music was understood increasingly through the opposition of youth and adulthood, I show how each of Lynn's DJ programs expressed different valences of domesticity to address different intimate publics: a family audience for *Records at Six*, mature men and their wives in *Evening Record Album*, and (obviously) housewives in *Housewives' Choice*. A through line in these discussions is how Lynn, as a mature, respectable, and mainstream performer, negotiated the radical shifts underway in the music industry at the time, as well as the forces that threatened to marginalize her as old-fashioned and irrelevant—forces that ultimately did contribute to her marginalization in histories of postwar popular music.

WOMEN'S VOICES, PUBLIC DOMESTICITY, AND THE POPULAR MAINSTREAM AT THE BBC

In order to understand the cultural significance of Vera Lynn's stints as BBC DJ, we must begin by examining three hidden and interconnected narratives. First, we must acknowledge the work of women DJs at the BBC before and during the 1950s when there were considerable institutional and cultural constraints placed upon women who spoke on the air. Second, we must uncover how ideologies of public domesticity shaped broadcasting practices during the 1950s and set the terms under which women might gain a voice on air. And, finally, we must ask why the BBC supported the adult-oriented popular music mainstream during the rise of rock, and what its audience might have found in it.

Women DJs and the BBC Mic

Women's participation in the public sphere has long been the object of special scrutiny, and the sound of their voices on radio is no exception. Critiques of women broadcasters sometimes referred to technical matters—equipment designed for lower voices—but they almost always returned to the social: women sounded shrill, nagging, or patronizing. In its early decades, the BBC restricted women from many announcing roles, especially those involving authority or expertise, such as news reading, giving records recitals on topics like jazz, and even announcing variety performances.[10]

During World War II, the BBC increased the number of women announcers; their voices embodied how "women are doing men's jobs these days" and made audible the BBC's commitment to the war effort.[11] The BBC's Overseas Entertainments Unit promoted women announcers and singers, like Lynn, as "radio girlfriends" for forces listeners overseas, building up a wartime intimate public around their ability to evoke reassuring images of home. Largely, these "girlfriends" were white English women, who spoke with upper-middle-class accents, and the Britain they evoked as home was widely understood as the white metropole of a multiracial empire. But there were exceptions, most notably the Jamaican writer Una Marson, who in 1942 began producing (and sometimes announcing) *Calling the West Indies*, which connected West Indian men stationed in the United Kingdom (both as soldiers and as specialized workers in industries like forestry) with listeners in the Caribbean.[12]

It was through her broadcasting with the Overseas Entertainments Unit that Vera Lynn became known as the Forces Sweetheart, a status that is still core to her public persona. After the war, however, the BBC reduced women's announcing roles, even barring women newsreaders in January 1951.[13] Thus, when Lynn announced her own live music programs, both during and after the war, she was unusual not only because few musicians announced their own shows but also because she was a woman in an announcing role—despite the fact that her script and delivery were normatively feminine.

Although the BBC limited announcing opportunities for women, they played an active role behind the scenes. As Catherine Murphy has shown, during the 1920s and 1930s, women headed a few departments,

> ran libraries, sold advertising space [in BBC print publications], auditioned variety stars and produced science programmes. Women were the backbone of the organization, answering telephones, typing news bulletins, cataloguing gramophone records and scheduling diaries; without women buildings wouldn't have been cleaned nor meals served.[14]

This contrast in possibilities—a potential for advancement behind the scenes but few opportunities at the microphone—was abundantly evident in the Gramophone Department, which was headed by a woman, Anna Instone, for twenty-five years, from 1947 until her retirement in 1972.

A musician trained at the Royal Academy of Music, Instone joined the BBC in 1933 and became the department's director in 1947.[15] Instone and her staff rarely appeared on air, but they played a critical role in determining which records would be played. In 1951, the DJ Jonah Barrington described his own weeks of intensive preparation for a series before acknowledging

> the real work . . . lies within the BBC's own gramophone library. For it is here, among the librarians, that one encounters the zealots of discography: men and women who, once they sense that your enthusiasm matches their own, will go to the ends of the earth . . . to find the record you want.[16]

By 1958, when Lynn was airing her DJ programs, Instone's department had "the largest collection of commercial records in the world, over 50,000 discs."[17]

There were two important exceptions to the unwritten rules that kept women away from the microphone as regular hosts for gramophone programs.[18] Doris Arnold compiled and announced the light classical program *These You Have Loved*, which aired intermittently from 1938 to 1963. A "Cinderella," who had started out as a secretary, Arnold's sympathetic delivery made her popular with forces listeners during the war.[19] Likewise, Jean Metcalfe came to fame in 1942 as a radio girlfriend and DJ for the records request show, *Forces Favourites*. She remained with the postwar version of the program, *Family Favourites* (renamed *Two-Way Family Favourites* in 1955), until 1967, sharing hosting duties with a series of male announcers based in Germany.[20] The notions of domesticity and white femininity that framed the BBC's radio girl friends as morale boosters during the war would transform into a new form of public domesticity after the war.

Public Domesticity

One of the most counterintuitive aspects of Vera Lynn's career during the 1950s is the seeming contradiction between her professional accomplishments during what she called "the busiest period of my whole life" and publicity that emphasized her strong domestic orientation.[21] Lynn's success in the 1950s was remarkable: she had several hit records in the United Kingdom and United States; starred in the West End revue *London Laughs* (1952–54); and starred in several series on radio and television. Meanwhile, her publicity emphasized her family-mindedness, love of cookery, and skill at curtain making—while downplaying her role as breadwinner.[22] Lynn could not just be an exceptional voice; to remain legible as a sincere, relatable star, she also had to be seen as an ordinary wife, mother, and homemaker.[23]

The notion of public domesticity appears most frequently in scholarship on the nineteenth century examining how domestic values—and with them, women, especially white middle- and upper-class women—found their way into the public sphere. Amy Richter writes, "At its most basic, public domesticity attempted to bring the cultural associations and behaviors of home life to bear upon social interactions among strangers, to regulate public interactions and delineate the boundary of Victorian respectability."[24] Radio extended the project of public domesticity, bringing it back into the home and to its intimate public. Beginning in the interwar years, the BBC approached broadcasting as a tool for cultural uplift, not only through programming but by encouraging a respectable, middle-class mode of family life—of families gathered together around a "radio hearth," rather than dispersed to the pub or street.

The values of public domesticity found their apotheosis in the postwar era. Claire Langhamer observes, "In Britain, as elsewhere in Europe, the modern home and its inhabitants were represented as the symbolic, and actual centre of postwar reconstruction."[25] Indeed, the 1950s are often evoked with images of single-family dwellings, homemaker mothers, breadwinner fathers, and Baby Boom children—embodying postwar affluence and white heteropatriarchy, as well as the conformity against which the counterculture would eventually rebel.

However, as feminist historians have argued, this postwar narrative is far more complicated. Langhamer has shown that, by the early 1960s, "only a quarter of married couples were able to begin their married life living independently"; postwar housing shortages meant that single-family homes remained only a dream for many in the United Kingdom.[26] Pervasive housing discrimination made the situation even more difficult for Black and Asian Britons, whose rates of immigration to the United Kingdom increased from 1948 into the 1960s.[27] Beyond housing, the postwar period was defined not only by the transformation of what had been imagined as a white nation, but also by Britain's loss of status as a global imperial and economic power, with independence movements throughout the Commonwealth, an ascendant United States, and ongoing austerity policies, under which consumer goods and food were rationed until July 1954. In this context, the embrace of domesticity bound together concerns of gender, race, and national belonging.

Women, as broadcasters and as an audience, played an important role in the BBC's project of public domesticity during the postwar period. Whereas in the United States postwar consumerism fueled the rapid expansion of television ownership, few in austerity Britain owned televisions; "radio was still the universal medium" until well into the 1950s.[28] In contrast to the rise of mobile and individualized listening in the United States, memorialized in *American Graffiti*'s soundscape of car radios and cruising, the availability of cars and transistor sets meant that radio listening in 1950s Britain "was a *domestic* activity."[29]

The BBC engaged with domesticity in highly gendered ways through both programming and scheduling. Evenings were devoted to ambitious cultural, educational, and entertainment programming, which was aimed at an attentive audience, represented since the 1920s by the figure of "tired businessman." Post–WWII, this figure was supplemented by the more domestically engaged "family man," who devoted much of his leisure to his companionate marriage, his family, and maintaining his home.[30] Daytime programs, particularly those on the BBC's Light Programme, were directed to women listening at home, an audience that the BBC approached with new seriousness after the war.[31] The BBC introduced new daytime programming, ranging from serials like *Mrs. Dale's Diary* to magazine shows that covered a mixture of serious, practical, and entertaining topics, most notably *Women's Hour*, which is still on the air. Broadcast daily at 2:00 p.m., *Women's Hour* aligned with the break between morning chores and the return of children from school, enabling women to listen as they ironed, mended, or fed an infant.[32]

Programming like *Women's Hour* represented only one manifestation of the new status enjoyed by women in domestic roles after World War II. As Langhamer has observed, concerned about employment, declining birthrates, and high "rates of marriage failure," "the British Welfare State placed family maintenance at its centre" during the postwar period.[33] In this environment, mothers were recognized for their role in maintaining family stability and children's wellbeing, and housewifery was recognized "as a profession." Even for married women who worked outside the home (around 25 percent of married women in 1951, a number that continued to grow), their "domestic role was considered to be of paramount importance." For women participating in public life, the home became a source of authority.[34]

The BBC's postwar embrace of public domesticity was thus a double-edged sword for women broadcasters, who tended overwhelmingly to be white and middle class. It helped women's programming gain a greater foothold, but it limited how women could be represented. Metcalfe was paired with a male cohost for the daytime *Family Favourites*, Arnold offered soothing female companionship in the evening with *These You Have Loved*, and Lynn starred in homely (or, homey, in US parlance) variety shows aimed at a family audience. For women who broadcast at the BBC after the war, the clearest road to success involved embracing respectability, normative femininity, and public domesticity.

The Popular Mainstream at the BBC

Lynn, in her pose as a DJ, was not the only artist pictured on page 4 of the January 12, 1957 issue of *Melody Maker*. The other photograph featured the Chas McDevitt Skiffle Group—smiling, youthful, apparently white—with a guitar strumming Nancy Whiskey at its center.[35] Rooted in the traditional jazz revival, skiffle was a youth-oriented music that helped pave the way for rock 'n' roll in Britain. The page, with its stories and ads oriented to big band– and crooner-based mainstream pop on one hand and skiffle and traditional jazz "groups" on the other, demonstrated the growing bifurcation (or age-grading) of popular music during the period between genres aimed at adults and those aimed at youth. Adults may have been the dominant audience of the 1950s, but popular music historians have tended to focus on the rise of the youth audience and rock 'n' roll.[36] A recurrent trope in these histories is the BBC's failure to adequately engage with youth-oriented popular music, in striking contrast to US radio. The contrast is rooted in the distinct radio systems of the two nations, the differing role of recorded music on the radio, and the BBC's ongoing commitment to respectability.

In the United States, television's rise transformed radio into a secondary medium that provided recorded music, which was cheaper to program than live shows and was well suited to semi-distracted listening. Meanwhile, the number of locally owned stations grew; they targeted narrower demographics with new formats, most notably Top 40.[37] By the time that rock 'n' roll emerged in the mid-1950s, a number of DJs and stations were available to promote the style.[38]

In Britain, where radio remained the primary domestic medium, the situation was very different. With its monopoly on broadcasting within the United Kingdom and noncommercial, public service mandate, the BBC had little incentive to develop specialized formats like Top 40. Instead, the BBC continued as a mixed service, targeting different audiences throughout the day, with gender as a particularly salient category (as described in the preceding section). This approach left little space for the relatively small youth audience, and what programming there was had to take the sensibilities of the broader audience into account.[39] Thus, whereas the BBC promoted the live performance of skiffle as a respectable form of youth music making, it restricted the "regular or repeated broadcasting" of rock 'n' roll records, such as Elvis Presley's "Heartbreak Hotel."[40] Such restrictions recalled its sensitivities about jazz and crooning in earlier decades, which had been motivated both by moral concerns (including racist and problematic notions that jazz was primitive and crooning was effeminate) and by a commitment to protecting British culture from becoming Americanized.[41] However, the restrictions on rock 'n' roll records were also the product of policies limiting how much airtime the BBC could devote to recorded music. These policies meant that most of the music aired on the BBC after the war continued to be live, and gramophone records programs stood out.

Additionally, a persistent concern during the period involved how best to reintegrate veterans (usually imagined as men) into the family circle.[42] We might productively consider the vogue for sweet music in the late 1940s and 1950s in light of Kip Pegley's finding, in their ethnographic work with post-deployment Canadian forces, that returning soldiers often turn to familiar music from before their deployment and to soothing music in order to deal with post-traumatic stress disorder (PTSD) and the challenges of reintegrating into civilian life.[43] In a period when PTSD went unnamed, might soothing, sentimental music performed by beloved singers like Lynn have done similar things, not just for World War II veterans but also for a civilian population that had endured bombing and privations from six years of war?[44] The adult audience's taste for "sugary" music—as well as the broader cultural embrace of domesticity—was eventually framed by the counterculture as a form of conformity and cultural conservatism, but these orientations also emerged from trauma and hardship experienced on a national scale.

It was in this context that Vera Lynn, a recording artist popular with mature audiences, signed her exclusive contract with the BBC in late 1956. While she was not the first woman to DJ for the BBC—both Arnold and Metcalfe were important pioneers and contemporaries—she did have to operate, like them, within the frameworks of respectability, gender normativity, and public domesticity. What occurred during Lynn's stints as DJ, however, was a reckoning with the status of youth-oriented popular music and the question of who was included in radio's intimate public, both of which challenged the terms through which women had gained a voice on postwar radio.

VERA LYNN, BBC DJ

In 1956, the year—for us in Britain—of rock 'n' roll, cinema-seat-ripping, Bill Haley, Elvis Presley and Tommy Steele, there was, surprisingly enough, still room for me. Within the space of a few weeks I began both radio and television shows for the BBC, the fruits of an exclusive two-year contract with the corporation. It was an unprecedented offer allowing me TV shows, radio shows and separate series of record programmes with me as disc jockey. I was back and it meant a lot to me.[45]

In her autobiography, Vera Lynn described her late 1950s contract with the BBC in terms of age-grading—between adult-oriented mainstream pop and the youthful rebellion of rock 'n' roll. That there was still space for Lynn in 1956 was probably not as surprising as she recalled. Although she had not had a regular show on the BBC since 1952, she was a highly regarded recording artist and entertainer, and rock 'n' roll still seemed like a fad. But still, why did the BBC ask the singer to host a DJ series as part of her exclusive contract? And how can we understand the intimate publics hailed by her two series, *Records at Six* and *Evening Record Album*, their relation to ideologies of public domesticity, and the ways that they reinforced Lynn's persona of sincerity and respectability?

Despite her popularity, Lynn, with her sincere and sentimental repertory and speaking style, had been an ambivalent figure for the BBC. During World War II, BBC staff had periodically "rested" her because they identified her as the catalyst for complaints that the BBC was unmanning the forces with too much sentiment.[46] For a few years after the war, BBC Variety set aside these concerns, and Lynn starred in a number of Light Programme series. By late 1950, however, the contracts dried up. J. H. Davidson, assistant head of Variety, wrote to Lynn's agent: "If Vera Lynn is prepared to 'brighten' her programmes we shall be pleased to give the matter our immediate consideration. Meanwhile, I am afraid it is impossible for us to give you a date upon which a series is likely to commence."[47] Lynn turned instead to Radio Luxembourg, which carried her weekly series until BBC radio and television took a renewed interest in her in 1956.[48]

If Lynn was a difficult figure for BBC radio, BBC television producers recognized that her mastery of both radio's intimate address *and* the variety stage made her an ideal performer for a live audiovisual medium with a domestic viewership. Lynn appeared regularly on BBC television in the decade after the war, most notably in 1955 when she starred in a VE-Day anniversary show, for which Audience Research reported that a phenomenal 70 percent of respondents had liked her appearance "very much."[49]

Lynn's popularity was rooted in her fans' memories of her role as a reassuring voice during World War II, a role extended in the postwar "sweet revolution." She also embodied the respectable glamor, public domesticity, and white femininity that the leadership for both BBC Television and its new commercial competitor, Independent Television (ITV), considered crucial for courting women audiences, the group in charge of family viewing schedules.[50] In late 1955, the newly established ITV won the first round of competition for Lynn's talents when it booked her for *The Vera Lynn Show*, an evening variety series aimed at a family audience.[51] But when Ronnie Waldman, the head of BBC Television Light Entertainment, learned that Lynn was interested in working with BBC Television, he moved quickly, lunching with the singer on May 31, 1956, and contacting his radio counterpart the next day.[52]

Lynn, Waldman reported, wanted stability: a break from touring, a predictable income stream, and a schedule that would enable a better work-life balance for her tight-knit family and school-aged daughter.[53] If the BBC could make an offer that approximated her income from Radio Luxembourg, ITV, and her variety contracts—£8,000 a year—she would agree to exclusivity. Waldman was eager to sign, but the contract required a commitment from BBC Sound (radio). Its leadership was open to booking Lynn, but they worried about the expense—and whether they could use her for thirty bookings a year. Including six DJ shows in the mix made the deal feasible for BBC Sound, both because records shows were cheap to produce and because they helped avoid overwhelming listeners with too much of Lynn's distinctive singing.[54]

The decision to include a DJ series in Lynn's contract did not come out of the blue. Metcalfe, who had also come to popularity with a wartime forces audience, was currently earning plaudits for her DJ work on *Two-Way Forces Favourites*, and, only a few months earlier (in April 1956), Lynn herself had done a week's stint as a DJ for a BBC show called *The Song's the Thing*, in which popular singers served as guest DJs.[55] Economics and scheduling aside, Lynn was apparently a good DJ. Although only contracted for six DJ shows, she ended up airing seventeen DJ shows in the first year of her contract, and in subsequent years, she was contracted to DJ more.

When the first year of what became a multiyear contract went into effect in August 1956, it became clear that Lynn's television and radio audiences differed. On television, *Vera Lynn Sings* offered its broad family audience big-budget variety, featuring performers from a range of genres and song selections for Lynn that emphasized her more recent recordings. On the Light Programme, *Yours Sincerely—Vera Lynn* reminded listeners "of songs you will want to remember," including only "one new song in each programme."[56] Addressing a narrower and older audience, the radio show offered a continuation of the soothing radio persona Lynn had developed in the war. Meanwhile, Lynn's DJ shows preserved her intimate connection with her audience while expanding the musical range beyond what she would herself sing. *Records at Six* was scheduled in the early evening, whereas *Evening Record Album* aired later in the evening; respectively, they traced a path from a mixed family audience to a narrower adult audience.

ENTERTAINMENT FOR FAMILIES: *RECORDS AT SIX* (JANUARY–APRIL 1957)

Records at Six aired weekly at 6:30 p.m. on Thursdays from January to April 1957 during the "toddlers' truce," when both BBC Television and ITV went off the air (supposedly to allow mothers to put young children to bed). The toddler's truce embodied how 1950s broadcasting in the United Kingdom reinforced normative domestic routines: early bedtimes for young children, tea for everyone else.[57] It also represented a liminal moment in the broadcasting day. Whereas television went off the air for an hour, creating a dividing line between daytime programming for women and children and evening shows for adults, radio stayed on the air; shows that aired during the toddlers' truce aimed to please both youth and adults.

The half-hour *Records at Six* featured a broad selection of current pop hits, a template that continued even when the toddlers' truce ended in February and television became a continuous service from 3:00 p.m. to 11:00 p.m. daily.[58] Lest listeners forget that their host was Vera Lynn, each show started (and sometimes ended) with a fifteen-second excerpt from her recording of "Yours," the song that had become her signature tune during World War II and also opened *Vera Lynn Sings* on television. Lynn's famously sincere personality threaded through *Records at Six* in her spoken introductions and in selections from her extensive postwar discography, which opened and closed each show. The selections may have built upon her long-standing reputation for sincerity, respectability, and stylistic conservatism, but they were not old wartime or prewar songs: nearly a third had been recorded in the past year. *Records at Six* was not retrospective in the manner of *Yours Sincerely—Vera Lynn*, its live Light Programme counterpart.

Records at Six was not only a promotional vehicle for Lynn; it promoted a wide range of artists and even the idea in general of records as a form of entertainment. Out of the usual ten records per episode, eight featured other artists. Light instrumental music was a significant presence in recognition of the teatime airing, which recalled the tradition of light music that blossomed in public eating establishments during the interwar period.[59] With at least three instrumental records an episode, listeners could hear a wide sampling of British light music: beyond the inevitable Mantovani, there was Frank Chacksfield, Robert Farnon, and Norrie Paramor featuring Eddie Calvert (the man with the golden trumpet, who also guested on Lynn's television show), along with famous show bands led by Ted Heath, Billy Cotton, and Joe Loss. The selections tended to the colorful and upbeat, helped by a healthy dose of Latin numbers, from the Habanera from *Carmen* to "Rum-Ba Ba, Mambo Quickstep." Popular, melodic British singers—the youthful hitmakers Joan Regan, Ruby Murray, and cheeky Alma Cogan (known as "the girl with a giggle in her voice"); wartime favorite Anne Shelton, hit crooners like Dickie Valentine, David Whitfield, and Jimmy Young; the comedian-singer Max Bygraves, and the working-class Beverley Sisters—were also well represented.

The show's other selections ranged more widely to include records by mainstream US singers and vocal groups: Bing Crosby and Louis Armstrong's duet, "No, You Has Jazz," from the film *High Society* (1957), and selections from Nat "King" Cole, Sammy Davis Jr., Tennessee Ernie Ford, Les Paul and Mary Ford, and Doris Day. About one record a week appealed directly to youth listeners, with hit US crooners like Pat Boone and the Platters; calypso, including Shirley

Bassey's hit "The Banana Boat Song"; and a handful of "rock and roll" records: instrumentals by Winnifred Atwell, the Trinidadian-born, Royal Academy–trained piano virtuoso, who had come to popular fame when she played boogie woogie on a semi-out-of-tune upright, along with two selections from Bill Haley, "Hook, Line, and Sinker" and "Don't Knock the Rock." As Lynn had announced in the first episode of her TV series, she liked "the rock and roll"—although she never sang it.[60] The tincture of recordings by Haley in this family-oriented records program was especially noteworthy given the moral panic about the *Rock Around the Clock* riots, when the film featuring Haley had reportedly inspired seat-ripping, aisle-dancing teenaged mobs.[61]

Meanwhile, the token representation of respectable Black British artists like Atwell and Bassey and African American artists like the Platters, Cole, and Davis (there was no Chuck Berry or Little Richard) offered a slightly expanded sense of a more inclusive intimate public to a nation that prided itself on avoiding US-style segregation while still discriminating against Black British citizens in housing and employment. Indeed, African American artists featured regularly in British entertainment during the period; however, Black British musicians were marginalized or had to frame their work through an American lens.[62] Atwell, who starred in her own BBC television series in 1957, and Bassey, who was breaking through as a major artist, were the exceptions that proved the rule.[63] Given that, at the same time, the BBC had also devoted an entire television series to blackface minstrelsy (the highly popular *Black and White Minstrels*), which ran well into the 1960s, even such minimal representation is notable.[64]

Lynn's role as DJ for a cheerful teatime records show contributed to her sincere, domestic persona. The DJ show represented a more intimate counterpoint to Lynn's role in her popular television variety show: in contrast to elaborate production numbers, there was simply convivial chat; in contrast to guest performers, there were recordings of other musicians; in contrast to the vision of Lynn in a set dressed as a sitting room, listeners heard Lynn while seated around their own tables. In wartime, she had been a radio girlfriend, but by the late 1950s she had become a radio friend of the family.

ENTERTAINMENT FOR ADULTS: *EVENING RECORD ALBUM* (MARCH 1958–MARCH 1959)

Lynn had become a fixture of family-oriented BBC television, but BBC radio had positioned her on the adult side of the generational divide. Thus, when Television Light Entertainment moved to renew her contract, BBC Sound was increasingly reluctant to participate. Finding space for nearly thirty broadcasts featuring Lynn seemed incompatible with their efforts to better serve youth listeners while also transitioning into the role of secondary medium, as television ownership expanded (a majority of households owned a television by 1959).

The solution was to reduce the number of retrospective *Yours Sincerely—Vera Lynn* episodes and have Lynn DJ more. BBC Sound filled nearly half its share of her contract with DJ spots—thirteen shows each in 1958 and 1959—but it moved Lynn's half-hour records show from teatime to the evening: first 8:30 p.m. on Mondays and then 10:30 p.m. on Tuesdays. Much as *Records at Six* had done, *Vera's Evening Record Album* was framed around Lynn's personality, opening again with "Yours" but now closing with "Goodnight, God Bless," a soothing song by Ray Mack and Martin Lewis, complete with the chimes of Big Ben. The relaxing mood continued with selections from Lynn's recent discography that leaned heavily on her lush, mood music-inspired album, *If I Am Dreaming*, from 1956.

As had been the case with *Records at Six*, most of the program's records were by artists other than Lynn. There were still up-tempo and novelty records—Atwell's boogie woogie, a large dose of Latin numbers, and aggressively cheerful novelties like "The Chipmunk Song"—but the program was most committed to singers of jazz standards and traditional pop. The selections spanned the Atlantic with Sarah Vaughan, Johnny Mathis, Perry Como, Nat King Cole, Anne Shelton, Sammy Davis Jr., Frank Sinatra, Peggy Lee, and Bing Crosby, as well as the Nashville Sound exponent George Hamilton IV and younger pop crooners like Paul Anka, Pat Boone, and David Whitfield. Chris Barber's traditional jazz group made an appearance, but there was no rock 'n' roll. The repertory was unapologetically adult in orientation, drawing on Lynn's mature, intimate appeal to create a mood of sophisticated relaxation for men and women who had the time to enjoy the music guided by the voice of a familiar peer. If Lynn's singing and announcing during World War II had helped build up her persona as an unthreatening Sweetheart to the Forces, her DJ role in the 1950s situated her as a proxy for another romantic institution: the companionate but still patriarchal marriage, in which wives were expected to cater to their husbands' emotional needs.[65] It was an intimate public built on the ideals of heteronormative marriage and the stable, comfortable life that was the focus of public domesticity in the 1950s.[66]

But BBC radio was reckoning with changing times—the rise of consumer society, the growth of television, a youth culture with radically different music tastes, and an emerging sense that Britishness could not be assumed to be exclusively white. By 1959 the assertion by a *New Musical Express* correspondent, that "[m]any of her [Lynn's] fans do not care to reveal their feelings for fear of being labeled an 'old-timer,'" had come to pass.[67] There might have been room for Lynn at the BBC in 1956, when Haley was the rage, but with the arrival of youth-oriented music television shows like *Oh Boy!* and *Top of the Pops*, *Vera Lynn Sings* was finally judged to be "outmoded," and her exclusive contract with the BBC came to an end.[68] But BBC Sound had been treating her as old-fashioned radio—or at least adult radio—for over two years. Lynn's mastery of public domesticity, mature femininity, and respectable glamor had finally become a liability.

CONCLUSION: A WOMAN'S PLACE, *HOUSEWIVES' CHOICE* (JUNE 1963)

In June 1963, the BBC's program guide *Radio Times* announced: "One male preserve—in a world where women are taking over men's jobs and doing them just as well—is the disc jockey spot on *Housewives' Choice*. But it is so no longer, for today Vera [Lynn] opens the programme's mailbags—the first woman since 1949."[69]

The DJ seat in *Housewives' Choice* had been an exclusively masculine role during the 1950s, but women had been DJs at the BBC going back to the late 1930s. Nonetheless, the announcement's liberatory tone evoked the new visibility of women in the public sphere, enabled by the recent introduction of the contraceptive pill (for married women only) and the 1964 Married Women's Property Act revision, which gave women legal ownership of the money they earned and allowed them to inherit property.[70] The gains were limited, however; women continued to marry young, have large families, and be understood primarily through their domestic roles. The show featured the requests of "housewives," not "women," after all, even if Betty Friedan's challenge to the cult of feminized domesticity, *The Feminine Mystique*, had inspired debate only a few months before Lynn appeared on *Housewives' Choice*.[71]

By the time Lynn hosted *Housewives' Choice* for two weeks in late June 1963, she had not broadcast regularly on BBC television or radio for nearly three years. In her autobiography, she described the early 1960s—dominated by the Beatles and "beat" music—as a personal "song drought" in which she found it hard to find "new songs of a kind I wanted to sing and could sound true to myself in."[72] The shift prompted her move to EMI from Decca, the company with which she had recorded for twenty-five years, and her decision to pursue international touring in the Netherlands and Antipodes. For BBC Radio in 1963, as it grappled with deep changes in pop music, Lynn was a historic, not a contemporary, performer.[73] In fact, the BBC Home Service aired *The Vera Lynn Story*, the first of many retrospective documentaries about the singer, in July 1961. Lynn's booking as host for *Housewives' Choice* aligned with this retrospective status: since its inception in October 1946, the records request show had featured a string of older crooners, bandleaders, and—almost always—male DJs.

Why were the DJs for *Housewives' Choice* men? The answer lies in the housewife-oriented daytime schedule of the Light Programme during the 1950s.

Although female hosts like Metcalfe gained an enthusiastic following among women listeners, they did not entirely dominate the daytime schedule. Barnard suggests that daytime popular music radio aimed to validate women listeners at home while also satisfying their nostalgia for pre-marriage fun and romance; the conventional wisdom was that male presenters were more enjoyable and less threatening in this role than women.[74] When Annie Nightingale, the first woman DJ on Radio 1 (which replaced Light Programme in 1967), recalled the initial opposition to her hiring, she explained, "DJs were intended as 'husband substitutes.' BBC exact words. I kid you not."[75]

In contrast to the peer-oriented, taste-making address of youth-oriented DJs, the BBC's adult-oriented DJs were paired with their audiences in terms of heteronormative romance: cheerful men chivvying on housework-doing women during the day, reassuring women helping men relax in the evening. Indeed, this had been Lynn's role in *Evening Record Album*. This tradition—and small divergence from it that Lynn's *Housewives' Choice* booking represented—recalls the questions about the role of DJs, the intimate publics they addressed, and the place of women's voices on the air.

For Lynn to have been admitted into the fraternity of *Housewives' Choice* presenters in 1963 meant that she had crossed into Metcalfe's territory of friendly respectability as a daytime woman announcer who would not set the BBC's imagined housewife listeners on edge. The requests for Lynn's shows spanned the youth/adult divide, from Bing Crosby to the Beatles, Myra Hess to Petula Clark, Gracie Fields to Cliff Richard. If these choices represented nostalgia for pre-wedded life, they also demonstrated the broad age range that constituted the "housewife" demographic in a period when women married young. Frith's observation that women left the youth demographic when they married opens up a host of questions about the musical tastes of these young women; their requests suggest that marriage did not stop them from liking the Beatles, Tommy Steele, or Pat Boone.[76] In any event, their tastes apparently did not include Vera Lynn the singer, whose records were absent from the lists during the week she hosted.

The field of popular music studies has tended to focus on stories of revolution rather than incremental change and conservative tastes. Lynn's work as a DJ undoubtedly falls into the category of incremental change, in which women gained a voice as long as they were respectable, appropriately domestic, and (usually) white. However, her work also points to the ways in which the BBC had to negotiate the rising importance of recordings without playing too many records and an increasingly age-stratified popular music audience in which adults remained the majority. Lynn's DJ shows, particularly *Records at Six*, were sometimes more inclusive than one might assume, but ultimately they performed a commitment to connecting with and pleasing normative, mature audiences as they listened in the home. Her success as a DJ was not dramatic, but it required more labor than meets the eye.

It is telling about the BBC's and the media's attitudes toward Lynn that the most frustrating aspect of researching Lynn's DJ work was the paucity of materials that

I found in the archives. Except in the lead-up to *Records at Six*, which merited brief mentions in *Melody Maker* and *New Musical Express*, there was virtually no press coverage of Lynn's DJ work during the late 1950s. But there remains the photograph of Lynn on page four of the January 12, 1957, *Melody Maker*, which depicts the DJ at the start of her *Records at Six* series and tells us much. The photograph shows us the face of a woman who gets a seat at the table, her voice on the mic, her music made on her own terms. The intimate public she addresses is not composed of rebellious youth—that revolution is yet to come and she will not be part of it—but a larger, domestic audience, having their tea, putting children to bed, waiting for the television to come back on, and hoping she will play them something they like.

NOTES

I presented an earlier version of this chapter at the Leverhulme Trust-funded workshop, Connecting the Wireless World: Recreating Auditory Cultures, University of Denver, 2018; thank you to Simon Potter, Andrea Stanton, and the other organizers for the invitation and conversation. This chapter represents part of a larger project on Dame Vera Lynn's postwar career, funded by the Social Sciences and Humanities Research Council of Canada. My thanks to the research assistants who have worked on this project over several years: Nikki Brown, Rebecca Flynn, Christina Pellegrini, Frankie Perry, Whitney Thompson, and Rory Warnock. Finally, thank you to the BBC Written Archives Centre staff, especially Louise North and Els Boonen, for their insight and assistance. BBC copyright content reproduced courtesy of the British Broadcasting Corporation. All rights reserved.

1. "Vera Lynn on the Air," *Melody Maker*, January 12, 1957, 4.
2. B. Lee Cooper, "American Disc Jockeys, 1945–1975: A Bibliographic and Discographic Survey," *Popular Music and Society* 30, no. 3 (2007): 402.
3. Alice Bennett, "Radio DJs," *Encyclopedia of Contemporary British Culture*, ed. Peter Childs and Michael Storry (London: Routledge, 2013).
4. Cooper, "American Disc Jockeys, 1945–1975," 402.
5. See Robert Chapman, *Selling the Sixties: The Pirates and Pop Music Radio* (New York: Taylor and Francis, 2002); Cooper, "American Disc Jockeys, 1945–1975," 401–23; Susan J. Douglas, *Listening In: Radio and the American Imagination* (Minneapolis: University of Minnesota Press, 2004); Matthew Killmeier, "Voices between the Tracks: Disk Jockeys, Radio, and Popular Music, 1955–60," *Journal of Communication Inquiry* 25 (2001): 353–74; Paul Long, "The Primary Code: The Meanings of John Peel, Radio and Popular Music," *Radio Journal: International Studies in Broadcast and Audio Media* 3, no. 3 (2006): 25–48; Elena Razlagova, *The Listener's Voice: Early Radio and the American Public* (Philadelphia: University of Pennsylvania Press, 2011); Wes Smith, *The Pied Pipers of Rock 'N' Roll: Radio Deejays of the 50s and 60s* (Lanham: Longstreet Press, 1989).
6. There are a few exceptions. See Douglas, *Listening In*; Donna Halper, *Invisible Stars: A Social History of Women in American Broadcasting* (New York: Routledge, 2015); Elizabeth L. Wollman, "Men, Music, and Marketing at Q104.3 (WAXQ-FM New York)," *Popular Music and Society* 22, no. 4 (Winter 1998): 1–23; Ann Nightingale, *Wicked Speed* (London: Pan, 2000).

7. Andrew Crissell, *Understanding Radio* (London: Routledge, 1986), 65; Razlagova, *The Listener's Voice*, 136.

8. Jason Loviglio, *Radio's Intimate Public: Network Broadcasting and Mass-Mediated Democracy* (Minneapolis: University of Minnesota Press, 2005), xv.

9. Lauren Berlant, *The Female Complaint: The Unfinished Business of Sentimentality in American Culture* (Durham, NC: Duke University Press, 2008), 5–13.

10. Christina Baade, *Victory Through Harmony: The BBC and Popular Music in World War II* (New York: Oxford University Press, 2012), 106.

11. Cecil Madden, head of the BBC Overseas Entertainments Unit, quoted in Baade, *Victory Through Harmony*, 155.

12. Darrell M. Newton, *Paving the Empire Road: BBC Television and Black Britons* (Manchester, UK: Manchester University Press, 2011), 20–21. Newton asserts that the program represented some of the diversity of "West Indian culture . . . as a host of different, yet familiar forms of island music, dialect, and those individuals heralded by the BBC as worthy of association. The development of radio programmes for audiences of colour now moved beyond cricket matches, and often included pro-Empire propaganda and implications of racial tolerance" (19–20). Marson went on to produce *Caribbean Voices*, which presented the work of West Indian authors, including herself.

13. David Kynaston, *Family Britain, 1951–57* (London: Bloomsbury, 2009), 584.

14. Murphy, "'On an Equal Footing with Men?,'" 12. Beyond Marson's much-discussed work for the BBC and guest broadcasting spots by singers, performers, and other public figures, I have not found specific information from this period regarding the BBC's employment of women from racial and ethnic minorities.

15. Catherine Murphy, "Women in the BBC: A History, 1922–2002: Biographies" (unpublished manuscript, 2011), 31.

16. Jonah Barrington, "Who Would Be a Disc-Jockey?" *Radio Times*, December 12, 1951, 11.

17. Murphy, "Women in the BBC: A History, 1922–2002," 31.

18. A search of the BBC *Genome* reveals that Marson "of the BBC's West Indian Section" hosted an episode of *I Know What I Like*, a gramophone series that featured guest hosts drawn from entertainment and public life, on the General Forces Programme in April 1945.

19. "The Broadcasters," "Both Sides of the Microphone," *Radio Times*, April 19, 1940, 8; British Broadcasting Corporation, *Genome (Beta): Radio Times 1923–2009*, http://genome.ch.bbc.co.uk.

20. Dennis Barker, "Metcalfe [married name Michelmore], Jean (1923–2000), broadcaster," *Oxford Dictionary of National Biography*, October 16, 2018, http://www.oxforddnb.com.libaccess.lib.mcmaster.ca/view/10.1093/ref:odnb/9780198614128.001.0001/odnb-9780198614128-e-73684; BBC, *Genome*. During the Cold War, the British Army of the Rhine was stationed in Germany.

21. Dame Vera Lynn, *Some Sunny Day: My Autobiography* (London: Harper, 2009), 232.

22. Vera Lynn, script: *At Home*, March 6,1957, T14/119/Television/SF (Subject File)/At Home-Vera Lynn (1957).

23. Richard Dyer, *Stars*, rev. ed. (London: BFI Publishing, 2001), 43.

24. Amy G. Richter, *Home on the Rails: Women, the Railroad, and the Rise of Public Domesticity* (Chapel Hill: University of North Carolina Press, 2005), 60.

25. Claire Langhamer, "The Meanings of Home in Postwar Britain," *Journal of Contemporary History* 20, no. 2 (2005): 342.

26. Langhamer, "The Meanings of Home in Postwar Britain," 349.

27. Richard Weight, *Patriots: National Identity in Britain, 1940–2000* (London: Pan Books, 2003), 136–41.

28. By June 1955, only "40 per cent of middle-class households had a TV set [and] only 26 per cent of working-class households did." Kynaston, *Family Britain, 1951–57*, 464.

29. Stephen Barnard, *On the Radio: Music Radio in Britain* (Milton Keynes, UK: Open University Press, 1989), 35.

30. Langhamer, "The Meanings of Home in Postwar Britain," 354–55.

31. Barnard, *On the Radio: Music Radio in Britain*, 116.

32. Maggie Andrews, *Domesticating the Airwaves: Broadcasting, Domesticity and Femininity* (London: Continuum International, 2012), 18. As this schedule suggests, the BBC tended to address (and construct) a normative British audience that was implicitly white and middle class. Audience research reports sometimes broke down audiences by class, age, or gender (region was also a concern), but not race or ethnicity. Of course, this doesn't mean that working-class and racialized listeners didn't listen to the BBC; indeed, they had few alternatives given the BBC's monopoly on broadcasting within the United Kingdom. (Radio Luxembourg, the main commercial competitor, was based on the Continent; American Armed Forces Radio had limited geographical reach in Britain.)

33. Langhamer, "The Meanings of Home in Postwar Britain," 345.

34. Kristin Skoog, "Focus on the Housewife: The BBC and the Post-War Woman 1945–1955," *Networking Knowledge, Journal of the MeCCSA Post Graduate Network* 2, no. 1 (2009): 3–4; Angela Davis, *Modern Motherhood: Women and Family in England, 1945–2000* (Manchester, UK: Manchester University Press, 2012), 143.

35. "Groups Cash in on the Skiffle Craze," *Melody Maker*, January 12, 1957, 4.

36. Keir Keightley, "Reconsidering Rock," *The Cambridge Companion to Pop and Rock*, ed. Simon Frith, Will Straw, and John Street (Cambridge: Cambridge University Press, 2001), 112.

37. As William Barlow and other radio historians have shown, this period was critical in the development of Black-owned radio stations, which not only provided outlets for Black music and entertainers but also formed part of the media ecosystem that supported the civil rights movement in the United States. William Barlow, *Voice Over: The Making of Black Radio* (Philadelphia: Temple University Press, 1999).

38. Susan J. Douglas, *Listening In: Radio and the American Imagination* (Minneapolis: University of Minnesota Press, 2004), 256–67; Eric Rothenbuhler and Tom McCourt, "Radio Redefines Itself, 1947–1962," *Radio Reader: Essays in the Cultural History of Radio*, ed. Michele Hilmes and Jason Loviglio (New York: Routledge, 2002), 367–87.

39. Beyond women, youth, and particular taste categories (for example, jazz fans or the listeners served by the Third Programme with its high culture diet of modernist drama, chamber music, and scientific talks), there were a smattering of programs addressing more niche audiences. For example, Black British listeners seemed to have been the target audience for the music-centered *Caribbean Carnival*, billed as "The British West Indies Show," which aired Sundays on the Light Programme during summer 1957. BBC, *Genome*.

40. Barnard, *On the Radio: Music Radio in Britain* (Milton Keynes: Open University Press, 1989), 38.

41. Baade, *Victory Through Harmony*, 24–28, 151–52.

42. Lynn Spigel, *Make Room for TV: Television and the Family Ideal in Postwar America* (Chicago: University of Chicago Press, 1992), 40–41.

43. Kip Pegley, "Looking for 'Our Song': Canadian Soldiers and their Remembrance of War." Unpublished paper presented at Society for American Music meeting, Montreal, 2017.

44. There were also veterans from the Cold War and postcolonial conflicts; military service remained mandatory for British men until 1960.

45. Lynn, *Some Sunny Day*, 259–60.

46. Christina Baade, "*Sincerely Yours—Vera Lynn*: Performing Class, Sentiment, and Femininity in the 'People's War,'" *Atlantis, A Women's Studies Journal / Revue d'Etudes sur les Femmes* 30, no. 2 (2006): 36–49.

47. J. H. Davidson, letter to Leslie A. MacDonnell, November 28, 1950, BBC WAC RCONT/ Vera Lynn/Artists/File 2 (1944–50).

48. Lynn, *Some Sunny Day*, 233–34.

49. Audience research report, "Bless 'Em All," June 3, 1955, TV14/155/2 TV OB's/"Bless 'Em All"/ File 1B (May–June 1955).

50. Janet Thumim, *Inventing Television Culture: Men, Women, and the Box* (Oxford: Oxford University Press, 2004), 31.

51. "Vera Lynn," BBC Internal Circulating Memorandum (ICM), from Television Booking Manager (Holland Bennett) to HLE Tel. [Head of Television Light Entertainment, Ronald Waldman], December 1, 1955, BBC WAC TVART1/Vera Lynn/ File 1 (1938–62).

52. "Vera Lynn, Edmundo Ros, and Cyril Stapleton," BBC ICM from Television Booking Manager (Holland Bennett) to HLE Tel., May 17, 1956, BBC WAC TVART1/Vera Lynn/ File 1 (1938–62); "Vera Lynn," BBC ICM, from HLE Tel. to HV [Head of (Radio) Variety], June 1, 1956, BBC WAC TVART1/Vera Lynn/ File 1 (1938–62).

53. "Vera Lynn," BBC ICM, from HLE Tel. to HV, June 1, 1956.

54. "Long Term Contract: Vera Lynn," BBC ICM, from Assistant Head of Programme Contracts (GM Turnell) to C. Ent. (Sound), et al., September 19, 1956, BBC WAC TVART1/Vera Lynn/ File 1 (1938–62).

55. "Star Singers to Present Records Five Nights a Week in New BBC Series," *New Musical Express*, December 2, 1955, 7.

56. Programme Listings for August 23, 1956, *Radio Times*, August 17, 1956, 37; Gale Pedrick, "Our Vera," *Radio Times*, August 17, 1956, 6.

57. Janet Thumim, *Inventing Television Culture: Men, Women, and the Box* (Oxford: Oxford University Press, 2004), 24–25.

58. All information on the records played is drawn from the British Broadcasting Corporation Written Archives Centre, Programmes as Broadcast, Light Programme, 1957–63.

59. James Nott, *Music for the People: Popular Music and Dance in Interwar Britain* (London: Oxford University Press, 2002), 114–16.

60. BBC WAC TV Light Entertainment Scripts Sequence 1 1936–1964, reel 81/82.

61. Kynaston, *Family Britain, 1951–57*, 654–55.

62. Sarita Malik, *Representing Black Britain: A History of Black and Asian Images on British Television* (London: SAGE Publications, 2002). There has been far more scholarship on the history of Black British (and other racialized people) representations on television than on radio.

63. See McKay, "Winnifred Atwell."

64. For a discussion of Black representation in current events, drama, and other television (and, to a lesser extent, radio) genres, see Malik, *Representing Black Britain*; Newton, *Paving the Empire Road*.

65. Kynaston, *Family Britain, 1951–57*, 567. At least one listener did not find Lynn acceptably self-effacing: "My vote for the most big-headed disc jockey goes to Vera Lynn. Her record programme was ruined by too much self adulation in playing her own discs." R. H., letter to *Picturegoer*).

66. Lynn also continued to engage with active-duty troops. She broadcast at least one episode of *Evening Record Album* from Hamburg, where she "talk[ed] to servicemen . . . and play[ed] their particular favourites in records" ("Vera from Hamburg," *Disc*, February 7, 1959, 11).

67. "NME 1956–67 Nation-Wide Poll," *New Musical Express*, November 23, 1956, 7–9.

68. BBC ICM from Controller of Programmes, Television (Kenneth Adam) to HLE Tel., "Vera Lynn," February 2, 1959, BBC WAC TVART1/Vera Lynn/ File 1 (1938–62).

69. "Vera Lynn," *Radio Times*, June 13, 1963, 18.

70. "Timeline of the Women's Liberation Movement," *Sisterhood and After*, British Library, October 17, 2018, https://www.bl.uk/sisterhood/timeline.

71. Kira Cochrane, "1963: The Beginning of the Feminist Movement," *The Guardian*, May 7, 2013, https://www.theguardian.com/lifeandstyle/2013/may/07/1963-beginning-feminist-movement.

72. Lynn, *Some Sunny Day: My Autobiography*, 262.

73. Asa Briggs, *The History of Broadcasting in the United Kingdom, vol. V: Competition* (New York: Oxford University Press, 1995), 508. However, Lynn appeared regularly on ITV, returned to the Light Programme with *We Meet Again* in 1965, and starred in a variety show on BBC television variety show that ran 1969–77.

74. Barnard, *On the Radio: Music Radio in Britain*, 146–48.

75. Anne Nightingale, "Radio 1 Turns 50: Annie Nightingale on Pirates, Sexism and the Sound of the Underground," *The Telegraph*, September 25, 2017, https://www.telegraph.co.uk/radio/radio-presenters/radio-1-turns-50-annie-nightingale-pirates-sexism-sound-underground/.

76. Simon Frith, *The Sociology of Rock* (London: Constable, 1978), 135.

BIBLIOGRAPHY

Andrews, Maggie. *Domesticating the Airwaves: Broadcasting, Domesticity, and Femininity*. London: Continuum International, 2012.

Baade, Christina. "*Sincerely Yours—Vera Lynn*: Performing Class, Sentiment, and Femininity in the 'People's War.'" *Atlantis, A Women's Studies Journal / Revue d'Etudes sur les femmes* 30, no. 2 (2006): 36–49.

Baade, Christina. *Victory Through Harmony: The BBC and Popular Music in World War II*. New York: Oxford University Press, 2012.

Barker, Dennis. "Metcalfe [married name Michelmore], Jean (1923–2000), broadcaster." *Oxford Dictionary of National Biography*. October 16, 2018. http://www.oxforddnb.com.libaccess.lib.mcmaster.ca/view/10.1093/ref:odnb/9780198614128.001.0001/odnb-9780198614128-e-73684.

Barlow, William. *Voice Over: The Making of Black Radio*. Philadelphia: Temple University Press, 1999.

Barnard, Stephen. *On the Radio: Music Radio in Britain*. Milton Keynes, UK: Open University Press, 1989.

Barrington, Jonah. "Who Would Be a Disc-Jockey?" *Radio Times*, December 12, 1951, 11.

Bennett, Alice. "Radio DJs." In *Encyclopedia of Contemporary British Culture*, ed. Peter Childs and Michael Storry. London: Routledge, 2013.

Berlant, Lauren. *The Female Complaint: The Unfinished Business of Sentimentality in American Culture*. Durham, NC: Duke University Press, 2008.

Briggs, Asa. *The History of Broadcasting in the United Kingdom, vol. V: Competition*. New York: Oxford University Press, 1995.

British Broadcasting Corporation. *Genome (Beta): Radio Times 1923–2009*. Accessed September 22, 2017. http://genome.ch.bbc.co.uk.

British Broadcasting Corporation Written Archives Centre. Programmes as Broadcast, Light Programme, 1957–63.
British Broadcasting Corporation Written Archives Centre. RCONT/Vera Lynn/Artists/File 2 (1944–50).
British Broadcasting Corporation Written Archives Centre. TV Light Entertainment Scripts Sequence 1 1936–1964, reel 81/82.
British Broadcasting Corporation Written Archives Centre. T14/119/Television/SF (Subject File)/At Home-Vera Lynn (1957).
British Broadcasting Corporation Written Archives Centre. TV14/155/2 TV OB's/"Bless 'Em All"/File 1B (May–June 1955).
British Broadcasting Corporation Written Archives Centre. TVART1/Vera Lynn/ File 1 (1938–62).
"The Broadcasters," "Both Sides of the Microphone." *Radio Times*, April 19, 1940, 8.
Chapman, Robert. *Selling the Sixties: The Pirates and Pop Music Radio*. New York: Taylor and Francis, 2002.
Cochrane, Kira. "1963: The Beginning of the Feminist Movement." *The Guardian*, May 7, 2013, https://www.theguardian.com/lifeandstyle/2013/may/07/1963-beginning-feminist-movement.
Cooper, B. Lee. "American Disc Jockeys, 1945–1975: A Bibliographic and Discographic Survey." *Popular Music and Society* 30, no. 3 (2007): 401–23.
Crisell, Andrew. *Understanding Radio*. London: Routledge, 1986.
Curtis, Richard, dir. *Pirate Radio*. Working Titles Films, 2009.
Davis, Angela. *Modern Motherhood: Women and Family in England, 1945–2000*. Manchester, UK: Manchester University Press, 2012.
Douglas, Susan J. *Listening In: Radio and the American Imagination*. Minneapolis: University of Minnesota Press, 2004.
Dyer, Richard. *Stars*, rev. ed. London: BFI Publishing, 2001.
Frith, Simon. *The Sociology of Rock*. London: Constable, 1978.
"Groups Cash In on the Skiffle Craze." *Melody Maker*, January 12, 1957, 4.
Halper, Donna. *Invisible Stars: A Social History of Women in American Broadcasting*. New York: Routledge, 2015.
Keightley, Keir. "Reconsidering Rock." In *The Cambridge Companion to Pop and Rock*, ed. Simon Frith, Will Straw, and John Street, 109–42. Cambridge: Cambridge University Press, 2001.
Killmeier, Matthew. "Voices between the Tracks: Disk Jockeys, Radio, and Popular Music, 1955–60." *Journal of Communication Inquiry* 25 (2001): 353–74.
Kynaston, David. *Family Britain, 1951–57*. London: Bloomsbury, 2009.
Langhamer, Claire. "The Meanings of Home in Postwar Britain." *Journal of Contemporary History*, 20, no. 2 (2005): 341–62.
Long, Paul. "The Primary Code: The Meanings of John Peel, Radio and Popular Music." *Radio Journal: International Studies in Broadcast and Audio Media* 3, no. 3 (2006): 25–48.
Loviglio, Jason. *Radio's Intimate Public: Network Broadcasting and Mass-Mediated Democracy*. Minneapolis: University of Minnesota Press, 2005.
Lucas, George, dir. *American Graffiti*. Lucasfilm, 1973.
Lynn, Dame Vera. *Some Sunny Day: My Autobiography*. London: Harper, 2009.
Malik, Sarita. *Representing Black Britain: A History of Black and Asian Images on British Television*. London: SAGE Publications, 2002.
McKay, George. "Winifred Atwell and Her 'Other Piano': 16 Hit Singles and a 'Blanket of Silence,' Sounding the Limits of Jazz." In *Black British Jazz: Routes, Ownership and Performance*, edited by Jason Toynbee, Catherine Tackley, and Mark Doffman, 153–71. London: Ashgate, 2014.

Murphy, Catherine. "'On an Equal Footing with Men?' Women and Work at the BBC, 1923–1939." PhD diss., Goldsmiths College, University of London, 2011.

Murphy, Catherine. "Women in the BBC: A History, 1922–2002: Biographies." Unpublished paper, 2011.

Newton, Darrell M. *Paving the Empire Road: BBC Television and Black Britons*. Manchester, UK: Manchester University Press, 2011.

Nightingale, Anne. "Radio 1 Turns 50: Annie Nightingale on Pirates, Sexism and the Sound of the Underground." *The Telegraph*, September 25, 2017, https://www.telegraph.co.uk/radio/radio-presenters/radio-1-turns-50-annie-nightingale-pirates-sexism-sound-underground/.

Nightingale, Anne. *Wicked Speed*. London: Pan, 2000.

"NME 1956–67 Nation-Wide Poll." *New Musical Express*, November 23, 1956, 7–9.

Nott, James. *Music for the People: Popular Music and Dance in Interwar Britain*. London: Oxford University Press, 2002.

Pedrick, Gale. "Our Vera." *Radio Times*, August 17, 1956, 6.

Pegley, Kip. "Looking for 'Our Song': Canadian Soldiers and their Remembrance of War." Unpublished paper presented at Society for American Music Meeting, Montreal, 2017.

Programme Listings for August 23, 1956. *Radio Times*, August 17, 1956, 37.

Razlagova, Elena. *The Listener's Voice: Early Radio and the American Public*. Philadelphia: University of Pennsylvania Press, 2011.

R. H. Letter to *Picturegoer*, August 2, 1958, 3.

Richter, Amy G. *Home on the Rails: Women, the Railroad, and the Rise of Public Domesticity*. Chapel Hill: University of North Carolina Press, 2005.

Rothenbuhler, Eric, and Tom McCourt. "Radio Redefines Itself, 1947–1962." In *Radio Reader: Essays in the Cultural History of Radio*, ed. Michele Hilmes and Jason Loviglio, 367–87. New York: Routledge, 2002.

Skoog, Kristin. "Focus on the Housewife: The BBC and the Post-War Woman 1945–1955." *Networking Knowledge: Journal of the MeCCSA Post Graduate Network* 2, no. 1 (2009): 1–12.

Smith, Wes. *The Pied Pipers of Rock 'N' Roll: Radio Deejays of the 50s and 60s*. Lanham, MD: Longstreet Press, 1989.

Spigel, Lynn. *Make Room for TV: Television and the Family Ideal in Postwar America*. Chicago: University of Chicago Press, 1992.

"Star Singers to Present Records Five Nights a Week in New BBC Series." *New Musical Express*, December 2, 1955, 7.

Thumim, Janet. *Inventing Television Culture: Men, Women, and the Box*. Oxford: Oxford University Press, 2004.

"Timeline of the Women's Liberation Movement." *Sisterhood and After*, British Library, October 17, 2018, https://www.bl.uk/sisterhood/timeline.

"Vera Lynn." *Radio Times*, June 13, 1963, 18.

"Vera from Hamburg." *Disc*, February 7, 1959, 11.

"Vera Lynn on the Air." *Melody Maker*, January 12, 1957, 4.

Weight, Richard. *Patriots: National Identity in Britain, 1940–2000*. London: Pan Books, 2003.

Wollman, Elizabeth L. "Men, Music, and Marketing at Q104.3 (WAXQ-FM New York)." *Popular Music and Society* 22 (Winter 1998): 1–23.

Chapter 6

"A Belly Full of Spaghetti and Ears Full of Song": Felice Bryant and Country Music Songwriting in the 1950s

—Paula J. Bishop

Chet Atkins, the country music guitarist and producer, tells the story of arriving at the Hendersonville, Tennessee, home of Felice and Boudleaux Bryant, the Nashville songwriters, probably sometime in the 1950s or 1960s. With the smell of Felice's expert Italian cooking wafting through the air, Atkins recalled:

> You'd go into their house, and Felice'd be in the kitchen cooking supper maybe if I'd stayed for supper. And Boudleaux'd be fooling around on the guitar trying to get a melody started for a song he was writing. And she'd yell from in the kitchen, "That sounds like something else, Boudleaux, don't use that melody." [laughs] And he never talked back to her, but he'd change the melody 'til he got something that . . . she approved of.[1]

On the surface, this scene of domestic tranquility suggests a wife fulfilling the traditional role of that period by playing hostess for her husband's guests. But in fact, Atkins or any other Nashville musician or singer visiting was there to see both Felice and Boudleaux. The Bryants, who began writing songs together around 1946, had, by the mid-1950s, become two of the most sought-after songwriters in Nashville. They wrote songs that appealed to the Nashville artists and marketed them in their own unique way. Capitalizing on Felice's culinary abilities and outgoing personality, they invited artists to their home for dinner. They found that "a belly full of spaghetti and ears full of songs" made the artists more receptive to choosing their songs to record.[2] Felice's use of the domestic sphere allowed her to defy the gendered constraints of time, place, and industry to build a successful career, becoming what Mary Bufwack and Robert Oermann called the "woman who ignited the explosion of women writers on Music Row."[3]

Using published interviews, oral histories collected by the Country Music Hall of Fame, recollections of Felice's sons Dane and Del Bryant, as well as others, and autograph manuscripts, I examine Felice Bryant's songwriting career with her husband, focusing primarily on their formative years in the 1940s and '50s, when they were developing their skills as writers and honing their approach to marketing and managing their output, a period which also saw the coalescence of Nashville as the central site of country music production. At the same time, women's public roles in the workplace had yet to expand as they would with the rise of second-wave feminism in the 1960s. Women in this period often achieved their success not by directly challenging the system but by working within the social rules and understandings of gender roles. Through this examination of the early career of Felice Bryant, a key theme emerges that helps reposition our understanding of women at work in the music industry, and especially the country music industry, in the middle of the twentieth century. We have typically privileged the stories of women—particularly white women—who entered a male-dominated space and adapted to or defied the surroundings and behaviors, but I argue here that women like Felice understood how to bring that world into their own territory (both physical and gendered sociocultural spaces) and manipulate it to their ends, allowing them, in gradual but powerful ways, to contribute to the growth of the music industry.

COUNTRY MUSIC IN THE COLD WAR ERA

The country music industry has largely controlled the historical narrative of the genre, presenting it and its practitioners in a rustic authenticity that adheres to and upholds traditional, conservative values, particularly in regard to gender roles. As Kristine McCusker and Diane Pecknold argue, even the work of historians has been influenced by and contributed to the idea that men created or innovated and women acted in support roles, with the occasional female singer rising to the top.[4] This approach is particularly apparent when examining the history of country music through the 1950s, and ignores the important creative contributions made by women who worked off the stage, such as Felice Bryant. For example, in his seminal work *Country Music U.S.A.*, first published in 1968, Bill Malone included short biographical references to the white women who rose to the top of the charts in the early decades of the industry (1920s through the early 1960s).[5] The descriptions simply identify these performers as women and recognize their participation, but do not engage in any analysis of how their presence might have shaped the definition and understanding of what country music was in that time and place, or how their work (both process and product) affected the construction of meaning by communities of listeners. The assumption by Malone, and subsequent authors, has largely been that a female star was the rare exception to the male-dominated narrative rather than instrumental in the success of the industry. Furthermore, Malone is primarily interested in women as performers and entertainers rather than creatives, producers, and business people, and hence the women songwriters in this period receive scant attention. Mary Bufwack and Robert Oermann, in 2003, produced an encyclopedic volume that included women involved in various aspects of the industry, including Felice Bryant, but as a work of recovered narratives, the authors do not attempt to draw larger meaning from the roles of these women. Scholarship in country music has, however, begun to tackle these issues (though still primarily through a white racial lens), particularly through research and editing by Diane Pecknold, Kristine McCusker, Pamela Fox, Nadine Hubbs, Francesca Royster, and others.[6]

While World War II brought a surge of women working outside the home, the revival of conservative ideals in the Cold War years drew women back into the home and out of the workplace, reestablishing to some degree the nineteenth-century Victorian ideals of piety, purity, submissiveness, and domesticity for women. Elaine Tyler May has connected this idea of domestic containment with the ideology of the Cold War, arguing that establishing a normative family unit defended Americans against subversive social forces such as communism while also providing the foundation for the American aspirations of prosperity and fulfillment.[7] While May's study focuses mostly on white middle-class women and therefore presents a narrow view of women in this period, some aspects of her findings resonate with the lives of the performers and fans of country music in the middle of the twentieth century. For instance, each member of the family unit had a role to play in order to maintain the stability: the man provided the income and security necessary to maintain the idealized white middle-class life, typically working outside of the home, while the woman worked at home, rearing the children, taking care of the household chores such as provisioning, cooking, and cleaning, and providing for the needs of the man. The wife of the Cold War era did not typically seek employment outside of the home because her job *was* the home, and she was expected to be fulfilled by that.

Historical narratives of containment such as May's have been contested by others, including Joanne Meyerwitz, who notes that these depictions reduce the women of the postwar era to victims of societal norms. She and the authors in her collection *Not June Cleaver: Women and Gender in Postwar America, 1945–1960* highlight "pockets of resistance" and the numerous ways that women challenged various systems to bring about change for women.[8] Felice Bryant, a traditional stay-at-home wife and mother, challenged the system by working, albeit not in one of the traditional, "acceptable" roles for women such as a secretary, teacher, or nurse. The real story for many American women like Felice lies in some middle ground that allows them to conform while finding ways to resist and ultimately make changes.

The world of country music fully embraced the postwar conservative notion of the "ideal woman," incorporating it into the social and cultural framework of the industry in two important ways: one was the division of labor and the other was performative. Men worked the technical and managerial jobs, and women were secretaries. As musicians, men played instruments as session musicians or in a band. If they could sing, they could build a career as a solo artist or work as a backup singer. Women typically performed as a lead or backup singer but rarely played instruments. Most songwriters working in country music in the 1950s were men, in part because of gendered expectations but also because of the business of songwriting itself, which had yet to crystallize into a profession that stood apart from performance. Many singers still wrote their own songs, and since most of the country music artists at the time were male, it stands to reason that more men were songwriters than women.

Women performers reenacted and reinforced the gender expectations of country music during the 1950s, foremost by dressing conservatively and behaving "properly." Kitty Wells, who recorded one of the most defiant honky-tonk anthems of the period, "It Wasn't God Who Made Honky-Tonk Angels," regularly appeared on stage on *The Grand Ole Opry* in gingham dresses with high, ruffled collars. These women deferred to their husbands, whether they were musical partners or the husband was an off-stage figure who helped authenticate the woman in the eyes of the industry and the fans. Acting outside of the social and cultural norms—for instance, getting a divorce, acting provocatively toward a man, using crude language, challenging male authority—risked record sales. At the least, it could leave one in a precarious social and historical position in the world of country music, as was the case for Patsy Cline. Shunned by many in Nashville for her resistance to the expectations of a female singer in country music, her legacy was not secured until nearly two decades after her 1963 death, when feminists privileged and honored narratives of rebellious women challenging the system.[9]

These gendered expectations of women were articulated and sustained through fan magazines such as *Country Song Roundup*, which had a regular feature called "Meet the Mrs." that sought to "look into the activities and interests of wives of famous folksingers," many of whom were also musicians, singers, songwriters, and business owners in their own right. The wives were routinely praised for sacrificing their ambition to stay home, raise the children, and maintain an efficient and orderly home in order to make their famous husband's careers possible. Peter La Chapelle noted in his study of country music and the Okie migrant community of Southern California that this conservatism replaced a more liberal and egalitarian approach of the preceding decade, when a woman might be featured as a working cowgirl or celebrated for her skills outside the home.[10] He further notes, however, that while this recontainment of women progressed, Meyerwitz's pockets of resistance still existed within the world of country music and reflected the ongoing negotiation of women's roles in the broader society. La Chapelle argues that the country songs of this era reinforced notions of gender while at the same time providing opportunities for women to transcend those boundaries as performers.

Not unlike its pop and R&B counterparts, country music was dominated by men in the 1950s. In fact, only a handful of women appear on the top singles *Billboard* charts from 1944 to 1960: Margaret Whiting (in a duet with Ferlin Husky), Jean Shepard (as a solo performer and in a duet with Ferlin Husky), Kitty Wells, the Davis Sisters, and the Browns (two women and a man). Aside from attitudes about female performers in country music and restrictions on their activities and behaviors, the dearth of women in country music in this period can also be attributed to limited access to performance outlets such as the stage and radio. Without those, it was more difficult to draw the attention of the record labels, cut a record, and then sell it. Likewise, there were few female songwriters during this period. Performers like Kitty Wells and Martha Carson wrote songs that they would perform or record, but few women wrote mainly for other performers, and those that did typically spent some portion of their career as singers. For instance, Cindy Walker recorded with Decca Records in the 1940s before turning more exclusively to songwriting in the 1950s. She wrote a number of hits for Gene Autry, Eddy Arnold, Webb Pierce, and Bob Wills. Jenny Lou Carson started out performing with her sisters, then recorded in the late 1930s with the Prairie Ramblers. Her songwriting credits include hits for Tex Ritter, Roy Acuff, Eddy Arnold, and Red Foley. Marijohn Wilkin toured with Red Foley in the early 1950s before turning to songwriting. In the 1950s, her songs were recorded by Wanda Jackson, Jimmy C. Newman, Lefty Frizzell, and others. While Felice spent some part of her early years as a performer, she quickly came to focus on songwriting as her career choice.

BECOMING A SONGWRITING TEAM

Felice Bryant (1925–2003) was born Matilda Genevieve Scaduto in Milwaukee, a city filled with the musical influences of recent European immigrants, including Italians, Poles, and Germans.[11] Her father emigrated from Palermo, Sicily, around 1912–13 to Milwaukee and became a barber. Her mother was a second-generation Sicilian American originally from Pennsylvania. Though many of her family members played instruments, Felice claimed she was not a musician: "I play nothing—I don't play the first thing, not even the doorbell. I don't know any of the rules. I can't read music. I can't pick [guitar]."[12] Instead she loved to sing. She sang on a Saturday morning radio show on WEMP and WISN in Milwaukee, performed in musicals at the Riverside Theater, where she was later an usherette, and sang on a USO show during World War II. As a young girl, Felice turned to writing poems and songs as a refuge from the turmoil of her working-class neighborhood and her family. She recalled, "My home life was such that if I had anything on my mind, I couldn't spill it to anybody. And so I wrote."[13] Her treasured copy of *The Best Loved Poems of the American People*, as well as the Italian folksongs of her family and the hymns and sacred songs of the Catholic Church, helped her develop her lyrical writing skills.

Boudleaux (1920–1987) was born in Shellman, Georgia, and grew up near Moultrie, Georgia.[14] He began studying violin at age five, and played for the Atlanta Philharmonic Orchestra for the 1937–38 season. Though classically trained, he absorbed the musical influences around him, including hillbilly music and jazz. Boudleaux used his talents to get fiddling jobs with hillbilly and cowboy bands, notably Hank Penny's Radio Cowboys, who performed on radio station WSB in Atlanta, and Gene Steele and His Sunny Southerners in Memphis. By 1945 he had quit the hillbilly bands and joined a jazz group that toured the United States.

Felice and Boudleaux's life together began on Valentine's Day 1945, when Boudleaux's jazz combo performed at the Schroeder Hotel in Milwaukee. Felice worked there at night as an elevator operator, and, from her vantage point, was able to see the band members when they left the lounge. As a young girl, she had dreamed of dancing with a tall man with a beard when she was eight years old, and when she saw Boudleaux at the water fountain in the lobby, she knew he was literally the man of her dreams: "When I saw Boudleaux, I recognized him! I don't know if you call that love at first sight or 'My God, [my] friend! I was wondering when you'd come along.' . . . He didn't know who the hell I was, but I somehow knew who he was."[15] She got his attention by offering to buy him a drink at the water fountain but accidentally showered him with the stream of water from the fountain. Boudleaux was charmed by her and introduced her to the band as his fiancée later that evening. Five days later, they embarked on their life together, though the marriage would not be official for several months. In the meantime, he gave her the nickname of Felice, which she used for the remainder of her life.[16]

Together Boudleaux and Felice traveled around to his gigs at clubs and state fairs, spending time in Green Bay, Wisconsin; Cincinnati; Oakland, California; Boise, Idaho; Chicago; and Selma, Alabama. Between engagements they often returned to Boudleaux's hometown of Moultrie, eventually settling there. From there Boudleaux often traveled to gigs, leaving Felice at home. Out of boredom and loneliness, she turned to writing songs, poems, and stories. She explained, "My God, it took half an hour to clean this damned apartment. There is nowhere to go. I mean what could you do?"[17] Her efforts eventually led to their songwriting collaboration: "We started writing in Moultrie because we had no money. We were married a year before we wrote together.... Boudleaux would come home and ask, 'What did the little woman do today?'—that old jazz. And I'd say, 'Well, I wrote this and I wrote that' and some of it I would sing, because sometimes the words were melodies in themselves."[18] Eventually they amassed about eighty coauthored songs, at which point, they began contacting publishers, though they did not receive any positive responses.

Finally, in 1949 they met Fred Rose of Acuff-Rose Publishing in Nashville, who arranged to have Little Jimmie Dickens record their song "Country Boy." It rose to #7 on the *Billboard* chart and became an instant favorite at the Grand Ole Opry. Boudleaux and Felice continued to travel, perform, and write, getting three more of their songs recorded. Rose arranged for Boudleaux to work as a song plugger for Tannen Music, a New York–based publishing company owned by Nat Tannen.[19] Song pluggers presented a publisher's song to recording artists and their record companies, hoping to "place" the song with the artist, meaning the artist recorded it and the publishing company collected royalties. Boudleaux negotiated an arrangement with Tannen that allowed him to focus solely on his and Felice's songs. Though Tannen paid him less than what Boudleaux and Felice made as performers, they felt it was the right direction for them. "Everybody thought we were crazy," Felice later noted, "but we saw the far vision."[20] They packed up their two young sons, Del and Dane, and moved to Nashville in 1950 to pursue their dream. Boudleaux continued to represent Tannen until at least the end of 1953. After a two-year attempt at running their own publishing house, they signed a ten-year exclusive deal with Acuff-Rose in 1957, after they had firmly established themselves as hit-making songwriters.[21]

The Bryants recognized that to support themselves and their family as songwriters, they would require a catalog of good songs that had hit potential. Quantity was important, and as Felice held, "you had to write all the garbage out before you got to the jewel."[22] In order to consistently produce enough material to cull through, the Bryants developed a routine at home that allowed them to focus on songwriting while still honoring the requirements of their family. In their early years, they would put their two sons to bed and write all night, without the distraction of the children or the telephone. In the morning they would get Del and Dane ready for school, then sleep during the day while the boys were away. After they built a house on Old Hickory Lake outside of Nashville, they kept more conventional hours, working at least three hours during the day. Being together at home, they could, as Felice recalled, "feed ideas back and forth while I did the housework."[23] Boudleaux acted as scribe, capturing their collaborative ideas on paper while she moved about completing her household chores. In this way, Felice was able to balance the demands of both career and home.

In the early years of their collaboration, they were not very organized in collecting and cataloging their output, but, as Felice recounted, Chet Atkins helped them find a solution:

> Chet noticed that Boudleaux and I were writing on paper napkins, torn pieces off of brown paper bags. Boudleaux'd be going like this [mimes searching pockets], "I got a song right here," you know, and just searching for it, and I'd have my purse open. And Chet said to me, he said, you know, he said, no telling how many good tunes he's losing. Why don't you get him these ledgers like Stephen Foster used to write in. And so I got 500-page ledgers. And Boudleaux and I got up to sixteen of these things. And we didn't lose any material after that.[24]

The first ledger, a gift from Felice to Boudleaux, is inscribed, "To my adorable husband on his 31st birthday. You're a wonderful father and a very loving husband. I thank God for you." She inscribed each ledger after that, sometimes with a loving message, and other times with thoughts about the process or their career ("oil for the House of Bryant," reads the inscription of the book that contains their smash hit "Rocky Top"). As the "keeper of the books," Boudleaux wrote out the melody, lyrics, and chords of any new song, regardless of who had composed it, though I observed several pages in the volume corresponding to 1958 with her handwriting.[25]

Though Felice and Boudleaux collaborated together on their songs, they often started a song individually, then joined forces to finish. Boudleaux described their songwriting process this way:

> Each of us composes music. Each of us writes lyrics. Each of us writes alone from time to time. There's hardly a day that goes by that we don't get some sort of an idea for a song. A lot of days we get five or six ideas for songs and finish them all. Other days we don't finish anything. Most of the time we write together. She might write a song; she might write a piece of lyric that suggests something to me, or she might have a little tune.[26]

Felice wrote constantly, working out her ideas on yellow legal pads or sometimes singing them into a tape recorder. Her compulsion to write led her to once say that "I'll write in a puddle of mud if I can get a stick to make a dent."[27] Boudleaux claimed she had "enough lyrics material to satisfy . . . twenty collaborators."[28] When she had material ready or hummed a tune that Boudleaux thought was promising, he would enter work into the book.

Working together required cooperation and an understanding of each person's unique viewpoint and working process. She was the idea person, practical and grounded in reality, whereas Boudleaux was more cerebral and excelled as the craftsman and polisher of their work: "When we write, if it works Boudleaux lets me go. If it's bad, he lets me go and fixes it later."[29] He had strict ideas about rhyming, grammar, the use of the vernacular, and avoiding artificiality in the lyrics, whereas she was more flexible. The following exchange both demonstrates their differences and the way they interacted:

> FELICE: This is where we argue. His idea of what sounds phony doesn't necessarily sound phony to me. Now we will have a discussion on that.
> INTERVIEWER: Do you believe in leaving it in, too?
> BOUDLEAUX: If it absolutely expresses a thing or if it's in the vernacular of the rest of the song.
> FELICE: Oh, see, there's another point now. If it's in the vernacular of the rest of the song, which could be a perfect piece of grammar but then all of a sudden the word "ain't got no time" wouldn't fit. We would argue, because—
> BOUDLEAUX: I think that if you're writing a song, whenever, especially, it's hopefully going to be a sophisticated type song, then you would want the whole thing to have that flavor. But if the song isn't that sort of song, then—
> FELICE: But sometimes it's very human sounding, too, when it's going along in a sophisticated manner. If it becomes very human, you leave it alone.
> BOUDLEAUX: What you're getting now is a very—
> FELICE: If you stick to a precise sophistication, you become phony.
> BOUDLEAUX: What we're doing—
> FELICE: Then the word "phony" fits.
> BOUDLEAUX: What we're doing now is an example of exactly the way we write together.[30]

This exchange demonstrates that within their working relationship, Felice maintained a unique creative identity that was valued and important to their success as songwriters. And though their differences in style could lead to "some knockdown and drag-out verbal battles over the lyrics of a song,"[31] they found ways to resolve those differences, often through compromise and bargaining.

Felice conceived of songs from a lyrical perspective: "I'm lyrics, and so I start with lyrics. My lyrics have a musical value . . . the words do. And so I compose my melody around my lyrics. But to compose a melody right off the bat, that's not my shtick."[32] She drew inspiration from what was around her: "I'm inspired by the snow. I like snow clouds and white caps on Lake Michigan. And did you know that a drive out Dickerson Road inspires me more than anything else in Middle Tennessee?"[33] She was a keen observer and listened to what was going on around her, whether it was the rhythm of the vacuum as she cleaned house or snippets of conversation that she overheard in the grocery store. Her sons recalled that she eventually had to be more circumspect about jotting down ideas when out in public because people noticed. She was also attuned to current trends and historical moments and could incorporate them into lyrics in a way that could be both specific and timeless. At the same time, she understood the social expectations and constraints of pop and country music in the 1950s and knew what would draw fire and what would not. For example, when Boudleaux was working on "Wake Up, Little Susie," the Everly Brothers 1957 hit, he created racy lyrics. She recognized that those lyrics were not going to be appropriate for those two young boys and fixed it by adding a bridge that clarified and sanitized the scene for listeners.[34]

Stories of love, loss, family, home, and nostalgia have always been central to the lyrical identity of country music, and Felice was a natural storyteller with a sense of the arc needed to captivate listeners and draw them into the narrative. She was adept at performing that task in the miniature form required to write song lyrics, where the story must be conveyed in three minutes, two or three verses, a chorus, and maybe a bridge. For example, the Everly Brothers' 1959 hit "Take a Message to Mary," written primarily by Felice, tells the story of a man in jail asking someone to get word to his fiancée that he will not be returning, but pleading with the messenger not to reveal the truth of his whereabouts.

The Bryants were always careful about attribution. If one contributed even the slightest idea to the song, the name would be carefully inscribed in the ledger books and the copyrights filed accordingly. In her recollection of the creation of "Wake Up, Little Susie," she rushes to be included because she senses a hit in the making: "I was upstairs and I hadn't gotten out of bed yet. And Boudleaux was on the main floor which wasn't carpeted and so the acoustics were just feeding up to the bedroom section. And I hear this, [sings] 'Wake up, little Susie, wake up.' And I thought, 'Man, that sounds great, just that much.' And so I thought, 'I'd better get downstairs' because Boudleaux was most capable of finishing stuff on his own and I had to jump in when I thought we've got something here and I want a piece of this."[35] While she provided more suitable lyrics for this song, Boudleaux wrote the opening prologue of "Take a Message to Mary" because he felt her composition needed something more.[36] Though each of these songs had one main writer, both are credited, reflecting their collaborative approach and sense of fairness.

To get songs into the hands of the artists, publishers in New York and Nashville in the 1950s relied on song pluggers, who were often not the song's composer. These company representatives visited recording studios or record labels and pitched songs as artists came and went. The Bryants *did* pitch songs in the small demo studio of their publisher Acuff-Rose, and occasionally made demo tapes that could be circulated, though they had less success placing a song that way.

According to Felice, if she sang, Boudleaux would be dissatisfied because she might be off-pitch or not sing something the way he wanted it, and when he sang on the demos, he sounded "bad."[37] Instead, the Bryants took a more personal and direct approach, one that capitalized on Felice's personality and domestic skills. Their early efforts centered on two places: their home(s) in the Nashville area and the Grand Ole Opry, the metaphorical home of country music. In both environs, Felice tapped into and resisted gendered assumptions and networks.

From the moment they arrived in Nashville in 1950, the Bryants started going to the Opry on Saturday nights. Boudleaux, whom many of the musicians knew from his playing on radio station WSB and his work with Hank Penny, would go backstage and jam with the (mostly male) musicians while Felice chatted with the women backstage. Developing backstage relationships with the singers allowed them to gather information on what the artists needed, as well as develop a sense of that person's style. Boudleaux recalls, "People found out that we wrote songs and they'd ask us if we had anything and we never said no. If we didn't have anything, we'd rush home and write it in a hurry and invite them out to dinner."[38] Felice used their time at the Opry to help ensure the success of their songs that were being performed on stage that night. As Del remembers it, "Mom was always running around and going out to the stage area to get in the audience to scream and yell and hopefully encourage an encore from the audience because if you got an encore your song was sung again or you had another verse that Mom and Dad had written and sung again. It was better exposure for your song. And if you had three or four or five or six encores on a song, it might help launch it into that next level of whatever that it took to become a hit."[39] To work the audience at the Opry required that Felice tap into the network of women backstage—singers and wives of musicians—to find someone to watch their two young sons.

Early in their days in Nashville, Felice and Boudleaux began inviting singers to their house for dinner, a tactic that proved to be their most effective sales tool. Felice would fix spaghetti, veal scaloppini, or chicken cacciatore (relatively exotic in Nashville in the 1950s). Boudleaux would suggest songs, singing the tune while accompanying himself on the guitar. Felice would offer commentary from the kitchen and generally charm the visitors. Fred Foster, founder of Monument Records, remembers the scene: "When they were showing songs, it was like a party. She was always bringing something to eat or drink, and he's singing or looking through the book [one of the song ledgers]. And he comes on a song, 'Oh, this might be good.' And she'd say, 'No, Boudleaux, how about so-and-so?' because that would trigger something in her mind, you know."[40] Felice once humorously noted that they fed the artists "until they couldn't move and Boudleaux would have a captive audience. They had to listen, and to get out, they had to take something. We'd trap 'em!"[41] Once a song was chosen, Boudleaux and Felice might teach the artist the song while he was still at the house, though they sometimes made demo tapes for that purpose. They could also discuss and give advice on the arrangement of the song for the record. When they moved to their lakeside house in Hendersonville, their home became a popular destination, with people like the Everly Brothers, Eddie Arnold, Jimmy Dickens, Bob Luman, and others visiting for dinner and to hear songs. The convivial setting for these meetings helped build personal relationships between the Bryants and most of the people involved in country music.

Working at home this way served multiple purposes. They could keep the ledger books safe at home yet still present songs directly to artists. It also solved some of the logistical problems of raising two young children while working as professional songwriters. When Dane and Del were very young and the family was living in the trailer on Dickerson Road in Nashville, Felice and Boudleaux would put the boys to bed in the only bedroom in the trailer while they worked with the artists. After the guests left, they would move the boys to the pullout sofa in the living room. Dane and Del recall hearing singers such as Cowboy Copas and Hawkshaw Hawkins working on songs with their parents.[42] Felice also recognized that in order to be active in their songwriting career in Nashville and country music at that time required tactics that differed from what a male songwriter might do: "[T]hat was one of the reasons I stayed home a lot because it aggravated the good old boys. And you sort of tried pretty much to stay out of their way because you were an uppity woman, whatever the hell that was. But what I did at home was my business. I'm glad that Boudleaux enjoyed what we did at home and it became a business. It started out as a hobby, but it became our livelihood. But I still had to stay out of the way of the boys."[43] The men did not want her in their space, but she could get them into hers and use her skills and tools to create a working business relationship.

FELICE AS COUNTRY MUSIC PIONEER

An article in the June 22, 1952, edition of *The Tennessean* drew readers' attention to the fact that "everybody's writing songs," from schoolteachers to cabdrivers.[44] The article featured two housewives, Marjorie Marlow and Estelle Friedman, of Nashville. An accompanying photograph shows the two women sitting on a couch in what appears to be a home (as opposed to an office), notebooks and pencil in hand, presumably working on a new song together, visually signifying a tranquil and casual domestic setting for these writers. The author notes that Nashville has become a "hopeful paradise for amateurs," and consequently, the reader understands that the songwriting efforts of these two women is a hobby or amusing diversion, although at least three of their songs had been recorded by this point.

Furthermore, in a dismissal of both the writers and country music in one stroke, the author notes that these women, who studied poetry and music in college, have set that training aside to write for the folk music industry (as country music was sometimes called at the time). Instead, their lyrics rely on simple constructions and clever phrases to capture the listener's attention. The article also describes the work of Helen Hudgins, who had some relatively significant writing credits during the 1950s. The wife of a US district attorney, Hudgins has "four children to care for and an eleven-room house in Franklin to supervise. Her songs have been written between household chores."[45] The author positions songwriting as a secondary activity for women that must be balanced against the demands of being a wife and mother, an idea that was echoed in the "Meet the Mrs." series that appeared in *Country Song Roundup* in the early 1950s.

While Felice embraced the domestic expectations of a wife and mother in the 1950s, she also bent the system to her own needs and desires. She cooked meals for her family and for guests because that was what was expected, but she also loved to cook. She arose at six o'clock in the morning "to a bundle of surprises . . . Whatever happens I go along with it. The only thing I'm sure of is breakfast at 6:15 a.m. and dinner at 4:30 p.m. I get the kids their breakfast and they're off to school. Then bedlam starts. Boudleaux and I may sit down to write or have people in to play some tunes for, or drive out to our farm on the other side of town. We never remember to eat lunch."[46] At the same time, she integrated her children into her professional aims: "[W]orking and raising kids came easy for me. When we're writing, we're at home. I never carried the usual mama-load. And we took 'em with us everywhere. . . . They were never shooed away when company came."[47] Dane and Del helped prepare the house and dinner for guests, and were encouraged to participate in the creative exchange with artists. Del recalls Boudleaux allowing him to select songs that might be appropriate for a visiting artist, and Felice told a story once of Del singing one of the Bryant songs for Kitty Wells ("she didn't cut it!").[48] Both Dane and Del remember helping their parents record demos; they were usually charged with turning on and off the tape recorder.

Working in the country music industry in the 1950s meant facing certain expectations about appearance, behavior, and deportment. A feature piece on songwriter Cindy Walker in 1950 described her this way: "here's a gal that looks good, sounds good, is good. Well, she's got everything, and brains besides!"[49] The writer "admire[s] modesty" (presumably Walker's) and declares her to be "sweet," hoping she will always stay that way. Other articles throughout *Country Song Roundup* describe women in similar fashion, sometimes even listing their height and weight, and often expressing surprise at their skills and accomplishments outside of the home. It is against this backdrop that Felice made her way as a songwriter. As many people described to me, she spoke her mind and was willing to vigorously promote and defend her work. She said of herself, "Direct from brain to mouth—no censoring action, that's me. But I'll tell you something, if I censored myself I'd lose 9½ ballgames out of 10. Sometimes I hear myself saying something before I know I'm saying it."[50]

Though she was forthright and ambitious, Felice faced obstacles. As their younger son Del explained, some artists liked the idea of a song that Boudleaux had written and were not as receptive to one that Felice had written or participated in writing. Rumors swirled that Boudleaux had given her songwriting credits just to make her happy.[51] Felice was aware of these sentiments, and it aggravated her because it was decidedly not the case. In addition to being a woman and being the wife of a songwriter, Del also thought part of the problem was that Felice did not play an instrument.[52] The assumption was that if you were not a musician (and vocalists—therefore many women performers—are excluded from the cadre of musicians), you could not write a melody. Another strike against Felice in the South of the 1950s was her ethnic heritage: she was a petite woman from the North with strong Italian features in a Nashville that was dominated by women from long-standing white Southern families who could trace their roots to the British Isles, hence she was cast as an outsider.[53] In spite of this, Felice knew she was a trailblazer: "I've been opening new doors all my life. I really believe ignorance is best. You can break rules if you don't know there are any—innovators are just rule breakers—the guy with a little knowledge is the one who's limited. In music, in this business, you need to know a lot of nothing, Boudleaux knows a lot . . . I don't know any of the rules . . . I can't quit now, though—I'm a star!"[54] Lionel Cartwright, a country music artist who met the Bryants in the early 1980s, got the impression from her that in the face of opposition, she felt compelled to produce the best work she could and a lot of it.[55] She watched out for herself, but Del explains that she was also willing to champion the work of other women and advise them on surviving in the business and in life.

CONCLUSION

It is estimated that by the end of their careers, the Bryants had written thousands of songs, of which an estimated 800 have been recorded multiple times and in other genres besides country. Some of their biggest hits came in the late 1950s with the rock 'n' roll duo the Everly Brothers, but other early hits included recordings by Little Jimmie Dickens, Cowboy Copas, Carl Smith, Ernest Tubb, Kitty Wells, and others. Later recording artists included Emmylou Harris, Gram Parsons, Bob Dylan, the Osborne Brothers, and many more. Their song "Rocky Top" became one of the official state songs of Tennessee and is regularly performed at sporting events by the University of Tennessee's marching band. Though Felice only had seven copyrighted solo songwriting credits, she coauthored over four hundred songs with Boudleaux. They were inducted as a team into the Nashville Songwriters Hall of Fame (1972), National Songwriters Hall of Fame (1986), National Academy of Popular Music (1986), and the Country Music Hall of Fame (1991). Felice was also awarded the Nashville Arts Foundation's Living Legend Award in 1991.

When Boudleaux died in 1987, Felice retreated from the world and from songwriting for a period of time. She did attempt another songwriting partnership with Dennis Morgan, writing five songs in two days in 1990, but she told an interviewer in 1995 that she and Boudleaux could write as many as ten songs a day. Without him, she found the songwriting "stopped being fun."[56] She continued to write, however, creating more songs, poems, stories, plays, and monologues.

In retelling their life story, Boudleaux often implied that if it were not for Felice's strong drive to write, he might have continued as a working musician, leading the family from job to job, town to town. Felice created a model for women who wished to maintain agency over their work and home lives while working as professionals in the country music business. She was deeply engaged in the writing of their songs, and enjoyed that aspect of it tremendously. She was grateful to have success at doing what she loved while still raising a family. She actively constructed the identity that she wanted and needed under the real and changing constraints of the time and place in which she lived. She inspired later generations of both male and female songwriters, including Gail Davies, who draws attention to Felice's influence in her own autobiography.[57] Davies shared with me that when Felice was near the end of her life and gravely ill, Davies "sent her a card telling her how much she had influenced other female writers, what a great role model she had been."[58] Finally, we can wonder if Felice's presence on Music Row and at her home entertaining (mostly male) recording artists and industry leaders acclimated people to the idea of women as full participants in the creation and production of country music outside of their traditional roles as singers and secretaries.

NOTES

1. Lee Wilson, *All I Have to Do Is Dream: The Boudleaux and Felice Bryant Story*, DVD (Nashville: House of Bryant, 2011).

2. Boudleaux Bryant and Felice Bryant, interview by John Rumble, March 26, 1983, 47, Frist Library and Archive, Country Music Hall of Fame and Museum.

3. Mary A. Bufwack and Robert K. Oermann, *Finding Her Voice: Women in Country Music, 1800–2000* (Nashville: Country Music Foundation Press and Vanderbilt University, 2003), 327.

4. See especially Kristine M. McCusker and Dianne Pecknold, ed., *A Boy Named Sue: Gender and Country Music* (Jackson: University Press of Mississippi, 2004); Dianne Pecknold and Kristine M. McCusker, ed., *Country Boys and Redneck Women: New Essays in Gender and Country Music* (Jackson: University Press of Mississippi, 2016); Kristine M. McCusker, "Gendered Stages: Country Music, Authenticity, and the Performance of Gender," in *The*

Oxford Handbook of Country Music, ed. Travis Stimeling (New York: Oxford University Press, 2017), 355–73.

5. Bill C. Malone, *Country Music U.S.A.: A 50-Year History* (Austin: University of Texas Press, 1968). The first edition was based on his 1965 dissertation. The second edition was published in 1985 with new material and revised in 2002. A third revised edition was published in 2010, with additional material provided by Jocelyn Neal regarding the first decades of the twenty-first century.

6. McCusker and Pecknold, *A Boy Named Sue*; Pecknold and McCusker, *Country Boys and Redneck Women*; Pamela Fox, *Natural Acts: Gender, Race, and Rusticity in Country Music* (Ann Arbor: University of Michigan Press, 2009); Nadine Hubbs, *Redneck, Queers, and Country Music* (Berkeley: University of California Press, 2014); Nadine Hubbs and Francesca Royster, "Uncharted Country: New Voices and Perspectives in Country Music Studies," *Journal of Popular Music Studies* 32, no. 2 (June 2020): 1–10.

7. Elaine Tyler May, *Homeward Bound: American Families in the Cold War Era* (New York: Basic Books, 2008). May's study focuses mostly on white middle-class women and, thus presents a narrow view of women in this period.

8. Joanne Meyerowitz, "Introduction: Women and Gender in Postwar America, 1945–1960," in *Not June Cleaver: Women and Gender in Postwar America, 1945–1960*, ed. Joanne Meyerowitz (Philadelphia: Temple University Press, 1994), 4.

9. Joli Jensen, "Patsy Cline's Crossovers: Celebrity, Reputation, and Feminine Identity," in *A Boy Named Sue: Gender and Country Music*, 107–31.

10. Peter La Chapelle, *Proud to Be an Okie: Cultural Politics, Country Music, and Migration to Southern California* (Berkeley: University of California Press, 2007), 163.

11. Wilson, *All I Have to Do Is Dream: The Boudleaux and Felice Bryant Story* (Nashville, TN: House of Bryant Publications, 2011); Bobbie Malone and Bill C. Malone, *Nashville's Songwriting Sweethearts: The Boudleaux and Felice Bryant Story*, Illustrated ed. (Norman: University of Oklahoma Press, 2020).

12. Quoted in Wilson, *All I Have to Do Is Dream*, 25.

13. Quoted in Wilson, *All I Have to Do Is Dream*, 23.

14. Wilson, *All I Have to Do Is Dream*; Malone and Malone, *Nashville's Songwriting Sweethearts*.

15. Quoted in Lee Rector, "Writers Felice & Boudleaux Review 30 Years," *Music City News*, February 1980, 7.

16. Wilson, *All I Have to Do Is Dream*, 26–30.

17. Boudleaux Bryant and Felice Bryant, interview by Patricia A. Hall, November 19, 1975, 16, Frist Library and Archive, Country Music Hall of Fame and Museum.

18. Quoted in Wilson, *All I Have to Do Is Dream*, 35, 38.

19. Bryant and Bryant, interview, November 19, 1975, 27.

20. Quoted in Rector, "Writers Felice & Boudleaux Review 30 Years," 7.

21. At the end of the Acuff-Rose deal, the domestic rights to all of the Bryants' tunes reverted back to them and are now held by their publishing company, House of Bryant.

22. Dane, quoting his mother, in Wilson, *All I Have to Do Is Dream* (DVD).

23. Quoted in Jack Hurst, "Hit-Writing Song Pros Still Don't Know 'Why,'" *Nashville Tennessean*, March 22, 1971, 27.

24. Wilson, *All I Have to Do Is Dream* (DVD).

25. At the time I originally wrote this, the ledgers were in the possession of the Bryants' sons and housed in a bank vault. Del and Dane allowed me to view the ledgers in the offices of the bank. The ledgers have since been digitized by the Country Music Hall of Fame and the images are available in their digital archive, https://digi.countrymusichalloffame.org/.

26. Quoted in Wilson, *All I Have to Do Is Dream*, 39.
27. Quoted in Paula Schwed, "Making It in Nashville," *Kingsport* (TN) *Times*, April 8, 1978, 2.
28. Quoted in Wilson, *All I Have to Do Is Dream*, 39.
29. Quoted in Lee Wilson, "Meet Felice and Boudleaux Bryant, Writers of 'Rocky Top' and Many Other Hit Songs," *Knoxville Magazine*, July 1981, 20.
30. Bryant and Bryant, interview, November 19, 1975, 8.
31. Boudleaux Bryant, quoted in H. B. Teeter, "Boudleaux & Felice: The Whole Nation Sings Their Songs," *Nashville Tennessean*, January 8, 1956, 9.
32. Quoted in Wilson, *All I Have to Do Is Dream*, 25.
33. Quoted in Teeter, "Boudleaux & Felice: The Whole Nation Sings Their Songs," 9.
34. Wilson, *All I Have to Do Is Dream* (DVD).
35. Wilson, *All I Have to Do Is Dream* (DVD).
36. Michael Kosser, "The Everly Brothers and the Bryants: A Husband-and-Wife Team Launches the Greatest Duo in the History of Pop Music," in *How Nashville Became Music City U.S.A.: 50 Years of Music Row* (Milwaukee: Hal Leonard, 2006), 93.
37. Wilson, *All I Have to Do Is Dream* (DVD).
38. Wilson, *All I Have to Do Is Dream* (DVD).
39. Wilson, *All I Have to Do Is Dream* (DVD).
40. Wilson, *All I Have to Do Is Dream* (DVD).
41. Quoted in Wilson, *All I Have to Do Is Dream*, 68.
42. Wilson, *All I Have to Do Is Dream* (DVD).
43. Wilson, *All I Have to Do Is Dream* (DVD).
44. Bill Woolsey, "Everybody's Writing Songs," *Tennessean*, June 22, 1952.
45. Woolsey, "Everybody's Writing Songs," 8.
46. "Bryant Home Is Alive with Sound of Music," *Sandusky* (Ohio) *Register*, January 27, 1965.
47. Ed Ward, "Country Music's Roots Wrapped around Couple," *Austin American-Statesman*, October 23, 1981, E5.
48. Ward, "Country Music's Roots Wrapped around Couple."
49. "Life Is a Song for Cindy Walker," *Country Song Roundup*, February 1950.
50. Wilson, "Meet Felice and Boudleaux Bryant," 21.
51. Del Bryant, interview with author, July 17, 2017.
52. Del Bryant, interview with author, July 17, 2017.
53. Del Bryant, interview with author, July 17, 2017.
54. Wilson, "Meet Felice and Boudleaux Bryant," 20.
55. Lionel Cartwright, interview with author, July 12, 2017.
56. Sylvia A. Nash, "All You Have to Do Is Dream," *Southern Reader*, Summer/Fall 2009, 21.
57. Gail Davies, *The Last of the Outlaws: The Life and Music of Gail Davies* (Gail Davies, 2011).
58. Gail Davies, interview with author, July 27, 2017.

BIBLIOGRAPHY

Bryant, Boudleaux, and Felice Bryant. Interview by John Rumble, March 26, 1983. Frist Library and Archive, Country Music Hall of Fame and Museum.
Bryant, Boudleaux, and Felice Bryant. Interview by Patricia A. Hall, November 19, 1975. Frist Library and Archive, Country Music Hall of Fame and Museum.
Bufwack, Mary A., and Robert K. Oermann. *Finding Her Voice: Women in Country Music, 1800–2000*. Nashville: Country Music Foundation Press and Vanderbilt University, 2003.

Davies, Gail. *The Last of the Outlaws: The Life and Music of Gail Davies*. Gail Davies, 2011.
Fox, Pamela. *Natural Acts: Gender, Race, and Rusticity in Country Music*. Ann Arbor: University of Michigan Press, 2009.
Hubbs, Nadine. *Rednecks, Queers, and Country Music*. Berkeley: University of California Press, 2014.
Hubbs, Nadine, and Francesca Royster. "Uncharted Country: New Voices and Perspectives in Country Music Studies." *Journal of Popular Music Studies* 32, no. 2 (June 2020): 1–10.
Hurst, Jack. "Hit-Writing Song Pros Still Don't Know 'Why.'" *Nashville Tennessean*, March 22, 1971.
Jensen, Joli. "Patsy Cline's Crossovers: Celebrity, Reputation, and Feminine Identity." In *A Boy Named Sue: Gender and Country Music*, 107–31. Jackson: University Press of Mississippi, 2004.
Kosser, Michael. "The Everly Brothers and the Bryants: A Husband-and-Wife Team Launches the Greatest Duo in the History of Pop Music." In *How Nashville Became Music City U.S.A.: 50 Years of Music Row*, 87–94. Milwaukee: Hal Leonard, 2006.
La Chapelle, Peter. *Proud to Be an Okie: Cultural Politics, Country Music, and Migration to Southern California*. Berkeley: University of California Press, 2007.
"Life Is a Song for Cindy Walker." *Country Song Roundup*, February 1950.
Malone, Bill C. *Country Music U.S.A.: A 50-Year History*. Austin: University of Texas Press, 1968.
Malone, Bobbie, and Bill C. Malone. *Nashville's Songwriting Sweethearts: The Boudleaux and Felice Bryant Story*. Illustrated ed. Norman: University of Oklahoma Press, 2020.
May, Elaine Tyler. *Homeward Bound: American Families in the Cold War Era*. New York: Basic Books, 2008.
McCusker, Kristine M. "Gendered Stages: Country Music, Authenticity, and the Performance of Gender." In *The Oxford Handbook of Country Music*, edited by Travis Stimeling, 355–73. New York: Oxford University Press, 2017.
McCusker, Kristine M., and Dianne Pecknold, ed. *A Boy Named Sue: Gender and Country Music*. Jackson: University Press of Mississippi, 2004.
Meyerowitz, Joanne. "Introduction: Women and Gender in Postwar America, 1945–1960." In *Not June Cleaver: Women and Gender in Postwar America, 1945–1960*, edited by Joanne Meyerowitz, 1–18. Philadelphia: Temple University Press, 1994.
Nash, Sylvia A. "All You Have to Do Is Dream." *Southern Reader*, Summer/Fall 2009.
Pecknold, Dianne, and Kristine M. McCusker, ed. *Country Boys and Redneck Women: New Essays in Gender and Country Music*. Jackson: University Press of Mississippi, 2016.
Rector, Lee. "Writers Felice & Boudleaux Review 30 Years." *Music City News*, February 1980.
Schwed, Paula. "Making It in Nashville." *Kingsport* (TN) *Times*, April 8, 1978.
Teeter, H. B. "Boudleaux & Felice: The Whole Nation Sings Their Songs." *Nashville Tennessean*, January 8, 1956.
Ward, Ed. "Country Music's Roots Wrapped around Couple." *Austin American-Statesman*, October 23, 1981.
Wilson, Lee. "Meet Felice and Boudleaux Bryant, Writers of 'Rocky Top' and Many Other Hit Songs." *Knoxville Magazine*, July 1981.
Wilson, Lee. *All I Have to Do Is Dream: The Boudleaux and Felice Bryant Story*. Nashville, TN: House of Bryant Publications, 2011.
Wilson, Lee. *All I Have to Do Is Dream: The Boudleaux and Felice Bryant Story*. DVD. Nashville, TN: House of Bryant, 2011.
Woolsey, Bill. "Everybody's Writing Songs." *The Tennessean*, June 22, 1952.

Chapter 7

Goldie and the Gingerbreads: A Case Study of the All-Girl Band in 1960s Rock 'n' Roll

—Brittany Greening

In 1962 Goldie Zelkowitz landed on the idea of an all-female rock and roll group following her introduction to drummer Ginger Panebianco at the Cinderella Club in Greenwich Village.[1] Zelkowitz was a Jewish R&B singer with an eye for commercial branding and was impressed by Panebianco's simultaneous talent and sex appeal. She recognized the possibilities of a white, female rock and roll band whose members not only looked alluring but who could also competently play their instruments, as this combination was all but unheard of at the time. The two women combined their names to form Goldie and the Gingerbreads and began the tedious process of recruiting other female musicians to the project.[2] The music industry rewarded their efforts when the Gingerbreads were offered a record contract with Decca in 1963, earning the distinction "the first all-female rock and roll group to be signed to a major label."[3] With the addition of pianist Carol O'Grady and the support of a major label, the trio toured West Germany and Switzerland with Chubby Checker.[4] In 1964 they provided entertainment for the Mods and Rockers' Ball, a birthday party for recent Warhol discovery Baby Jane Holzer.[5] While performing at the party, the Gingerbreads attracted the attention of Atlantic Records founder Ahmet Ertegun, who quickly signed them to the Atlantic subsidiary label Atco.[6]

Rock and roll music histories often overlook the Gingerbreads or mention them only briefly. In this essay I propose several reasons for this absence. The first reason is that the Gingerbreads fell between dominant popular music genre categories because they lacked a bass player to round out their standard rock and roll lineup, because the group was comprised only of white women, and because of contextual specificities of the music industry at the time. Secondly, rather than subverting gender and performance conventions of the period, the group prioritized their own commercial success by playing up their novelty status and hyper-performing their femininity. Consequently, those feminist musicological histories that privilege female performers who resisted or subverted rock and roll's masculinist ethos, rather than those who worked within it, tend not to pay heed to the Gingerbreads. Finally, the masculine ideals that historically informed rock and roll criticism fundamentally impacted both the ways popular musicians were evaluated at the time and how they have been historicized and retrospectively located within (or excluded from) the canon.[7]

This work emerges from my consideration of whether documenting the experiences of artists and groups like the Gingerbreads can serve as one way to contest the enduring hegemony of a rock and roll canon that depends on and perpetuates masculine ideals of aesthetic criteria and engagement.[8] While the Gingerbreads have not been canonized because they did not necessarily redefine or reimagine the field of rock and roll music and culture, their experiences and challenges reveal much about the mess of tensions and contradictions in which female popular musicians find themselves ensnared. I am occupied with a feminist enterprise of not simply applying those same masculine canonical ideals to female popular musicians and retrospectively asserting their place within the canon. Instead, I imagine a mode of feminist musicological scholarship that takes as its starting point the experiences of individual female musicians or groups on a case-by-case basis. I posit that doing so allows us to begin to untangle that mess of tensions and contradictions while also acknowledging the important and impactful experiences of those women who worked within the preexisting confines of rock and roll conventions to build careers for themselves.

This essay examines the experiences of Goldie and the Gingerbreads as white women in the male-dominated field of rock and roll and attempts to locate those experiences within the shifting political and social landscape of the mid-1960s. It emphasizes the group's historical and social contexts as a means of highlighting the racial, gendered, and genre-related tensions which informed the careers and experiences of the Gingerbreads' members. My discussion herein builds from Maureen Mahon's assertion that "all musicians must negotiate the dynamics of race, gender, and sexuality as they intersect with historical context and questions of musical genre, artistic voice, commercial viability, and mainstream views of race-and gender-appropriate expression."[9]

THE GINGERBREADS, FEMALE PROPRIETY, AND MIDDLE-CLASS RESPECTABILITY

The same year that Goldie and the Gingerbreads signed to Decca Records, Betty Friedan envisioned a greater potential for American women in *The Feminine*

Mystique. To some, Friedan's text is a benchmark for the emergent second-wave feminism movement because of its thorough unpacking of the disservices done to educated white American women by their limited social roles.[10] To others, the text homogenizes the experiences of American women and, as Jo Gill writes, takes "as a norm a white, middle-class, heterosexual, suburban experience."[11] There is consensus, however, that *The Feminine Mystique* entered prominently into discourses about white American femininity in the 1960s and contributed to shifting conceptualizations of gender roles in the United States.[12] Still, it wasn't until the latter half of the decade that second-wave feminism cumulated into a fully realized social movement; so, as of 1963, the experiences of white women in the United States were still informed, if not defined, by 1950s expectations of feminine propriety and middle-class respectability. For this reason, when temporary Goldie and the Gingerbreads bass player Nancy Peterman became pregnant while on tour, bandleader Goldie Zelkowitz felt she had no choice but to attempt to procure Peterman an illegal abortion. "In the 1960s, birth control for unmarried women was still illegal in certain states," journalist Claire Fallon explains.[13] "*Roe v. Wade* was not yet a glimmer in the Supreme Court's eye, and an attempt to get [Peterman] an illicit procedure fell through."[14] As a result, Peterman had to leave the band and the Gingerbreads were left, not for the first time, without a bassist.[15]

Throughout their short career, the Gingerbreads reorganized their lineup several times as members left and were replaced. They achieved relative lineup stability in 1964 with the addition of guitarist and backup singer Carol MacDonald, and with the exchange of Carol O'Grady's piano for Margo Lewis's B-3 Hammond organ. In her memoir *Lollipop Lounge*, Zelkowitz (who now writes and produces records under the name Genya Ravan) recalls the difficulty of filling the band's all-female roster:

> [F]inding other Gingerbreads was always going to be difficult. In the 1960s, it was really unusual for girls to pick up instruments unless they were somewhat strange to begin with. What mother would encourage her little darling to play drums or bass or trombone back then? The same went for music classes. Back then the piano, or even the violin, was considered a suitable instrument for a young girl, but the notion of training to play rock 'n' roll was unimaginable. Rock 'n' roll was what juvenile delinquents did, not young ladies.[16]

Zelkowitz's comments regarding the musical practices of women at the time are consistent with Mavis Bayton's observations that classical training on typically feminine instruments such as violin, piano, and flute works to "affirm hegemonic femininity," and so is an acceptable musical vehicle for young women, while playing rock instruments is not.[17] The Gingerbreads remained bassless throughout the majority of their career, adapting to the limited availability of female bass players and Zelkowitz's exacting band member selection by opting to have the bass material played on the Hammond B-3 organ. The organ consequently became a prominent timbre in the group's sound, as it was with many bands of the decade, and it developed into a sonic signifier of the Gingerbreads' adaptability to the inherently masculinist nature of rock and roll, a genre that explicitly discouraged the participation of women on electric instruments such as the bass.[18] Even as the rock and roll band lineup cohered into the now-standard iteration of guitar, bass guitar, drums, and vocals, the Gingerbreads utilized their nonstandard instrumentation to amplify their sonic femininity and solidify their novelty status.[19] This strategy differentiated the Gingerbreads from other all-female rock and roll bands of the era such as the Pleasure Seekers, the Liverbirds, Ace of Cups, and Fanny, all of which adhered more firmly to the standard rock and roll lineup. However, as I will demonstrate, it also undermined their status as a legitimate rock and roll band.

The challenge of finding and maintaining a full Gingerbreads roster continued to dog Zelkowitz and Panebianco. Zelkowitz's observations on the topic demonstrate that the band's experiences were informed by tensions of competing modes of 1960s white female subjectivity and reveal how gendered tensions among band members became incorporated into concerns about the band's genre categorization and marketability. Their first guitar player, Shuggie Q, "walked and talked like a truck driver" and was too "obviously butch" for the band's aesthetic, according to Zelkowitz, who preferred members to adhere to conventionally feminine modes of gender performance.[20] Bass player Nancy Peterman was a short-lived asset because her unplanned pregnancy forced her to leave the band in 1964.[21] The band's original pianist, Carol O'Grady, was deemed "not 'rhythm and blues' enough" for the group and her domestic priorities became equally problematic. This reveals Zelkowitz's inherent awareness of the potential for popular music genres to powerfully affect the direction of an artist's career and suggests tensions among the band members regarding their competing ideals of female subjectivity.[22] Zelkowitz recollects that "Ginger and I discovered that Carol really was different from us. She had different dreams: she wanted to get married, have a home and raise children."[23]

For some women of the era, such as Zelkowitz and Panebianco, rock and roll provided an escape from the domesticity that, for others such as O'Grady, defined the experience of womanhood. "The life plan set out for these girls was unacceptable to them," Wini Breines observes in her analysis of the 1950s white female experience.[24] The Gingerbreads developed into women during the fifties, so norms and mores from that decade continued to inform their experiences. "Their society's expectations and, closer to home, those of their parents, did not coincide with their own yearnings. . . . They rebelled against the bourgeois respectability and timidity of middle-class conventions that included domestic gender expectations."[25] Though several of the one-time Gingerbreads succumbed to the comfort of family life, Zelkowitz and Panebianco viewed domesticity as the anticlimax to their musical careers and sought explicitly to avoid it. However, middle-class respectability proved difficult to overcome, especially for the Gingerbreads' parents, who held particular views about gender propriety and attempted to exert varying degrees of control over their daughters' careers.

Zelkowitz, the daughter of Jewish-Polish refugees, remembers her acute awareness of the discrepancies between her own desires and her mother's. Zelkowitz recalls, "My mother had an image of the perfect little girl she wanted, and . . . I could not be that girl—the girl who agreed with everything, smiled and was polite, who wore frilly bows in her hair and lace on her clothes."[26] In this passage she names the gendered signifiers that, as a child, made her aware of the confines of female propriety. Gretchen Lemke-Santangelo explains that during the 1950s, "working-class girls were more tightly controlled by their families than at least some of their brothers and more affluent female peers. Their parents, particularly those aspiring to middle-class status, were often more concerned about preventing moral lapses among their daughters than in fostering girls' independence and freedom."[27] As Polish immigrants, the Zelkowitz family's aspiration for middle-class status and adherence to its norms may have been heightened by their desire to assimilate, which subsequently amplified Zelkowitz's feelings of social suffocation.

This parental preoccupation with respectability similarly affected Zelkowitz's fellow Gingerbreads Susan MacDonald and Ginger Panebianco. In an interview with Gillian G. Gaar, MacDonald recounts her feelings of being "torn" between wanting her parents to remain ignorant to the "improper" places where she was spending time and desiring their permission to travel to Philadelphia to record a single.[28] Gaar writes that, "armed with her parents' permission, MacDonald traveled to Philadelphia and made her first record, 'I'm in Love'/'Sam, Sam, Sam, My Rock and Roll Man,' for a local label before starting college."[29] For Panebianco, the tension between her family's respectability and her desire to make rock and roll formed a rift between her and her parents. At the prospect of a Miami gig with the otherwise all-male band Devlin and the Premiers, she requested her parents' permission to travel south. She was promptly informed that it was unacceptable for a seventeen-year-old girl to travel unsupervised to Miami in the company of four boys. Music historian Angela Smith writes, "Ginger was devastated, [s]o she did what any rebellious girl from an Italian Catholic family from Long Island would do. She wrote a good-bye note, packed a bag, jumped into her '62 Ford XL 500, and drove away into the night."[30]

Despite her own willful resistance to the constraints of female propriety and middle-class respectability, Zelkowitz was not immune to the anxiety of social stigmatization. Her discomfort with Shuggie Q's "butch" appearance and her insistence that Nancy Peterman leave the band following the revelation of her pregnancy suggests Zelkowitz was aware that social stigmatization could destroy the careers of an all-female group. Lemke-Santangelo explains that "[m]aintaining appearances was, in fact, a major preoccupation of 1950s middle-class households," and that "image and appearance, secured through consumption and adherence to middle-class behavioural norms, held the key to respectability and status."[31] Zelkowitz's middle-class upbringing, combined with her determination to front a successful rock and roll group and her awareness of commercial expectations for female performers, influenced her to make several decisions for the sake of the band's public respectability, some of which were unpopular with her bandmates. For example, in one excerpt from *Lollipop Lounge*, Zelkowitz defends her insistence that guitarist Susan MacDonald's lesbian sexuality remain unknown to the public for the sake of the band's commercial success.

> Back then—remember, this was the 1960s—I was very sensitive about any risk of Goldie and the Gingerbreads being labeled a "lezzy group." My concern had nothing to do with anyone actually *being* gay—I had no problem with that—it was just that I didn't want anything to stand in the way of success for the band, and I knew all it would take was one gay band member coming out of the closet for us all to be *branded* . . . and that would be bad for business. After all, this was long before being out was in. The idea was to get guys to fantasize about sleeping with the band; they weren't going to dream those dreams—well, probably not—if they thought we were all lesbians. In the 1960s the club owners and managers in New York City all knew each other; half the clubs in NYC were owned by the same people. It was a tight little Italian clique. I wanted to make musical history, not become history. If we got a reputation for being a "lezzy group" our bookings would dry up, and it could be the end of us.[32]

As Zelkowitz astutely observes, the Gingerbreads needed to navigate a set of tensions unique to the all-female band at the time to simultaneously pursue their careers in popular music, maintain their individual reputations, and balance their social and familial obligations. While the novelty of the band stemmed from their unprecedented ability to lay claim to their own sexual and musical autonomy, the marketability of the Gingerbreads also depended on audience perception of their feminine respectability. Jacqueline Warwick summarizes this tension thus: "Girls who participate in youth culture and popular music . . . are expected to be pretty enough to attract male attention and societal approval, but they must also be able to suppress their own sexual desires in order to maintain a patriarchal social order."[33]

THE GINGERBREADS NAVIGATE GENRE, NOVELTY, AND GENDER

It was not unusual for female recording groups of the 1960s to regularly reorganize their lineups. Consequently, doing this did not undermine the Gingerbreads' commercial marketability. For the decade's girl groups, the interchangeability of their members was a purposeful marketing strategy that emphasized belonging and girl-to-girl friendships to female teen consumers.[34] This visual collectivity was achieved through the construction of a uniform group image characterized by matching hairstyles, clothing, and accessories in a strategy that appealed to the "self-consciously female teen market of the period," all of which are explored by Cynthia C. Cyrus in her survey of the girl group image.[35] While the expression of female collectivity was not a priority for Zelkowitz during the days of the Gingerbreads, she believed that the male-centric rock and roll industry would welcome a foursome of attractive women in matching outfits, so she adapted this particular girl group strategy.[36] Zelkowitz remembers that she did not always make these decisions democratically: "Ginger and I would go to costume-hire shops in Times Square and rent sparkly slutty outfits, some with fringe, some with rhinestones and sequins. The other girls didn't like my taste in costumes, but I made them wear the things anyway."[37] For Zelkowitz, the priority was first and foremost the commercial and monetary success of the band, more so than the individual preferences or subjectivities of the band's members.

Perhaps because of their matching uniforms, or perhaps simply because they were an attractive foursome of women, albeit white women, performing popular music during the early and mid-1960s and there were no other existent genre categories into which the band readily fit, the genre of "girl group" is often ascribed to Goldie and the Gingerbreads despite it being at odds with their instrument playing. Further, Zelkowitz was preoccupied with the deliberate construction of the Gingerbreads' image. In her work about Led Zeppelin, Susan Fast explains that "the consideration of 'image' is antithetical to ideas about rock authenticity: it suggests that there might be something constructed (artificial) about the band, that they might have commercial interests in mind—as if any rock or pop artist did not."[38] While Zelkowitz's interest in heightening the novelty status of the band contributed to their short-term success, it may also have resulted in the band's subsequent dismissal by rock and roll fans and critics.

In what scholarship there is about them, there is some discrepancy about whether the Gingerbreads ought to be considered a "girl group." For example, they appear in the "Girl Groups" chapter of Gaar's *She's a Rebel*, primarily because of the band's image and "their dependence on the manager/songwriter/producer teams around them," a characteristic of their career that I will explore in more depth later in this essay.[39] On the other hand, Warwick argues that the girl group is defined by a number of distinct characteristics such as "an emphasis on the concerns and interests of teenage girls in its lyrics," "an instrumental sound often dominated by orchestral instruments" rather than the traditional rock and roll instrumentation, "and above all, the audibly adolescent voices of girls interacting in dialogues between lead and backing vocalists."[40] "Thus," Warwick argues, "Little Eva and Lesley Gore are part of the girl group sound, while all-female 60s bands such as the Liverbirds and Goldie and the Gingerbreads are not, because they were self-contained units of instrumentalists/songwriters/singers and also because they did not present identities understood strictly as adolescent."[41] This discrepancy in scholarship about whether or not the Gingerbreads ought to be considered a "girl group" is worth interrogating because, as Mahon asserts, "genre labels have a powerful effect on the shape and direction of an artist's career."[42] This discussion demonstrates Mahon's point that each female recording artist must navigate a unique landscape of race and gender dynamics that play out in the recording industry through genre categories.[43]

Several feminist scholars have explored the fraught relationship between women and the performance of rock and roll. For Lisa Rhodes, the exclusive nature of the genre stems from its interaction with technology. "For a woman to decide to harness technology in the pursuit of artistic expression is as subversive as if she were to paste on a beard and dress in drag," Rhodes posits.[44] In a different vein, Mina Carson, Tisa Lewis, and Susan M. Shaw describe the traditionally acceptable roles of women in rock and roll. They write that, "[f]or women, learning to play a rock instrument [was] an especially bold gesture because of rock'n'roll's usual association with masculinity," and that "[o]n those occasions when women were allowed entrée into this masculine domain, only the role of vocalist was truly open for women's participation. On the whole, men just didn't want to listen to women play bass, drums, or electric guitar. Women were welcome only on the sidelines—as fans and groupies."[45]

Thus, one can argue that simply by performing on the instruments of the typically masculine rock and roll group, Goldie and the Gingerbreads challenged the traditional discourse of the genre in a way that was not easily reconciled by rock and roll gatekeepers of the era. In her essay on the discursive categories "groupie" and "teenybopper," Norma Coates explains "that sexy female stars needed to be physically and discursively put in a position where they did not undermine or threaten masculinity as normalized by rock culture (and in the mainstream culture from which the notion was imported)."[46] Within Coates's framework, the term "girl group" works to place Goldie and the Gingerbreads "in a subservient or at least lesser position than their male counterparts," undermining their authority as rock and roll musicians.[47] It is not my intention here to deride the girl group genre. Rather, my goal is to examine whether, by locating the Gingerbreads and subsequent all-female bands like the Go-Go's and the Bangles within the girl group genre, critics and music historians have maintained the rigid gender categories that have permeated rock and roll culture from its conception. As Coates states, "[s]exy, successful women in rock were fine as long as they could be placed in gender-normative categories."[48] For female musicians trying to build careers in rock and roll in the 1960s, the genre category of "girl group" may have served just the normative purpose that Coates describes.

However, as Fast argues, the essentialism that informs the construction and maintenance of rigid genre categories overlooks the fact that, "far from being static, the way in which popular music is consumed/interpreted is dynamic, ever-changing, dependent on the individual doing the consuming and interpreting."[49] David Brackett, too, "emphasizes the temporal, experiential, functional, and fleeting quality of genres" while acknowledging the "the importance of the genre concept for communicating about texts."[50] He continues that "genres are not static groupings of empirically verifiable musical characteristics, but rather associations of texts whose criteria of similarity may vary according to the uses to which the genre labels are put," and argues that groupings "include more than musical-style features" but also "hinge on elements of nation, class, race, gender, sexuality, and so on."[51] In her work about Black female rock and roll recording artists such as Big Mama Thornton, Betty Davis, Tina Turner, and others, Mahon teases out the dynamism and complexity of popular music genre categories and the impact that being included in or excluded from genres can have on the careers of female recording artists:

> In the American recording industry, music genres facilitate the marketing and promotion of music, identifying artists and their perceived audiences with particular musical sounds and performance styles. Genre categories and the practices and discourse that maintained them created some of the most significant boundaries that these women confronted. One challenge was that their work combined stylistic impulses and performance practices with what were viewed as separate and distinct music genres. This, coupled with their race and gender identities, made their fit within dominant Black or white genres imperfect and caused them to stand betwixt and between genres, either in their historical moment or in retrospect.[52]

Like the artists that Mahon discusses, the Gingerbreads are difficult to locate within dominant popular music genres, and this has complicated their position in rock and roll history. While all four members of the Gingerbreads were white, their being conspicuously and explicitly female was sufficient, it seems, to exclude them from rock and roll's dominant narratives, which have tended not to account for the "temporal, experiential, functional, and fleeting quality of genres" that Brackett describes and instead tend to build from a static and essentialist notion of what is and is not rock and roll.[53] Interrogating the career of a band such as the Gingerbreads demonstrates inconsistencies in genre categorization and suggests that rigid genre conceptualizations are at odds with the messy realities of popular music performance.

Though they toured Europe with all-male rock and roll groups like the Animals, the Yardbirds, the Hollies, and the Kinks, which implies that they were billed as a rock and roll act by their record labels, the Gingerbreads were often included on these bills as little more than a novelty act.[54] The Gingerbreads were thoroughly aware of the limited expectations about their musicianship and mobilized the novelty of their all-girl lineup to book gigs. Susan MacDonald recalls to Gaar that the Gingerbreads "got more jobs because they were exploiting the hell out of us. All Girl Band! They'd do the whole thing, tits and ass. And we didn't care. We were happy because we knew we could play, and we were knocking the socks off of most of the male bands."[55] The club owners' low expectations about "girl bands" became the butt of a recurring joke for the Gingerbreads, but also gained them the upper hand on several occasions. Gaar recounts a story told by Zelkowitz when the latter spoke on a New Music Seminar panel in New York in 1990:

> We'd walk into a club with all our instruments and you could see the owner going "Oh my God, these broads? They know how to play? They really know how to play?" We'd set up and have a sound check and play totally out of tune, and I would sing the wrong lyrics. And the guy'd be chewing on his cigar going "Oh my God! Oh my God! Oh my God!" And by the time we went on and counted off the song, we were cookin'. You could see the cigar drop and the guy had a heart attack . . . We had fun with this.[56]

The experiences of the Gingerbreads are consistent with Bayton's observation that "a women's band is expected to be sexy and incompetent, expectations which form a de facto hurdle facing women musicians and, especially, all-women bands," and must be "coped with or combated in some way."[57] The Gingerbreads coped. They utilized the sexist preconceptions of club owners in New York City as a form of personal entertainment, which subverted the power structures at play between all-female band and band booker, but they also capitalized on the surprise that club owners experienced at their musical ability by successfully building a reputation for themselves. Though their music and playing abilities were "viewed through a lens of patriarchal assumptions," as Bayton emphasizes, Goldie and the Gingerbreads were comfortable working within these patriarchal confines, navigating tensions and challenges as they arose.[58]

Conversely, even while the Gingerbreads were successful in navigating the sexist landscape of band booking and promotion, they faced what would prove to be insurmountable difficulty in their dealings with record label officials. "Every record company we ever had except Ahmet Ertegun's Atlantic label screwed us out of royalties," Zelkowitz laments in *Lollipop Lounge*.[59] As well as the mismanagement of their money, all-female bands such as Goldie and the Gingerbreads received little label support in the way of promotion, relegated instead to being a "novelty" act and added to bills of five or more popular all-male bands to pique the interests of male rock and roll fans.[60] In the studio, the musical preferences of the band members were paid little attention by producers. Both Zelkowitz and MacDonald were displeased with the song selection of "Can't You Hear My Heart Beat?" by Decca Records management team Mike Jeffries and Mickie Most. "In truth," writes Zelkowitz, "we girls actively disliked the song, which we thought was sappy. Chas [Chandler] and Eric [Burdon] didn't understand us at all, not musically. . . . Chas and Eric tried very hard to make us sound like a girls' pop group. . . . I resented them trying to make us sound like something other than what we were. Eric kept saying, 'Sing it like Diana Ross would sing it,' to which I'd reply, 'But I'm *not* Diana Ross.'"[61]

Upon complaining to Zelkowitz about "Can't You Hear My Heart Beat?" MacDonald recalls receiving the response, "We gotta do what they say!"[62] In her interview with Gaar, MacDonald grudgingly recollects having to "do everything they [the record label] said or we were not going to be successful. So we record this stupid song, and they shove us off to the Star Club in Germany because we don't have our working visas yet."[63] Nor was this the last time that "Can't You Hear My Heart Beat?" would be problematic for the Gingerbreads. Though the song became a British Top 10 in 1965, political turmoil between the two members of their management team, Mike Jeffries and Mickie Most, undermined its American release. When a dispute between Most and Jeffries caused them to part ways, they each claimed the recording rights to the song for themselves. This resulted in the nearly simultaneous recording and release of the song by two different bands: first by Goldie and the Gingerbreads, managed by Jeffries, who initially released the song in the UK, and then by the already popular all-male band Herman's Hermits, managed by Most. The latter version hit the US charts only two weeks prior to the proposed US release date of the Gingerbreads' version and promptly rose to #2, removing any chance that the Gingerbreads would have a hit with the song.[64] "Can't You Hear My Heart Beat?" was the Gingerbreads' only opportunity for a hit single in the United States, a goal that remained unrealized with the disbanding of the group in 1966.

DOCUMENTING THE GINGERBREADS

Despite some chart success in the UK and regional popularity in Europe, Goldie and the Gingerbreads failed to make a lasting impression on the rock and roll culture of the United States and have all but faded from collective rock and roll memory. When recounted, the tale of the Gingerbreads is typically accompanied by the phrase "first all-girl rock band to be signed to a major label," some description of the group's "novelty" status, and discussion of their professional and personal relationships with British Invasion bands such as the Animals, the Hollies, and the Rolling Stones.[65] It is unclear whether the difficulties faced by the Gingerbreads during their navigation of the recording industry simply proved too challenging to overcome, as is the case with more than 80 percent of artists—only 5 percent of whom ever make enough profit to repay their record companies' financial investments in them—or whether the Gingerbreads fell victim to a more precise form of gender discrimination at the hands of their management.[66] Zelkowitz cites jealousy and insecurity among band members as the source of the initial cracks in the Gingerbreads' foundation.[67] In reality, some combination of these factors was likely at play. While it is possible to infer why the band may have failed to achieve chart success in the 1960s, I am also interested in unpacking the Gingerbreads' relative absence from popular music histories to demonstrate how the career success and subsequent historicization of a band depends on a particular blend of historical and social contexts, gender identities and performances, and genre discourses, among other factors.

Feminist media studies scholar Christine Feldman-Barrett addresses the question of the absence of bands such as Goldie and the Gingerbreads from rock and roll histories and posits that more scholarly attention has been paid to "harder-hitting groups of the 1970s, like Fanny and the Runaways," and "late-1970s punk bands, like the Slits, Raincoats, and Au Pairs" than to the all-girl bands of the mid-1960s. This is due, argues Feldman-Barrett, to the fact that these latter bands did not conform to rock and roll's masculinist narrative, but instead undermined it.[68] "This narrative of the rock genre, solidified in the 1970s and further perpetuated, has subsequently placed the 1960s all-girl bands in a 'pre-rock' category," claims Feldman-Barrett, and so these bands have "not been institutionalized in the rock canon."[69]

In the late 1960s, rock and roll critics became invested "in the long-standing rhetoric that the Romantics and modernists had used to establish cultural capital for their music," Matthew Gelbart explains.[70] It is from this cultural shift that highbrow acceptance of rock music manifested itself, and words such as "authenticity," "genius," and "masterpiece," as well as concepts such as "selling out" and "aesthetic autonomy," became commonplace in rock and roll culture.[71] Production of albums that might warrant such praise became the priority of rock artists, labels, and producers, and critics no longer deemed artists worthy of attention for releasing a series of chart-topping singles.[72] It is not coincidental that this change occurred nearly simultaneously with the introduction of publications like *Rolling Stone* and *Crawdaddy: The Magazine of Rock*, magazines that have served as primary tastemakers and gatekeepers of the rock and roll industry in North America since their establishment in 1967 and 1966, respectively.⁷³ The preoccupation with album-oriented rock dominated the content of these magazines, excluding popular music that did not meet their standards of artistry or progressiveness. Norma Coates writes that by this time, too, "the girl groups and 'British Bird' singers of the early and mid-1960s were long gone, out of memory and out of rock and roll culture," and as the masculinist ethos of rock criticism solidified under the example of *Rolling Stone*, the musical accomplishments of the Gingerbreads and their all-female contemporaries remained undocumented.⁷⁴ Furthermore, the Gingerbreads' bassless interpretation of the rock and roll lineup, as well as their output of only six singles, proved insufficient to attract retroactive recognition as a rock and roll group.

When popular music analysis developed into a field of scholarship in the 1990s, it took many of its cues from rock and roll criticism, perpetuating the erasure of bands such as Goldie and the Gingerbreads. Warwick observes that both popular music scholars and rock critics alike have tended to ignore songs with romantic narratives, as well as "those pop songs that make use of conventional harmonic language, clichéd grooves, and standard instrumentation," such as the music foisted upon the Gingerbreads by their management teams.⁷⁵ This situation, according to Warwick, is further aggravated by the pervasive "fascination with the Beatles, the Rolling Stones, Bob Dylan, Jimi Hendrix, and the Grateful Dead" in popular music scholarship regarding the 1960s.⁷⁶ "Even within the realm of histories explicitly addressing popular music," she explains, "most begin their narratives of the 1960s with the so-called British Invasion of the North American music charts by artists such as the Beatles and the Rolling Stones and conclude with the counterculture festivals at Monterey (1967) and Woodstock and Altamont (both 1969)."⁷⁷ Because the music of Goldie and the Gingerbreads never charted in the United States and the success of the group is limited to regional recognition in the UK and Europe, the narratives that Warwick describes typically exclude them; they are eclipsed instead by the rock and roll supergroups of the decade. As Feldman-Barrett contends, "mid-1960s all-girl bands have had to vie for attention during the time they were active and, also, in subsequent rock scholarship."⁷⁸

Even within the realm of feminist scholarship regarding female performers of the 1960s, scholars and critics have overlooked the music of Goldie and the Gingerbreads, perhaps due to its less-than progressive nature. Some effort has been made by feminists such as Gretchen Lemke-Santangelo to give voice to the women of the counterculture movement, including all-girl groups the Ace of Cups and Fanny. The counterculture has been of particular interest to modern feminist scholars because of its contradictory nature; despite the movement's ethos of progressiveness, women of the counterculture continued to be restricted to the rigidly defined gender roles of the 1950s and early '60s.⁷⁹ The music of the Gingerbreads, however, is distinctly non-countercultural and participates instead in established popular music conventions of the era.[80] Feminist music historians Sheila Whiteley and Alice Echols pay particular attention to the era's frontwomen, dwelling at length on the music and experiences of Janis Joplin of Big Brother and the Holding Company, Grace Slick of Jefferson Airplane, and "Big Mama" Cass Elliott of the Mamas and the Papas fame, perhaps because, as Feldman-Barrett observes, "the female singing voice is allowed some inclusion, especially if it is deep, powerful, and non-typically feminine."[81] Scholars have afforded attention to the decade's female folk singers Joni Mitchell and Joan Baez, the former for her songwriting prowess and unconventional expression of femininity, and the latter within the context of the urban folk revival and the decade's subsequent protest movements.[82] Warwick explores the relevance of the 1960s girl groups to both the history of rock and roll and to the broader conceptualization of feminist discourse in popular culture, although, as discussed, she maintains that Goldie and the Gingerbreads are not a girl group.[83]

Thus, even from a feminist perspective, groups who owe some amount of their success to the foundation laid by the Gingerbreads tend to outshine the accomplishments of the band. Fanny built directly on the achievements of the Gingerbreads, earning themselves the accolade "the first all-female band to release their album from a major label and have a top 40 hit."[84] Bands such as the Go-Go's and the Bangles continued to normalize the all-girl band in rock and roll culture, achieving considerable commercial and critical success throughout the 1970s and '80s, and dominating the "all-girl band" narrative that resulted.[85] Gaar, however, acknowledges the significance of the group in her enduringly important *She's a Rebel: The History of Women in Rock & Roll*, asserting that "[t]he Gingerbreads, while receiving little recognition themselves, helped to lay the groundwork that enabled other female performers to break out of the conventional roles women were still expected to play in the music industry."[86] In her contribution to Barbara O'Dair's *Trouble Girls: The Rolling Stone Book of Women in Rock*, Deborah Frost cites Goldie and the Gingerbreads as the launching point for the history of the all-girl rock band, solidifying their contributions within the documented history of rock and roll. So, while the relative absence of the Gingerbreads from musical scholarship seems to have resulted from a combination of factors, there are also those who have begun the process of reinserting them into the ever-evolving rock and roll narrative. However, as I have explained, it is not my intention here to vie for the inclusion of the Gingerbreads in the rock and roll canon as I have explained, but to imagine a mode of scholarship that circumnavigates the enduring dominance of the rock and roll canon by spotlighting artists and groups who are excluded. Highlighting the careers and challenges faced by bands and artists on a case-by-case basis, as I have done here, can reveal much about the entanglement of various social, historical, and cultural characteristics and the ways that these characteristics affect the lives and careers of female popular music artists.

CONCLUSION

The all-girl band is a unique entity, one in which the perspectives and personalities of women can define artistic decision making in a fashion that is uncommon within the realm of rock and roll. No two are the same, as each all-girl band is as dynamic a body as the women themselves who constitute it. As such, the strategies they employ in their navigation of the minefield of the rock and roll industry readily lend themselves to individual analyses and discourage the application of blanket statements and stereotypes. Goldie and the Gingerbreads built a tentative career, not by subverting industry expectations of femininity or by producing music that might be labeled as progressive but by recognizing an unfilled niche in the market of 1960s rock and roll and taking active steps to fill it. For some members of the Gingerbreads, rock and roll offered an alternative to the constraints of domestic life, and though it was a pursuit often fraught with challenges, especially for a group of young white women in the early 1960s, the group proved themselves sufficiently flexible to adapt to many of these difficulties.

The continued relevance of the all-girl group, however, is a somewhat contentious topic. Following her exploration of the history of the all-girl band, Deborah Frost argues that the concept itself is "as quaint a notion as the single-sex college."[87] Though, as she acknowledges, "[r]eaders of riot acts—from the Slits to Bikini Kill—have no doubt helped redress some of the wrongs done gurls since Eve got stuck with the apple," Frost maintains that anyone "primarily concerned with growing as an artist" must overcome the tendency to select bandmates based on the limiting category of gender, a process that she insists is "fatal to the openness, spontaneity, and experimentation that the process of genuine creation simply demands."[88] Perhaps, then, the Gingerbreads' preoccupation with gender remains their ultimate downfall, despite it also being the characteristic that has come to retrospectively define the group. Or perhaps the fault lies with the music industry's inability to see past the gender of the Gingerbreads, to the musical talent and potential that remained unrealized underneath. "No one was inspiring us or pushing us to write our own music," laments Zelkowitz.[89] She continues, "Andrew Loog Oldham did the right thing when he forced the Stones to start doing so; it might have been interesting if we'd had an Andrew Oldham to do the same for us."[90]

Regardless, the prerogative of this essay is not to determine the ongoing relevance of the all-girl band as a musical body. Rather, I have attempted to demonstrate the productive nature of interrogating the experiences of artists or groups on a case-by-case basis with an emphasis on context to highlight the inherent tensions and contradictions that inevitably affect the experiences of women in the field of popular music. Goldie and the Gingerbreads may not have fundamentally altered rock and roll, but they were present at a singular moment in its history and the complexities of their career are worthy of documentation because they reveal much about rock and roll's enduringly gendered modes of categorization and historicization.

NOTES

1. Deborah Frost, "Garageland," in *Trouble Girls: The Rolling Stone Book of Women in Rock*, ed. Barbara O'Dair (New York: Random House, 1997), 416.
2. Frost, "Garageland," 416.
3. Lucy O'Brien, *She Bop II: The Definitive History of Women in Rock, Pop and Soul* (London: Continuum, 2012): 129.
4. Genya Ravan, *Lollipop Lounge: Memoirs of a Rock and Roll Refugee* (New York: Billboard Books, 2004), 63.
5. O'Brien, *She Bop II*, 95.
6. O'Brien, *She Bop II*, 95.
7. Ann Werner, Tami Gadir, and Sam De Boise, "Broadening Research in Gender and Music Practice," *Popular Music* 39, no. 3-4 (2020): 639–40.
8. Werner, Gadir, and De Boise, "Broadening Research in Gender and Music Practice."
9. Maureen Mahon, "They Say She's Different: Race, Gender, and the Liberated Black Femininity of Betty Davis," *Journal of Popular Music Studies* 23, no. 2 (2011): 148.
10. Stephanie Coontz, *A Strange Stirring: The Feminine Mystique and American Women at the Dawn of the 1960s* (New York: Basic Books, 2011), 105–6.
11. Jo Gill, "'Quite the Opposite of a Feminist': Phyllis McGinley, Betty Friedan and Discourses of Gender in Mid-Century American Culture," *Women's History Review* 22, no. 3 (2013): 425.
12. Gill, "'Quite the Opposite of a Feminist,'" 425.
13. Claire Fallon, "A History of All-Girl Bands and the Rock World That Tried to Keep Them Out," *Huffington Post*, April 26, 2017, http://www.huffingtonpost.com/entry/making-the-girl-band_us_58ed03a7e4b0df7e2045c149.
14. Fallon, "A History of All-Girl Bands and the Rock World That Tried to Keep Them Out."
15. Fallon, "A History of All-Girl Bands and the Rock World That Tried to Keep Them Out."
16. Ravan, *Lollipop Lounge*, 83.
17. Mavis Bayton, *Frock Rock: Women Performing Popular Music* (Oxford: Oxford University Press, 1998), 50.
18. Mary Ann Clawson discusses how the bass came to be identified as a female prerogative in "When Women Play the Bass: Instrument Specialization and Gender Interpretation in Alternative Rock Music," *Gender and Society* 13, no. 2 (1999): 193–210. However, this trend didn't begin until the 1990s.
19. Frost, 416.
20. Ravan, *Lollipop Lounge*, 83–84.
21. Ravan, *Lollipop Lounge*, 129.
22. Ravan, *Lollipop Lounge*, 73.
23. Ravan, *Lollipop Lounge*, 73.
24. Wini Breines, *Young, White, and Miserable: Growing Up Female in the Fifties* (Chicago: University of Chicago Press, 2001), 136.
25. Breines, *Young, White, and Miserable*.

26. Ravan, *Lollipop Lounge*, 4.

27. Gretchen Lemke-Santangelo, *Daughters of Aquarius: Women of the Sixties Counterculture* (Lawrence: University of Kansas Press, 2009), 38.

28. Gillian G. Gaar, *She's a Rebel: The History of Women in Rock and Roll* (New York: Seal Press, 1992), 57.

29. Gaar, *She's a Rebel*, 57.

30. Angela Smith, *Women Drummers: A History from Rock and Jazz to Blues and Country* (New York: Rowman & Littlefield, 2014), 72.

31. Lemke-Santangelo, *Daughters of Aquarius*, 40.

32. Ravan, *Lollipop Lounge*, 108–9.

33. Jacqueline Warwick, *Girl Groups, Girl Culture: Popular Music and Identity in the 1960s* (New York: Routledge, 2007), 145.

34. Cynthia J. Cyrus, "Selling an Image: Girl Groups of the 1960s," *Popular Music* 22, no. 2 (2003): 179.

35. Cyrus, "Selling an Image: Girl Groups of the 1960s," 176.

36. For further reading regarding the male gaze and the masculine ethos of the genre of rock and roll, see Simon Frith and Angela McRobbie, "Rock and Sexuality," in *On Record: Rock, Pop, and the Written Word*, ed. Simon Frith and Andrew Goodwin (New York: Routledge, 1990), 371–89; for discussion about gaze theory and rock and roll music, see Susan Fast, *The Houses of the Holy: Led Zeppelin and the Power of Rock Music* (Oxford: Oxford University Press, 2001.

37. Ravan, *Lollipop Lounge*, 79.

38. Fast, *The Houses of the Holy*, 180.

39. Gaar, *She's a Rebel*, 32.

40. Warwick, *Girl Groups, Girl Culture*, ix.

41. Warwick, *Girl Groups, Girl Culture*, ix.

42. Maureen Mahon, *Black Diamond Queens: African American Women and Rock and Roll* (Durham, NC: Duke University Press, 2020), 1.

43. Mahon, *Black Diamond Queens*, 7.

44. Lisa Rhodes, *Electric Ladyland: Women and Rock Culture* (Philadelphia: University of Pennsylvania Press, 2005), xv.

45. Mina Carson, Tisa Lewis, and Susan M. Shaw, *Girls Rock! Fifty Years of Women Making Music* (Lexington: University Press of Kentucky, 2004), 3.

46. Norma Coates, "Teenyboppers, Groupies, and Other Grotesques: Girls and Women and Rock Culture in the 1960s and Early 1970s," *Journal of Popular Music Studies* 15, no. 1 (2003): 81.

47. Coates, "Teenyboppers, Groupies, and Other Grotesques," 81.

48. Coates, "Teenyboppers, Groupies, and Other Grotesques," 81.

49. Fast, *The Houses of the Holy*, 163.

50. David Brackett, *Categorizing Sound: Genre and Twentieth-Century Popular Music* (Los Angeles: University of California Press, 2016), 5.

51. Brackett, *Categorizing Sound*, 5.

52. Mahon, *Black Diamond Queens*, 7.

53. Brackett, *Categorizing Sound*, 5.

54. Gaar, *She's a Rebel*, 65.

55. Gaar, *She's a Rebel*, 59.

56. Gaar, *She's a Rebel*, 59.

57. Bayton, *Frock Rock*, 122.

58. Bayton, *Frock Rock*, 122.

59. Ravan, *Lollipop Lounge*, 91.
60. Christine Feldman-Barrett, "From Beatles Fans to Beat Groups: A Historiography of the 1960s All-Girl Rock Band," *Feminist Media Studies* 14, no. 6 (2014): 1048.
61. Ravan, *Lollipop Lounge*, 155.
62. Gaar, *She's a Rebel*, 60.
63. Gaar, *She's a Rebel*, 60.
64. Gaar, *She's a Rebel*, 66.
65. Carson, Lewis and Shaw, *Girls Rock!* 85; Smith, *Women Drummers*, 73; Frost, "Garageland," 416.
66. Matt Stahl, *Unfree Masters: Recording Artists and the Politics of Work* (Durham, NC: Duke University Press, 2012), 11.
67. Ravan, *Lollipop Lounge*, 184.
68. Feldman-Barrett, "From Beatles Fans to Beat Groups," 1043.
69. Feldman-Barrett, "From Beatles Fans to Beat Groups," 1043.
70. Matthew Gelbart, "A Cohesive Shambles: The Clash's 'London Calling' and the Normalization of Punk," *Music & Letters* 92, no. 2 (2011): 231.
71. Gelbart, "A Cohesive Shambles," 231.
72. Gelbart, "A Cohesive Shambles," 231.
73. Coates, "Teenyboppers, Groupies, and Other Grotesques," 78; Kembrew McLeod, "1/2: A Critique of Rock Criticism in North America," *Popular Music* 20, no. 1 (2001): 49.
74. Coates, "Teenyboppers, Groupies, and Other Grotesques," 78.
75. Warwick, *Girl Groups, Girl Culture*, 6.
76. Warwick, *Girl Groups, Girl Culture*, 4.
77. Warwick, *Girl Groups, Girl Culture*, 4.
78. Feldman-Barrett, "From Beatles Fans to Beat Groups," 1043.
79. Lemke-Santangelo, *Daughters of Aquarius*, 38.
80. Lemke-Santangelo, *Daughters of Aquarius*, 29.
81. Feldman-Barrett, "From Beatles Fans to Beat Groups," 1043; Sheila Whiteley, *Women and Popular Music: Sexuality, Identity and Subjectivity* (New York: Routledge, 2000); Alice Echols, *Shaky Ground: The '60s and Its Aftershocks* (New York: Columbia University Press, 2002).
82. For example, Markus Jäger, *Popular Is Not Enough: The Political Voice of Joan Baez* (Stuttgart, Germany: ibidem, 2012); Anne Karppinen, *The Songs of Joni Mitchell: Gender, Performance and Agency* (New York: Routledge, 2016).
83. Warwick, *Girl Groups, Girl Culture*, 4.
84. Jessica L. Brown, "Fanny," *The Grove Dictionary of American Music*, 2nd ed. (Oxford: Oxford University Press, 2014).
85. Frost, "Garageland," 422; Peter Mercer-Taylor, "Songs from the Bell Jar: Autonomy and Resistance in the Music of the Bangles," *Popular Music* 17, no. 2 (1998): 188.
86. Gaar, *She's a Rebel*, 61.
87. Frost, "Garageland," 423–24.
88. Frost, "Garageland," 423–24.
89. Ravan, *Lollipop Lounge*, 82–83.
90. Ravan, *Lollipop Lounge*, 82–83.

BIBLIOGRAPHY

Bayton, Mavis. *Frock Rock: Women Performing Popular Music*. Oxford: Oxford University Press, 1998.

Brackett, David. *Categorizing Sound: Genre and Twentieth-Century Popular Music*. Los Angeles: University of California Press, 2016.

Breines, Wini. *Young, White, and Miserable: Growing Up Female in the Fifties*. Chicago: University of Chicago Press, 2001.

Brown, Jessica L. "Fanny." In *The Grove Dictionary of American Music*. 2nd ed. Oxford: Oxford University Press, 2014.

Carson, Mina, Tisa Lewis, and Susan M. Shaw. *Girls Rock! Fifty Years of Women Making Music*. Lexington: University Press of Kentucky, 2004.

Clawson, Mary Ann. "When Women Play the Bass: Instrument Specialization and Gender Interpretation in Alternative Rock Music." *Gender and Society* 13, no. 2 (1999): 193–210.

Coates, Norma. "Teenyboppers, Groupies, and Other Grotesques: Girls and Women and Rock Culture in the 1960s and Early 1970s." *Journal of Popular Music Studies* 15, no. 1 (2003): 65–94.

Coates, Norma. "Whose Tears Go By? Marianne Faithfull at the Dawn and Twilight of Rock Culture." In *She's So Fine: Reflections on Whiteness, Femininity, Adolescence and Class in 1960s Music*, edited by Laurie Stras, 183–202. Surrey, UK: Ashgate, 2010.

Coontz, Stephanie. *A Strange Stirring: The Feminine Mystique and American Women at the Dawn of the 1960s*. New York: Basic Books, 2011.

Cusick, Suzanne G. "Gender, Musicology, and Feminism." In *Rethinking Music*, edited by Nicholas Cook and Mark Everist, 471–98. Oxford: Oxford University Press, 2001.

Cyrus, Cynthia C. "Selling an Image: Girl Groups of the 1960s." *Popular Music* 22, no. 2 (2003): 173–93.

Echols, Alice. *Shaky Ground: The '60s and Its Aftershocks*. New York: Columbia University Press, 2002.

Fallon, Claire. "A History of All-Girl Bands and the Rock World That Tried to Keep Them Out." *Huffington Post*, April 26, 2017. http://www.huffingtonpost.com/entry/making-the-girl-band_us_58ed03a7e4b0df7e2045c149.

Fast, Susan. *The Houses of the Holy: Led Zeppelin and the Power of Rock Music*. Oxford: Oxford University Press, 2001.

Feldman-Barrett, Christine. "From Beatles Fans to Beat Groups: A Historiography of the 1960s All-Girl Rock Band." *Feminist Media Studies* 14, no. 6 (2014): 1041–55.

Frith, Simon, and Angela McRobbie. "Rock and Sexuality." In *On Record: Rock, Pop, and the Written Word*, edited by Simon Frith and Andrew Goodwin, 371–89. New York: Routledge, 1990.

Frost, Deborah. "Garageland." In *Trouble Girls: The Rolling Stone Book of Women in Rock*, 415–26. New York: Random House, 1997.

Gaar, Gillian G. "Girl Groups." In *She's a Rebel: The History of Women in Rock & Roll*, 31–62. New York: Seal Press, 2002.

Gelbart, Matthew. "A Cohesive Shambles: The Clash's 'London Calling' and the Normalization of Punk." *Music & Letters* 92, no. 2 (2011): 230–72.

Gill, Jo. "'Quite the Opposite of a Feminist': Phyllis McGinley, Betty Friedan and Discourses of Gender in Mid-Century American Culture." *Women's History Review* 22, no. 3 (2013): 422–39.

Jäger, Markus. *Popular Is Not Enough: The Political Voice of Joan Baez*. Stuttgart, Germany: ibidem, 2012.

Karppinen, Anne. *The Songs of Joni Mitchell: Gender, Performance, and Agency*. New York: Routledge, 2016.

Lemke-Santangelo, Gretchen. *Daughters of Aquarius: Women of the Sixties Counterculture*. Lawrence: University of Kansas Press, 2009.

Mahon, Maureen. *Black Diamond Queens: African American Women and Rock and Roll*. Durham, NC: Duke University Press, 2020.

Mahon, Maureen. "The Rock and Roll Blues: Gender, Race, and Genre in the Songwriting Career of Rose Marie McCoy." *Women and Music: A Journal of Gender and Culture* 19 (2015): 62–70.

Mahon, Maureen. "They Say She's Different: Race, Gender, Genre, and the Liberated Black Femininity of Betty Davis." *Journal of Popular Music Studies* 23, no. 2 (2011): 146–65.

Marcic, Dorothy. *Respect: Women and Popular Music*. New York: Texere, 2002.

McLeod, Kembrew. "1/2: A Critique of Rock Criticism in North America." *Popular Music* 20, no. 1 (2001): 47–60.

Mercer-Taylor, Peter. "Songs from the Bell Jar: Autonomy and Resistance in the Music of the Bangles." *Popular Music* 17, no. 2 (1998): 187–204.

O'Brien, Lucy. *She Bop II: The Definitive History of Women in Rock, Pop and Soul*. London: Continuum, 2012.

Powers, Ann. *Good Booty: Love and Sex, Black & White, Body and Soul in American Music*. New York: Harper Collins, 2017.

Ravan, Genya. *Lollipop Lounge: Memoirs of a Rock and Roll Refugee*. New York: Billboard Books, 2004.

Rhodes, Lisa L. *Electric Ladyland: Women and Rock Culture*. Philadelphia: University of Pennsylvania Press, 2005.

Smith, Angela. *Women Drummers: A History from Rock and Jazz to Blues and Country*. New York: Rowman & Littlefield, 2014.

Stahl, Matt. *Unfree Masters: Recording Artists and the Politics of Work*. Durham, NC: Duke University Press, 2012.

Stras, Laurie. "Introduction: She's So Fine, or Why Girl Singers (Still) Matter." In *She's So Fine: Reflections on Whiteness, Femininity, Adolescence and Class in 1960s Music*, edited by Laurie Stras, 1–32. Surrey, UK: Ashgate, 2010.

Stras, Laurie. "Voice of the Beehive: Vocal Technique at the Turn of the 1960s." In *She's So Fine: Reflections on Whiteness, Femininity, Adolescence and Class in 1960s Music*, edited by Laurie Stras, 33–56. Surrey, UK: Ashgate, 2010.

Warwick, Jacqueline. *Girl Groups, Girl Culture: Popular Music and Identity in the 1960s*. New York: Routledge, 2007.

Warwick, Jacqueline. "'He Hit Me, and I Was Glad': Violence, Masochism, and Anger in Girl Group Music." In *She's So Fine: Reflections on Whiteness, Femininity, Adolescence and Class in 1960s Music*, edited by Laurie Stras, 89–112. Surrey, UK: Ashgate, 2010.

Werner, Ann, Tami Gadir, and Sam De Boise. "Broadening Research in Gender and Music Practice." *Popular Music* 39, no. 3–4 (2020): 636–51.

Whiteley, Sheila. *Women and Popular Music: Sexuality, Identity, and Subjectivity*. New York: Routledge, 2002.

Chapter 8

Song and Sentiment in an Appalachian Woman's Private Lyric Notebook

—Travis D. Stimeling

In recent years, musicologists working to uncover details about the musical lives of women have looked to unconventional archives for more information on the ways that they have created, performed, listened to, and talked about music. Additionally, these scholars have turned to, for lack of a better term, "average" women in their work, thereby shedding light on the ways that music shapes everyday life. Kyra Gaunt's landmark study of the musical games that African American girls participate in during school recesses, for instance, highlights the power of oral tradition in developing key ideas about gender, sexuality, and race among the girls (and boys) who join in.[1] In an effort to open the bedroom doors of teen and preteen girls, Melanie Lowe's research on adolescent girls' reactions to pop superstar Britney Spears necessitated a series of semi-structured focus groups that allowed respondents to speak freely about a variety of musical and cultural issues.[2] Similarly, Candace Bailey's research on the ways that antebellum women used binders of published sheet music to articulate a desired identity to visitors required that she reconsider the binders volumes not simply as repositories of repertoire but as material culture objects that could reveal a great deal about the personality of binder volume's owner.[3] And Emily Hilliard's recent study of personal papers and recordings gathered by Eastern Kentucky musician and songwriter Nora Carpenter reveals how one woman used her personal archive to create a "self-curated life."[4]

This essay seeks to expand on this literature through a detailed examination of the musical life of one white Appalachian woman, Mary Olivia Smith, who was born in relative poverty and died a resident of a working-class community. Born in the rural Giles County, Virginia, in 1911, Smith witnessed a radical transformation of the Appalachian landscape from a primarily agricultural one to one that was shaped by the capital of the extractive industries that boomed during the first decades of the twentieth century.[5] Equipped with only a sixth-grade education (of which music likely played a minimal role), Smith maintained a remarkable document of her engagement with popular music of the 1930s and 1940s: a small notebook carefully laid out to hold her meticulous transcriptions of songs made popular by artists as stylistically diverse as Roy Acuff and Rudy Vallee. Spanning the course of several years, this small notebook was lovingly preserved, despite several relocations that could have damaged or destroyed the document; even today, the document shows only minimal wear and tear, especially for a cheap school notebook that is nearly a century old. This document was passed to her son Buddy Williams and came into my possession in the spring of 2016 thanks to a gift from Buddy and his wife, Kathleen. It provides a material example—what folklorist Barbara Kirshenblatt-Gimlett describes as a "material companion," or something that has "aged with [its] owners . . . [and that is] valued for [its] continuity"—that demonstrates the powerful role that popular song and popular song lyrics may have played in the class aspirations of one early twentieth-century Appalachian woman who followed the timber, coal, and defense industries and chased the "American Dream."[6]

This essay examines the traces of Smith's musical life that she left behind in her lyric notebook and explores what these traces might teach us about the ways she used music to make sense of the changing world in which she lived. In particular, this essay suggests that Smith's collection reflects her increasing class consciousness as she moved from a predominantly agrarian community to an industrial suburb over the course of her first three decades. Using her family's recollections and various genealogical data, this essay first documents Smith's life and considers the many sites where she could have developed a greater awareness of her class status, a class status that was inevitably inflected by her gender, race, and religion. Then, using the contents of her lyric notebook as evidence of her deliberate engagement with mass culture, it will be possible to consider the ways that popular music and its associated imagery reveal Smith's acceptance of and attempts to conform to white middle-class notions of "respectable" domestic femininity in the first half of the twentieth century. Taken together, then, this essay argues that, although men may have dominated many of the public spaces throughout the Appalachian region, girls and women played an important, if often undocumented role in both domestic and public affairs.

MARY OLIVIA SMITH: AN APPALACHIAN WOMAN IN MOTION

Mary Olivia Smith—known to everyone as Oleva, a name that is frequently found in official documents—was born in Hoges Store (Giles County), Virginia, to William Mahone Smith and Lily May Falls.[7] Little is known of her early years, but the 1920 census documented that she was living in the Pembroke District of Giles County with her sixty-seven-year-old grandfather, her sixty-four-year-old grandmother, her father, and two siblings.[8] According to a written statement provided by her daughter-in-law Kathleen Williams, Smith's mother died of pneumonia; her mother's absence from the 1920 census suggests that she passed prior to 1920.[9] The 1920 census, which documents the Smith neighbors as well, lists both her grandfather and her father as laborers on a "logging job."[10] According to a draft registration card that her father filed in 1917, however, William Mahone Smith had been employed as a "farm laborer" for J. L. A. Hoge of Hoges Store, Virginia only three years prior to the census.[11]

The nature of this agricultural labor was very much in flux during Smith's first years. As historians Ronald D. Eller and Ronald L. Lewis have demonstrated, central and southern Appalachia became the site of extensive economic development in the 1880s as industrialists set their sights on the virgin timbers that clung to the region's steep mountainsides and the coalbeds that laid beneath them. By the time Smith was born, an uneven but radical transformation of the region from a largely agrarian one to a market capitalist one was largely complete.[12] As such, laborers like William Smith, who likely had little land of his own, commonly left agricultural work behind in search of nearby work in the more lucrative timber industry. As Lewis notes of the nearby West Virginia timber industry, "Farmers often lived at home and walked to nearby logging sites each day, gradually increasing the radius of their work until they finally left home to stay in the logging camps."[13] Moreover, logging became a family business, Lewis notes, as families sought cash in an increasingly market-driven economy: "A larger labor recruitment process pushed farmers out of agriculture and pulled them into the timber industry as seasonal and then full-time workers. Cash was the most tantalizing lure. Young men either followed their fathers into the woods or were expected to find wage labor in the cash-scarce backcounties to assist their families in surviving the adjustment to a market economy."[14] Moreover, as Eller has observed, timber development also devastated traditional animal husbandry practices (including open forest grazing) and led to the expanded planting of row crops, which, on the mountain slopes, led to erosion and steadily decreasing soil productivity.[15] The impact of the industrialization of Giles County on young Smith is unclear, but it is possible that her parents struggled to adjust to the new world they were living in. As Eller has noted, "the migration from the family farm to the mining camp or mill village was for many mountaineers a difficult and traumatic move."[16] The transformation of the family farm from productive farmland to an industrial space could have been no less difficult and traumatic.[17]

Smith's early childhood, then, was already marked by rapid transitions. Her mother died prior to her ninth year, leaving her to assist with her two younger siblings. Without the help of a mother at home to tend the children and manage domestic affairs, Smith moved into her grandparents' home. And her father left his job as a farm laborer for a higher-paying but exponentially more dangerous job in the logging industry. But that would be just the first of a series of significant transitions that would mark Smith's early life. As Lewis's comments predicted, it was not long before the Smith family left Giles County altogether, eventually finding their way to Bluefield (Mercer County), West Virginia, a town that was in the midst of a major economic boom as a consequence of the timber and coal industries that flourished in the surrounding communities. A 1912 publication from the Bluefield Chamber of Commerce announced that the city was "the gateway to nature's storehouse of her greatest wealth," a boast that the city could support thanks to its exceptional rail connections to West Virginia's southern coalfields.[18] Additionally, the city was home to a substantial African American community, which flocked to the city in search of wage labor, educational opportunities at Bluefield State College, and West Virginia's more liberal attitudes toward racial segregation.[19] When Smith arrived in Bluefield, therefore, the city was home to a substantial professional class that sought domestic help to maintain their households; she would soon find herself filling that need, likely learning a great deal about middle-class respectability along the way.

To help care for her siblings, which eventually totaled twelve siblings after her father remarried, Smith left school at the end of her sixth grade year.[20] She did this for "about one a year, until Florence, her . . . sister was old enough to help" with the kids.[21] By her late teens, as Kathleen Williams recounted, she "was working as a mother's helper for a well off [sic] family in Bluefield."[22] There is no documentation to indicate who this "well off family" was, but it may have been one connected to the coal industry and its related industries.[23] Regardless, it is highly likely that this family had access to all of the modern utilities that found their way to the industrializing Bluefield in the first decade of the new century.[24] As a consequence, Smith may have had the opportunity to listen to radio broadcasts from regional and national stations during her daily activities. In his study of big band jazz in West Virginia's southern coalfields, Christopher Wilkinson noted that southern coalfield residents could pull in not only local and regional stations, such as Bluefield's WHIS, but such national clear-channel stations as Cincinnati's WLW; similarly, Ivan L. Tribe has noted that radio stations such as WHIS played a significant role in the proliferation of commercial country music throughout the state in the 1930s.[25] Bluefield was also the home to several theaters that showed films and presented concerts by local and traveling musicians, including predominantly African American acts such as Cab Calloway and Thomas "Fats" Waller.[26] Such exposure to regional and national media would reveal itself in the lyric book that Smith maintained.

Around November 1931, Smith—who, in her twentieth year was "considered ... to be an old maid"—married Robert Williams in the nearby town of Sophia, which was also home to an aspiring fourteen-year-old fiddler and future US Senator Robert C. Byrd.[27] A coal miner who worked the thick coal seams of the state's southern coalfields, Williams moved his young bride to several coal camps, where she gave birth to daughter Wanda in Helen (Raleigh County) in 1932 and and son Buddy in Holden (Logan County) in 1934.[28] To varying degrees, the coal camps—like the larger towns that served as county seats—also maintained modern utilities, especially electricity and telephone service. Still others provided mercantile and entertainment services to keep the miners and their families in the camps. The community of Tams (Raleigh County), for instance, has been "reputed to have ... one of the first theaters erected in the United States specifically for the showing of movies," the Golden Gate, which opened its doors in 1911.[29] Ronald D. Eller confirms this in his introduction to W. P. Tams Jr.'s memoir, noting additionally that Tams—the owner of the eponymous town—"had little respect for those operators who did not take an interest in providing good houses, sanitation, safe working conditions, good schools, and *proper amusements* for miners and their families."[30] Holden, which was named for the Harvard-educated coal baron who established the Island Creek mining operation, boasted a booming town, complete with a looming grade school building that educated the camp's youngest residents. As local historian Robert Y. Spence noted, "by 1912, most of Holden was built and then the town and the coal company became so much a part of each other that even now [1976] the people of Holden use phrases that refer to Island Creek operations that have disappeared."[31] The 1941 WPA guide *West Virginia: A Guide to the Mountain State* describes Holden as "a model coal town with a modern water system and recreational facilities, including a theater, tennis courts, Y.M.C.A. building, swimming pool, and a clubhouse in the English half-timbered style, on a landscaped lawn overlooking the main street of the town."[32] As such, it is clear that Smith was fortunate to live in some of the most progressive coal camps of the era, which likely helped her interact with the regional and national media. At the same time, as the work of historian Janet W. Greene suggests, Smith may have needed to take on occasional wage labor to supplement the family's income; if so, she may have had other opportunities to interact with popular culture through outside work in the coal camps.[33]

Little is known of the movement of the Williams family in the second half of the 1930s, but at some point before 1943, they moved from Holden to Monaville, another small coalfield community on the periphery of booming Logan, West Virginia.[34] In 1943, however, the Williamses moved to Columbus, Ohio, following many Appalachian migrants in search of more lucrative wages in the defense industry and related enterprises.[35] As sociologist Karida L. Brown notes in her study of the Black mining community of Lynch, Kentucky, "there were two gendered pathways for working-age blacks to take [during the 1940s and 1950s]—women could migrate to a city with a sibling or family member and find employment, or do so with a husband to start a family.... Men, on the other hand, had the choice of following the pre-carved path of a chain migration, joining the military voluntarily, or being drafted."[36] Many of the informants in Brown's study indicated that their time in the Appalachian coalfields was always intended to be a temporary stop in an ongoing migration from the Deep South, but, in Smith's case, it is possible to see that this migration to Columbus may reveal the power that patriarchal structures exerted in shaping her own life narrative.[37] That is, just as her father had moved her around the region in search of work, so, too, did her husband's employment uproot her from Appalachia, a region that, for her, was home.

Columbus brought full employment for the Williamses: "Robert took a job as a guard at the Ohio State Penitentiary[,] and Oleva was a 'Rosie the Riveter' at the Curtis[s]-Wright airplane factory."[38] The Columbus plant was responsible for the production of several significant aircraft, including most notably the Curtiss SB2C Helldiver, a state-of-the-art aircraft designed for use on aircraft carriers. As historians Louis R. Eltscher and Edward M. Young have noted, wartime production pushed the limits of the Columbus plant, particularly in terms of human resources: "The Columbus factory faced staggering challenges from the beginning, including the training of an unskilled workforce to produce the navy's most complicated carrier airplane. Only 2 percent of the first job applicants acknowledged any prior experience in aircraft production. A training program was quickly set up to teach the necessary skills to the new workers."[39] Smith was, undoubtedly, among those who received this specialized training.

By the end of the war, Smith had spent more than enough time in the industrial Midwest and was ready to return home. As scholars of Appalachian migration have documented extensively, Appalachian migrants then, as now, return to the "home place" as often as finances and work schedules allow in order to maintain kinship ties and often treat the region as a mythical pastoral retreat amid the chaos of urban life.[40] Williams was not alone, as Kathleen Williams noted directly: "Olivia missed West Virginia[,] and in 1945 the family moved back to Charleston...."[41] Like many "Rosies," Smith seems to have left the workforce after the war, while her husband Robert found work at the Union Carbide plant in South Charleston, where the postwar petrochemical boom was in full swing.[42] They remained in South Charleston's Spring Hill neighborhood until their respective deaths: Robert in 1960, Oleva in 1988. Smith's son Buddy and daughter-in-law Kathleen still live nearby.

Considering Smith's life on the whole, it is remarkable to consider the widespread and rapid social, cultural, environmental, and economic changes that she witnessed in her seventy-seven years. Born into a rural agrarian society, she spent her teens and twenties in the industrializing communities of the Appalachian timber and coal camps, where she experienced the first wave of sound films and wireless radio broadcasts. With the onslaught of global war in the 1940s, she left the relatively small—but cosmopolitan—coal camps of Logan County for the rapidly industrializing defense plants of Columbus, Ohio, where she undoubtedly encountered anti-Appalachian discrimination amid the urban chaos of the war effort.[43] And she returned to West Virginia in the postwar years to live the middle-class postwar dream in a semi-industrial suburb of the state capital, where her children earned high school diplomas and her grandchildren earned college degrees.[44] At the same time, it is worth noting that, for the overwhelming majority of her first three decades, Smith was active in the labor market, first as a domestic worker and later as a defense worker, taking a break from the public workplace only to rear her small children. Her return to West Virginia appears to have marked her return to domestic life, paralleling the economic lives of many white working-class women in the postwar era.[45] Looking back upon her early life, then, it seems that it was one of near constant dislocation. Yet, amid these rapid transitions and the constant need to negotiate new identities in changing environments, it appears that Smith found comfort in music. And it is to her early musical encounters that we now turn.

THE LYRIC BOOK

Smith maintained a small school composition notebook full of song lyrics over the course of at least fifteen years, if not longer. Smith's sixth-grade education—which mostly likely focused on reading, arithmetic, and penmanship—offered her some basic tools to elevate her class status, and her work as a domestic servant in a Bluefield home likely exposed her to a variety of "respectable" female activities, including the recitation of poetry and parlor music.[46] Moreover, the bustling coal towns and mercantile centers of the southern West Virginia coalfields provided Smith with opportunities to engage with national mass culture through radio, film, and possibly even the phonograph (although there is no evidence to suggest that she had access to a phonograph during the years that this book was compiled), as well as with African American, Italian, and Eastern European immigrants who had come to the region in search of work. As such, Smith would have been introduced to gendered, racialized, and classed notions of respectability through the characters she heard and saw in the mass media in addition to the people she interacted with in her daily life. And as a working-class mother in Columbus, Ohio, and South Charleston, West Virginia, she continued her celebration of sentimental popular song and its decidedly genteel attitudes toward gender and domesticity, even as she worked in defense plants and lived in the shadow of a major chemical plant. In sum, Smith's lyric book documents her efforts to use mass culture—and popular music specifically—to become a white, middle-class woman, even as those terms were being constantly redefined in the radical economic and cultural upheavals of the early twentieth century.

Smith's lyric book demonstrates a remarkable cursive script that is carefully laid out so as to maximize the amount of text that could be written on a page, but not to a point of cramming words onto the page. The book appears to have been compiled at three separate times and to unfold in a rough chronological order. Pages 1r–22r are written in blue ink, and, with the exception of page 6r, these pages are entirely in one hand. Pages 23r–25v are written in black ink, suggesting a separate copying. Pages 25v–54r are written in a firm lead pencil. The titles here occasionally appear to be in a different hand, but the lyrics are in the same hand as was found in the first two sections. There is no indication as to who may have written the titles in page 25v–54r; they may very well be the work of a less careful Smith or possibly one of the many children who was under her care during the time that she was compiling the book. Finally, pages 55r–56r return to blue ink. Text can be found on every page except pages 5v, 19v, and 54v, as well as the notebook's final eleven pages.

The book contains the lyrics to sixty-eight songs, including 1) sentimental songs such as "The Lover's Farewell" and "Little Rosewood Casket"; 2) gospel songs such as "Since Jesus Came Into My Heart" and "Farther Along"; 3) hillbilly favorites such as "East Virginia Blues," "Wabash Cannonball," and "Twenty-One Years"; 4) cowboy and western songs such as "Rose of San Antone" and "Springtime in the Rockies"; and 5) pop hits such as "Tip Toe through the Tulips" and "When My Blue Moon Turns to Gold." Such stylistic diversity mirrors the diversity that one would have encountered in the media landscape of the period during which Smith grew into adulthood. In fact, cross-referencing these songs with song folios held in the Southern Folklife Collection at the University of North Carolina at Chapel Hill; Tony Russell's discography *Country Music Records: A Discography, 1921–1942*; and Guthrie T. Meade, Richard K. Spottswood, and Douglas S. Meade's *Country Music Sources: A Biblio-Discography of Commercially Recorded Traditional Music*, sheds important light on the potential sources of Smith's musical and lyrical interests.[47] As shown in Table 1, the overwhelming majority of the songs appearing in Smith's book were recorded by Grand Ole Opry star Roy Acuff, with Jimmie Davis, the Carter Family, and Vernon Dalhart also offering significant contributions, as well. One song, "You're My Darling," even appears twice in the text, both times in the middle pencil section. Other notables include Gene Autry, the Delmore Brothers, and Wade Mainer.[48]

Dating most of the entries in the Smith lyric book poses several challenges. With the exception of page 6r, which appears to be the work of an aspiring suitor or a close friend and that presents the lyrics to Rudy Vallee and Leon

Table 1. Most Frequently Appearing Recording Artists in Mary Olivia Smith's Lyric Book

ARTIST	SONGS RECORDED	TOTAL NUMBER OF SONGS APPEARING IN SMITH BOOK
Roy Acuff	"Mother's Prayer Guides Me" "I Called and Nobody Answered" "Blue Eyed Darling" "Branded Wherever I Go" "Just to Ease My Worried Mind" "The Precious Jewel" "Old Age Pension Check" "Farther Along" "The Wreck on the Highway" "Lonely Mound of Clay" "Little Pal" ("Come Back Little Pal") "Stream Lined Cannon Ball" "You're My Darling" (x2) "Will the Circle Be Unbroken" "The Great Speckled Bird" "Wabash Cannon Ball" "Worried Mind"	17
Jimmie Davis	"Plant Some Flowers on My Grave" "You're My Darling" (x2) "A Sinner's Prayer" "I Told You So" "It Makes No Difference Now" "Last Letter"	6
Vernon Dalhart	"Among My Souvenirs" "The Convict and the Rose" "Little Rosewood Casket" "Home on the Range" "Mollie Darling" "When the Roses Bloom Again"	6
The Carter Family	"The Lover's Farewell" "Foggy Mountain Top" "Worried Mavn Blues" "Will the Circle Be Unbroken" "East Virginia Blues"	5

Zimmerman's "I'm Just a Vagabond Lover," a "foxtrot ballad" published by Leo. Feist in 1929.[49] The song appeared in the 1929 Florenz Ziegfeld film *Glorifying the American Girl*, in which Vallee sings it in a brief cameo appearance.[50] The film was released on 7 December 1929, and it likely made its way to a theater in Bluefield, West Virginia by January 1930, as the lyric transcription bears the date "January 15th, 1930."[51] No other text in the book bears a specific date, suggesting that this one was particularly important. Moreover, the lyrics transcribed are the ones that Vallee sang in the film, not the complete lyrics that he sang on the recording he made for Victor in 1929 nor from the sheet music published by Leo Feist.[52] All the more interesting, though, is that this lyric transcription is not in Smith's measured cursive handwriting, but is instead in a more random print. The lines of text are not laid out with the precision of a poem, but instead turn prosaic. And, finally, we know that this is not Smith's work because it is signed by its contributor, someone identified as "Dizzy." Dizzy's identity is entirely unclear. The contributor may have been a potential suitor or a close friend. Family members seem to think that Dizzy was "likely a girlfriend," but the heteronormative lyrics leave the lyric open to interpretation.[53] It could be an affirmation of a loving friendship, if Dizzy is assumed to be a female friend. But in a male suitor's hand, this contribution may have been a memento of a date gone well (at least in Dizzy's mind) and perhaps suggested Dizzy's desire to leave his "vagabond" ways behind to spend more time with a woman who he will "remember like last glowing embers / haunting your memory and dreams." But perhaps even more importantly, this contribution may very well suggest that Smith—who at nineteen, Kathleen Williams reminds us, was considered an "old maid" at the time—was opening her private world to a potential partner.[54]

In addition to Dizzy's contribution, it is possible to date at least two songs to World War II: "In Care of Uncle Sam" (26r) and "Smoke on the Water" (36r–36v). The war effort witnessed the widespread circulation of both sentimental songs addressing the losses on the home front and patriotic compositions intended to rally support for the war effort. The former, made famous by Denver Darling and His Texas Cowhands in a July 14, 1942, Decca recording, presents the perspective of a GI preparing to leave boot camp for a deployment somewhere in the midst of the global conflict.[55] "Smoke on the Water," on the other hand, is a jingoistic statement celebrating US military might and the apparently inevitable Allied victory over "the powers of dictators" and "the Heathen Gods" in Japan.[56] Popularized by country recording artist and Grand Ole Opry star Red Foley, who recorded the song for Decca, the song dominated the *Billboard* charts in 1944.[57] Yet, with the exception of these two songs, there is little trace of patriotism in the songs that Oleva selected for the volume. Rather, sentimental songs about deceased mothers ("Shake My Mother's Hand for Me"), deceased lovers ("Lonely Mound of Clay"), and modern technology ("Stream-Lined Cannonball") constitute the contents of the pages between these two overtly patriotic songs. Many of these songs were recorded by Roy Acuff, a prominent figure in the lyric book, suggesting that Smith may have been drawn to Acuff's particularly wholesome repertory rather than some of the more sexually adventurous numbers recorded by popular western swing bands or the minstrelsy-inflected songs that formed the core repertoire of the Grand Ole Opry and other barn dance programs at the time.[58]

If the war effort had little impact on Smith's selections, neither did her role as a defense worker.[59] A working-class woman who had always had to participate in the labor force, her move to Columbus likely did not signal a significant change in her class status.[60] Although Smith's financial capital undoubtedly grew significantly between her time in Bluefield and her move to Columbus, she was still working class, just like the many other women who migrated from Appalachia to the Midwest in search of gainful factory employment during the war.[61] Yet the topics and tone of the songs collected in her lyric book reveal a continued interest in sentimental songs—with the rare exception of more exuberant songs like "Stream-Lined Cannonball" or "Smoke on the Water." Of particular interest here are songs that reinforce what might be described as "good Christian values," that is, a belief in a respectable Christianity that shuns alcohol, tobacco, and other vices and that argues for the power of prayer as a tool for social reform. For example, "Wreck on the Highway," written by Dorsey Dixon and popularized by Roy Acuff, chastises people who pass by a fatal car accident without offering prayers for the souls of the departed or for the elimination of alcohol abuse and automotive daredevilry.[62] Similarly, "Farther Along" suggests that the mysteries of the universe will be revealed to the faithful after they pass from this life. Curiously absent, however, are songs dealing overtly with marital infidelity, divorce, and other ills of modern urban life that one might hear about in the increasingly popular honky tonk genre that emerged from urban working-class communities across the country.[63] Songs such as "Blue Eyed Darling" and "Last Letter" come closest, referring to lovers who have left, but these songs omit tawdry details and instead focus on the speaker's fidelity to the rambling beloved. As a married woman who was working as a wage-earner and raising a family, it seems that, even if she was witnessing marital infidelity, divorce, drunkenness, and other honky tonk activities in her daily life, her song selection focused on respectability and might be seen to reflect her efforts to build a respectable environment for her family, even in the midst of geographic and cultural dislocation.

In surveying the songbook as a whole, it is clear that Smith was exceptionally class-conscious throughout the period of its compilation. As a woman who worked in the homes of other, more privileged women, she was undoubtedly aware of the kinds of traits that were deemed to be socially acceptable among the moneyed classes of Bluefield and the southern West Virginia coal camps, and, despite her limited formal education, she includes markers of formal education in the material object itself, from her careful handwriting to the use of the French word *finis* to mark the end of each song. The subjects of the songs that she included seldom dealt with the harsh realities of daily life but with idealized (if sometimes tragic) love and the promise of heavenly reward. As such, we can read this lyric book not only as an effort to document favorite songs, but also as an effort to perform middle-class respectability. That occasional lapses into the realm of hillbilly music can be found from time to time—as evidenced by her inclusion of "Worried Man Blues" (10v–11v), "The Old Age Pension" (29r–30r), and "East Virginia Blues" (45v)—is likely a capitulation to taste that betrays her desire for upward mobility; it seems that, despite her best efforts, Smith was not always able to "get above her raisin." Such is often the case when working-class whites find their way into the middle class, hence the continued popularity of country music in suburban communities throughout the United States.[64]

Of course, these markers of class are inflected with markers of gender and race as well. Smith's musical selections are drawn heavily from repertories that are either explicitly or implicitly marked as white, whether the hillbilly music that occasionally makes an appearance or the popular songs that found their way into her book through films, radio broadcasts, and sheet music. The general absence of musical examples drawn from African American popular and vernacular music or songs drawn from the shadows of minstrelsy might seem especially striking in light of the southern coalfield's racial diversity or, conversely, to be typical of a presumed all-white rural Appalachia.[65] Yet, when viewed through the lens of middle-class white respectability, the absence of African American music and minstrel songs is not surprising in the least; white middle-class criticism of ragtime, jazz, and other African American musical forms was exceptionally common at the time, with critics frequently pointing to the ways that dance, timbre, and rhythm overstepped the boundaries of propriety.[66] Furthermore, as the defenders of domestic tranquility, it was often the responsibility of middle-class women of all races to do everything in their effort to promote virtuous entertainment and hobbies in their homes. As such, while it is possible that Smith simply did not like music with coarser themes, it is possible to see her frequent inclusion of gospel songs and other compositions dealing with romance in a genteel way as a decidedly feminine effort to shape the domestic environment and to banish the hardships of the broader world from her home.

Of course, the deliberate and self-conscious nature of this lyric book also reveals the precariousness of Smith's class status. For all of her aspirations and affinities with genteel white society, she was always intimately linked to the working class, whether as a domestic worker in Bluefield, a mother in the southern West Virginia coalfields, a Rosie in Columbus, or a middle-class wife in West Virginia's Chemical Valley. Even when her husband went to work at Union Carbide, her middle-class status was newly begotten and always at risk from a plant closure or workplace injury. But her children, including her son Buddy, were able to reap the benefits of the postwar middle class, seeking higher education and finding their ways into the managerial class. As such, Smith was undoubtedly pleased with her successes.

CONCLUSIONS

Smith was not a significant musician, nor is her name much known beyond the immediate circle of family and friends who knew her when she was living—a community that has diminished significantly in the three decades since her death. Furthermore, the songs that are included in this lyric book can be found in much more legible forms in a number of sheet music and song folio collections. Such documents are located in family archives in towns and cities around the world, and, for the most part, they are viewed as quaint reminders of loved ones or, more tragically, yet more papers to be shuffled off to recycling or the landfill in the wake of a loved one's passing. Yet, when read in the context of broader societal and musical trends, it is possible to discern patterns of behavior that help to explain how individuals may have navigated the world in which they lived.[67] As a consequence, such documents challenge "great man" narratives that grant an inordinate amount of narrative power to people who live in the public sphere, a sphere that, in the Western world, often favors male participants.

On a local and regional level, Smith's lyric book challenges the notion that Appalachian timber and coal camps were masculine homosocial spaces where the brute physical strength of lumberjacks and coal miners and the brute capital strength of timber and coal barons ruled. But the Smith lyric book points to the significant role that education played in the class aspirations of many people in the industrializing timber and coal communities of central Appalachia.[68] Although the grunt work of timbering, coal mining, and farming required relatively little formal education, supervisory positions required the ability to read, write, and cipher. The protagonist in Jean Ritchie's powerful song "West Virginia Mine Disaster," for example, laments that if she "had the money to do more than just feed [her children, she'd] get them good learning, the best could be found so that when they growed up they'd be checkers and weighers and not spend their life toiling in the dark underground."[69] And in a more practical sense, Smith would have been unable to construct a document such as this without her six years of formal education. As such, this humble document sheds important light on the ways that literacy helped spur the imaginations of young people throughout the region, just as the modern world came to their backdoors. Perhaps even more powerfully, then, this document demonstrates the remarkable power of the imagination—in this case an imagination that seems to be fascinated with gentility, honor, romance, and piety—in helping young people imagine a future for themselves and their families. Today, many of the communities that Smith lived in have almost disappeared as the extractive industries that led to their creation have sought more lucrative timber stands and coalfields. Towns like Holden, which was once a thriving community with modern amenities, barely merit a small, easily overlooked road sign that passes in a blur as coal trucks and passenger cars travel from one sprawling strip mall town to another, and the people who still inhabit these places have been left behind by an industry that promised them entry into a world of economic stability. Yet, as this relatively small document indicates, family archives and other personal papers may hold the key to recovering the histories of these places and the people who made them significant.

Table 2. Contents of Smith Lyric Book with Publication Dates[70]

Page #	Song Title (as recorded in Smith's book)	Date of Publication	Published Title
1r–1v	Let Him In	1881	
2r	Among My Souvenirs	1927	
2v–3r	Old Pal of Yesterday	1931	My Pal of Yesterday
3v	Tip Toe through the Tulips	1929	
4r	Springtime in the Rockies	1929	When It's Springtime in the Rockies
4v	Dark Eyes	1929	
5r	Lover Come Back to Me	1928	Lover, Come Back to Me!
5v	blank	---	
6r	I'm Just a Vagabond Lover	1929	
6v	Before the Rain	1928	
7r	Budded Rose	1927[71]	Down Among the Budded Roses
7v–8r	The Lovers Farewell	1930	The Lovers' Farewell
8v–9r	Foggy Mt. Top	1916[72]	Foggy Mountain Top
9r–9v	Lulaby Youdle	1928	Lullaby Yodel
10r–10v	Little Rose Wood Casket	1935	
10v–11v	Worried Man Blues	1930	
11v–12r	Red Wing	1907	
12v–13r	Carry Me Back to Dear Old Dixie	Unknown	
13v–14r	Twenty One Years	1931	
15r–15v	The Convict and the Rose	1925	

Page #	Song Title (as recorded in Smith's book)	Date of Publication	Published Title
15v–16v	When the Roses Bloom Again	1901	
17r–18r	Cowboy Jack	1935	
18v–19r	Welcome as the Flowers in May	1902	You're as Welcome as the Flowers in May
19v	blank	----	
20r–20v	Home on the Range	1935	
20v–21v	Mollie Darling	1872	
22r–22v	Since Jesus Came into My Heart	1914	
23r–23v	I Can Hear My Savior Calling	1894	
23v–24r	Mothers Prayer Guides Me	unknown	
24v–25r	I Called and Nobody Answered	1938	Nobody Answered Me
25v	Plant Some Flowers on My Grave		
26r	In Care of Uncle Sam	1942	
26v	Blue Eyed Darling	1940	
27r	Branded Where Ever I Go	1942	
27v	Just to Ease My Worried Mind	1940	
28r–28v	The Precious Jewel	1940	
29r–30r	The Old Age Pension	1939	
30v–31r	Farther Along	1911	
31v–32r	The Wreck on the Highway	1942	
32v–33r	Shake My Mother's Hand for Me	1947	
33r–33v	Little Pal	1938	Come Back Little Pal
33v–34r	Lonely Mound of Clay	1940	
34v	Stream Lined Cannon Ball	1940	
34v–35v	Left Me Up Above the Shadows	1922	
36r–36v	Smoke on the Water	1944	
37r	You're My Darling	1940	
37v–38v	Will the Circle Be Unbroken	1907	
39r	I Hang My Head and Cry	1942	I Hung My Head and Cried
39v	A Sinner's Prayer	1942	
40r	Hung Down My Head + Cried	1942	I Hung My Head and Cried

Page #	Song Title (as recorded in Smith's book)	Date of Publication	Published Title
40v	When My Blue Moon Turns to Gold	1941	When My Blue Moon Turns to Gold Again
41r	Just Pay Me No Mind	1941	Pay Me No Mind
41v–42v	I Told You So	1942	I Told You So!
43r	The Great Speckled Bird	1936	
43v–44r	Wabash Cannon Ball	1936	
44v–45r	Turn Your Radio On	1947	
45v	East Va. Blues	1935	
46r–46v	It Makes No Difference Now	1939	
46v–47v	Last Letter	1937	
47v–48r	Rose of San Antone	1940	New San Antonio Rose
48v	Worried Mind	1940	
49r–49v	Sweetheart or Stranger	1941	Sweethearts or Strangers
49v–50r	Any Old Time	1930	
50v–51r	When It's Time for the Whipporwill to Call	1940	
51v–52r	I'll Keep on Loving You	1921	
52v–54r	You're My Darling	1940	
54v	blank	----	
55r–55v	The Old Lamp Lighter	1946	
55v–56r	Rockin Alone	1932	Rockin' Alone (in an Old Rocking Chair)

NOTES

1. Kyra D. Gaunt, *The Games Black Girls Play: Learning the Ropes from Double-Dutch to Hip-Hop* (Philadelphia: Temple University Press, 2006).

2. Melanie Lowe, "Colliding Feminisms: Britney Spears, 'Tweens,' and the Politics of Reception," *Popular Music and Society* 26, no. 2 (June 2003): 123–40.

3. Candace Bailey, "The Antebellum 'Piano Girl' in the American South," *Performance Practice Review* 13, no. 1 (2008): 1–44; Candace Bailey, *Music and the Southern Belle: From Accomplished Lady to Confederate Composer* (Carbondale: Southern Illinois University Press, 2010); Candace Bailey, "Binder's Volumes as Musical Commonplace Books," *Journal of the Society for American Music* 10, no. 4 (November 2016): 446–69. See also Melanie Green's efforts to extend this discussion to the postbellum US South in "'The Whistling Wife': Women and Popular Song in the Postbellum American South," M.M. thesis, West Virginia University, 2015.

4. Emily Hilliard, "'Written and Composed by Nora E. Carpenter': Song Lyric Scrapbooks, Home Recordings, and Self-Documentation," *Southern Cultures*, accessed April 14, 2017, http://www.southerncultures.org/article/written-composed-nora-e-carpenter/.

5. John Alexander Williams, *West Virginia and the Captains of Industry* (Morgantown: West Virginia University Press, 1976); Ronald D. Eller, *Miners, Millhands, and Mountaineers: Industrialization of the Appalachian South, 1880–1930* (Knoxville: University of Tennessee Press, 1982); Ronald L. Lewis, *Transforming the Appalachian Countryside: Railroads, Deforestation, and Social Change in West Virginia, 1880–1920* (Chapel Hill: University of North Carolina Press, 2000); Chad Montrie, "Continuity in the Midst of Change: Work and Environment for West Virginia Mountaineers," *West Virginia History*, new series, 1, no. 1 (Spring 2007): 1–22. Appalachia was not alone in this transition, however, as David B. Danbom has traced in *Born in the Country: A History of Rural America*, 2nd ed. (Baltimore: Johns Hopkins University Press, 2006), 131–60.

6. Barbara Kirshenblatt-Gimlett, "Objects of Memory: Material Culture as Life Review," in *Folk Groups and Folklore Genres: A Reader*, ed. Elliott Oring (Logan: Utah State University Press, 1989), 330.

7. Delayed Certificate of Birth for Mary Oleva Smith, Virginia Department of Health, Bureau of Vital Statistics, Certificate #21056. The certificate indicates that she was born in Hage Store, Virginia, but that spelling has not been found elsewhere upon further research.

Although she was married for much of her life, I will refer to her by her maiden name for the sake of consistency.

8. 1920 US Census, Giles County, Virginia, population schedule, enumeration district (ED) 33, p. 15 (penned), dwelling 265, family 267, Smith, Olivia.

9. Kathleen Williams, email to author, July 9, 2017 (in author's possession).

10. 1920 US Census, Giles County, Virginia, population schedule, enumeration district (ED) 33, p. 15 (penned), dwelling 265, family 267, Smith, Russell S., and Smith, William.

11. "United States World War I Draft Registration Cards, 1917–1918," Virginia, image 148 of 614; citing NARA microfilm publication M1509, database with images, *FamilySearch*, National Archives and Records Administration, Washington DC, accessed May 14, 2014, https://familysearch.org/ark:/61903/3:1:33S7-9YT5-9ZYG?mode=g&i=145&wc=9F4C-16D%3A928355001%2C928542401&cc=1968530.

12. Eller, *Miners, Millhands, and Mountaineers*; Lewis, *Transforming the Appalachian Countryside*.

13. Lewis, *Transforming the Appalachian Countryside*, 157.

14. Lewis, *Transforming the Appalachian Countryside*, 155

15. Eller, *Miners, Millhands, and Mountaineers*, 230–31; Jerry Bruce Thomas, *An Appalachian New Deal: West Virginia in the Great Depression* (Lexington: University Press of Kentucky, 1998), 180–82.

16. Eller, *Miners, Millhands, and Mountaineers*, 232.

17. For a broad overview of the nature of farm life for West Virginia women during this period, consult Shirley C. Eagan, "'Women's Work, Never Done': West Virginia Farm Women, 1880s–1920s," *West Virginia History* 49 (1990): 21–36, http://www.wvculture.org/history/journal_wvh/wvh49-3.html, accessed May 7, 2019.

18. Bluefield Chamber of Commerce, *Bluefield, West Virginia: The Gateway to Nature's Storehouse of Her Greatest Wealth* (Bluefield, WV: Bluefield Chamber of Commerce, 1912).

19. See, for instance, Christopher Wilkinson, *Big Band Jazz in the Mountain State, 1930–1942* (Jackson: University Press of Mississippi, 2012), xiii, 25; H. Randall Poole, "From Black to White: The Transition of Bluefield State College from an Historically Black College to a Predominantly White Institution," PhD diss., University of Maryland at College Park, 1989; Joe William Trotter Jr., *Coal, Class, and Color: Blacks in Southern West Virginia, 1915–32* (Urbana: University of Illinois Press, 1990).

20. Williams, typescript family history.

21. Kathleen Williams, email to author, July 9, 2017 (in author's possession).

22. Williams, typescript family history.

23. Sadly, there is very little scholarly literature on domestic workers, and memoirs appear to be hard to come by. However, two significant books do offer some insight into the complexities of daily life, particularly for African American domestic workers: Susan Tucker, *Telling Memories among Southern Women: Domestic Workers and Their Employers in the Segregated South* (Baton Rouge: Louisiana State University Press, 1988); Rebecca Sharpless, *Cooking in Other Women's Kitchens: Domestic Workers in the South, 1865–1960* (Chapel Hill: University of North Carolina Press, 2013).

24. Lewis, *Transforming the Appalachian Countryside*, 384–85.

25. Wilkinson, *Big Band Jazz in the Mountain State*, 61–67; Ivan L. Tribe, *Mountaineer Jamboree: Country Music in West Virginia* (Lexington: University Press of Kentucky, 1984), 73–109, esp. 98–99.

26. William R. "Bill" Archer, *Bluefield* (Charleston, SC: Arcadia, 2000), 109; Wilkinson, *Big Band Jazz in the Mountain State*, 109.

27. Williams, typescript family history; Delayed Certificate of Birth for Mary Oleva Smith; Robert C. Byrd, *Child of the Appalachian Coalfields* (Morgantown: West Virginia University Press, 2015), 20–30.

28. Williams, typescript family history.

29. Wood, *Raleigh County, West Virginia*, 333.

30. W. P. Tams Jr., *The Smokeless Coal Fields of West Virginia: A Brief History*, 2nd ed. (Morgantown: West Virginia University Press, 2001), 2, 5 (emphasis added).

31. Robert Y. Spence, *The Land of the Guyandot: A History of Logan County* (Detroit: Harlo, 1976), 318, 328.

32. *West Virginia: A Guide to the Mountain State* (New York: Oxford University Press, 1941), 467n1.

33. Janet W. Greene, "Strategies for Survival: Women's Work in the Southern West Virginia Coal Camps," *West Virginia History* 49 (1990): 37–54, http://www.wvculture.org/history/journal_wvh/wvh49-4.html, accessed May 7, 2019.

34. Williams, typescript family history.

35. For more information on Appalachian out-migration to the Midwest, consult Kathryn M. Boran and Phillip J. Obermiller, ed., *From Mountain to Metropolis: Appalachian Migrants in American Cities* (Westport, CT: Bergin & Garvey, 1994); James N. Gregory, *The Southern Diaspora: How the Great Migrations of Black and White Southerners Transformed America* (Chapel Hill: University of North Carolina Press, 2005).

36. Karida L. Brown, *Gone Home: Race and Roots through Appalachia* (Chapel Hill: University of North Carolina Press, 2018), 169–70.

37. Brown, *Gone Home*, 29–52, 161–79.

38. Williams, typescript family history. For further discussion of the Rosies, consult Maureen Honey, *Creating Rosie the Riveter: Class, Gender, and Propaganda during World War II* (Amherst: University of Massachusetts Press, 1984).

39. Louis R. Eltscher and Edward M. Young, *Curtiss-Wright: Greatness and Decline* (New York: Twayne Publishers, 1998), 103.

40. Eller, *Miners, Millhands, and Mountaineers*, 237; Carl E. Feather, *Mountain People in a Flat Land: A Popular History of Appalachian Migration to Northeast Ohio, 1940–1965* (Athens: Ohio University Press, 1998), 223–31; Brown, *Gone Home*, 173–86.

41. Williams, typescript family history.

42. It should be noted that a recent study indicated that, although the short-term impact of the Rosie movement was limited, it "led to a permanent increase in blue-collar employment

and a permanent decrease in white-collar employment for cohorts of women who were of working age in 1940." Andriana Bellou and Emanuela Cardia, "Occupations after WWII: The Legacy of Rosie the Riveter," *Explorations in Economic History* 62 (2016): 125.

For a brief overview of Union Carbide's history in West Virginia, consult Union Carbide Corporation, "History," http://www.unioncarbide.com/History, accessed March 7, 2017.

43. West Virginia's coalfields were remarkably diverse communities, often boasting significant populations of African Americans, Italians, and Eastern Europeans who came to the area in search of gainful employment. In those areas where the United Mine Workers of America was particularly strong, interracial and interethnic solidarity was quite common.

For further discussion of the ethnic diversity of southern West Virginia coal camps, consult, among others, Trotter, *Coal, Class, and Color*; Deborah R. Weiner, "From Shtetl to Coalfield: The Migration of East European Jews to Southern West Virginia," in Ken Fones-Wolf and Ronald L. Lewis, ed., *Transnational West Virginia: Ethnic Communities and Economic Change, 1840–1940* (Morgantown: West Virginia University Press, 2002), 73–112.

44. Kathleen Williams, email to author, July 9, 2017 (in author's possession).

45. Alice Kessler-Harris, *Out to Work: A History of Wage-Earning Women in the United States* (New York: Oxford University Press, 1982), 273–319.

46. Marian Wilson Kimber has demonstrated the power of "elocution" in the class aspirations of US women in *The Elocutionists: Women, Music, and the Spoken Word* (Urbana: University of Illinois Press, 2017), 1–26.

For more on education in early twentieth-century Appalachia, consult, among others, J. R. LeMaster, ed., *Jesse Stuart on Education* (Lexington: University Press of Kentucky, 1992); Jess Stoddart, *Challenge and Change in Appalachia* (Lexington: University Press of Kentucky, 2002).

47. "Southern Folklife Collection Song Folios, circa 1882–1983," Southern Folklife Collection, Wilson Library, University of North Carolina at Chapel Hill Libraries, http://finding-aids.lib.unc.edu/30006/, accessed January 15, 2017; Guthrie T. Meade, Richard K. Spottswood, and Douglas S. Meade, *Country Music Sources: A Biblio-Discography of Commercially Recorded Traditional Music* (Chapel Hill: Southern Folklife Collection, University of North Carolina at Chapel Hill Libraries, 2002); Tony Russell, *Country Music Records: A Discography, 1921–1942* (New York: Oxford University Press, 2008).

48. Table 2 in this essay provides the book's complete contents, as well as the original publication date for each song.

49. Rudy Vallee and Leon Zimmerman, "I'm Just a Vagabond Lover" (New York: Leo. Feist, 1929).

50. "Glorifying the American Girl," https://en.wikipedia.org/wiki/Glorifying_the_American_Girl, accessed April 15, 2017. A clip of this performance can be found at YouTube, https://www.youtube.com/watch?v=eb36JID2jRA, accessed February 10, 2017.

51. Unfortunately, an examination of theater advertisements in the local newspaper did not turn up reference to this screening.

52. Rudy Vallee, "I'm Just a Vagabond Lover" (Victor 21967-A, 1929); *Discography of American Historical Recordings*, s.v. "Victor matrix BVE-51108. I'm just a vagabond lover / Connecticut Yankees; Rudy Vallée," http://adp.library.ucsb.edu/index.php/matrix/detail/800024265/BVE-51108-Im_just_a_vagabond_lover, accessed April 27, 2017.

53. Williams, email to author, July 9, 2017 (in author's possession).

54. Williams, typescript family history.

55. Denver Darling, "Care of Uncle Sam," Decca DE 6063 (July 14, 1942); Russell, *Country Music Records*, 296. According to Russell's discography, Denver recorded a number of wartime songs, including "Mussolini's Letter to Hitler," "Hitler's Reply to Mussolini," and "The Devil and Mr. Hitler."

56. Lyrics available at https://www.cowboylyrics.com/lyrics/foley-red/smoke-on-the-water-30897.html, accessed April 27, 2017.

57. Joel Whitburn, *The Billboard Book of Top 40 Country Hits: 1944–2006*, 2nd ed. (New York: Billboard Books, 2006), 122.

58. For more on minstrelsy's influences on barn dance programs, consult Pamela Fox, *Natural Acts: Gender, Race, and Rusticity in Country Music* (Ann Arbor: University of Michigan Press, 2009), 17–62.

59. This stands in stark contrast to Peter La Chapelle's discussion of the western swing boom among defense plant workers in southern California. Peter La Chapelle, *Proud to Be an Okie: Cultural Politics, Country Music, and Migration to Southern California* (Berkeley: University of California Press, 2007), 76–110.

60. In 1962, sociologists James S. Brown and George A. Hillery Jr. reported that, due to "a lack of vocational training (other than agricultural)[,] large proportions of migrants are obliged to enter the occupational structure at its lowest level. This level is the most vulnerable to economic fluctuation" ("The Great Migration, 1940–1960," in *The Southern Appalachian Region: A Survey*, ed. Thomas R. Ford [Lexington: University Press of Kentucky, 1962], 69).

61. In a 1994 review of sociological research on Appalachian migrant women, H. Virginia McCoy, Diana Gullett Trevino, and Clyde M. McCoy suggest that "the limited social science literature indicates that the social adjustment process required of Appalachian migrant women produces greater change in them than in the men. Appalachian culture requires that women fulfill the traditional roles of homemaker and mother, but the urban setting demands some transformation in decision making, in employment, and in marital relationships" ("Appalachian Women: Between Two Cultures," in Kathryn M. Borman and Phillip J. Obermiller, ed., *From Mountain to Metropolis: Appalachian Migrants in American Cities* [Westport, CT: Bergin & Garvey, 1994], 37).

62. Patrick Huber, "'A Blessing to People': Dorsey Dixon and His Sacred Mission of Song," *Southern Cultures* 12, no. 4 (2006): 111–31.

63. Joe W. Specht, "Put a Nickel in the Jukebox: The Texas Tradition in Country Music, 1922–50," in *The Roots of Texas Music*, ed. Lawrence Clayton and Joe W. Specht (College Station: Texas A&M University Press, 2003), 79–87.

64. See, among others, Jeffrey J. Lange, *Smile When You Call Me a Hillbilly: Country Music's Struggle for Respectability, 1939–1954* (Athens: University of Georgia Press, 2004); Diane Pecknold, *The Selling Sound: The Rise of the Country Music Industry* (Durham, NC: Duke University Press, 2007), 95–132.

65. Consult, for instance, Trotter, *Coal, Class, and Color*; Wilkinson, *Big Band Jazz in Black West Virginia, 1930–1942*; Brown, *Gone Home*. For a more extensive critique of Appalachia's presumed whiteness, consult Barbara Ellen Smith, "De-Gradations of Whiteness: Appalachia and the Complexities of Race," *Journal of Appalachian Studies* 10, no.1/2 (Spring/Fall 2004): 38–57; Mary K. Anglin, "Erasures of the Past: Culture, Power, and Heterogeneity in Appalachia," *Journal of Appalachian Studies* 10, no. 1/2 (Spring/Fall 2004): 73–84, esp. 77–78, 81.

66. Consider, for instance, Anne Shaw Faulkner, "Does Jazz Put the Sin in Syncopation?" *Ladies' Home Journal* (August 1921), 16, 34; reprinted in *Keeping Time: Readings in Jazz History*, 2nd ed., ed. Robert Walser (New York: Oxford University Press, 2015), 26–29.

67. For additional examples of useful studies that use personal and family archives to shed light on vernacular engagement with popular culture, consult Douglas B. Green, "The Blue Sky Boys on Radio, 1939–1940: A Newly Discovered Log of Their Daily Program, Kept by Ruth Walker," *Journal of Country Music* 4, no. 4 (Winter 1973): 108–58; Douglas B. Green, "Introduction," *Journal of Country Music* 5, no. 3 (Fall 1974): 91; "The Grand Ole Opry, 1944–45: A Radio

Log by Dick Hill, of Tecumseh, Nebraska," *Journal of Country Music* 5, no. 3 (Fall 1974): 92–122; Bob Pinson, "Introduction," *Journal of Country Music* 5, no. 4 (Winter 1974): 134; "Bob Wills and His Texas Playboys on Radio, 1942," *Journal of Country Music* 5, no. 4 (Winter 1974): 135–93; Charles Wolfe, "Up North with the Blue Ridge Ramblers: Jennie Bowman's 1931 Tour Diary," *Journal of Country Music* 6, no. 3 (Fall 1975): 136–45.

68. For a particularly moving exploration of the impact of education for Black coalfield residents, see Brown, *Gone Home*, 103–58.

69. Jean Ritchie, "West Virginia Mine Disaster," *Clear Waters Remembered* (Sire SES 97014 [1971]).

70. All publication information drawn from the UCLA Sheet Music Consortium, http://digital2.library.ucla.edu/sheetmusic/; *Discography of American Historical Recordings*, http://adp.library.ucsb.edu; hymnary.org; and Russell, *Country Music Records*, unless otherwise indicated.

71. Robert B. Waltz and David G. Engle, "Down Among the Budded Roses," in *The Ballad Index*, http://www.fresnostate.edu/folklore/ballads/RcDATBR.html, accessed July 2, 2017.

72. "Foggy Mountain Top" is a widely collected Appalachian song that was first published by Cecil Sharp in 1916. It is just as likely, though, that Smith encountered this song through the Carter Family, whose work figures considerably in this notebook. For more background on this song, consult Robert B. Waltz and David G. Engle, "Foggy Mountain Top," in *The Ballad Index*, http://www.fresnostate.edu/folklore/ballads/CSW042.html, accessed July2, 2017.

BIBLIOGRAPHY

Anglin, Mary K. "Erasures of the Past: Culture, Power, and Heterogeneity in Appalachia." *Journal of Appalachian Studies* 10, no. 1/2 (Spring/Fall 2004): 73–84.

Archer, William R. "Bill." *Bluefield*. Charleston, SC: Arcadia, 2000.

Bailey, Candace. "The Antebellum 'Piano Girl' in the American South." *Performance Practice Review* 13, no. 1 (2008): 1–44.

Bailey, Candace. *Music and the Southern Belle: From Accomplished Lady to Confederate Composer*. Carbondale: Southern Illinois University Press, 2010.

Bailey, Candace. "Binder's Volumes as Musical Commonplace Books." *Journal of the Society for American Music* 10, no. 4 (November 2016): 446–69.

Bellou, Andrianna, and Emanuela Cardia. "Occupations after WWII: The Legacy of Rosie the Riveter." *Explorations in Economic History* 62 (2016): 124–42.

Bluefield Chamber of Commerce. *Bluefield, West Virginia: The Gateway to Nature's Storehouse of Her Greatest Wealth*. Bluefield, WV: Bluefield Chamber of Commerce, 1912.

"Bob Wills and His Texas Playboys on Radio, 1942." *Journal of Country Music* 5, no. 4 (Winter 1974): 135–93.

Boran, Kathryn M., and Phillip J. Obermiller, ed. *From Mountain to Metropolis: Appalachian Migrants in American Cities*. Westport, CT: Bergin & Garvey, 1994.

Brown, James S., and George A. Hillery Jr. "The Great Migration, 1940–1960." In *The Southern Appalachian Region: A Survey*. Ed. Thomas R. Ford. Lexington: University Press of Kentucky, 1962. 54–78.

Brown, Karida L. *Gone Home: Race and Roots through Appalachia*. Chapel Hill: University of North Carolina Press, 2018.

Danbom, David B. *Born in the Country: A History of Rural America*, 2nd ed. Baltimore: Johns Hopkins University Press, 2006.

Discography of American Historical Recordings. http://adp.library.ucsb.edu. Accessed April 15, 2017.

Eagan, Shirley C. "'Women's Work, Never Done': West Virginia Farm Women, 1880s–1920s." *West Virginia History* 49 (1990): 21–36. Republished at http://www.wvculture.org/history/journal_wvh/wvh49-3.html. Accessed May 7, 2019.

Eller, Ronald D. *Miners, Millhands, and Mountaineers: Industrialization of the Appalachian South, 1880–1930*. Knoxville: University of Tennessee Press, 1982.

Eltscher, Louis R., and Edward M. Young. *Curtiss-Wright: Greatness and Decline*. New York: Twayne Publishers, 1998.

Faulkner, Anne Shaw. "Does Jazz Put the Sin in Syncopation?" *Ladies' Home Journal* (August 1921), 16, 34. Reprinted in *Keeping Time: Readings in Jazz History*. 2nd ed. Ed. Robert Walser, 26–29. New York: Oxford University Press, 2015.

Feather, Carl E. *Mountain People in a Flat Land: A Popular History of Appalachian Migration to Northeast Ohio, 1940–1965*. Athens: Ohio University Press, 1998.

Fox, Pamela. *Natural Acts: Gender, Race, and Rusticity in Country Music*. Ann Arbor: University of Michigan Press, 2009.

Gaunt, Kyra D. *The Games Black Girls Play: Learning the Ropes from Double-Dutch to Hip-Hop*. Philadelphia: Temple University Press, 2006.

"Glorifying the American Girl." https://en.wikipedia.org/wiki/Glorifying_the_American_Girl. Accessed April 15, 2017.

"The Grand Ole Opry, 1944–45: A Radio Log by Dick Hill, of Tecumseh, Nebraska." *Journal of Country Music* 5, no. 3 (Fall 1974): 92–122.

Green, Douglas B. "The Blue Sky Boys on Radio, 1939–1940: A Newly Discovered Log of Their Daily Program, Kept by Ruth Walker." *Journal of Country Music* 4, no. 4 (Winter 1973): 108–58.

Green, Douglas B. "Introduction." *Journal of Country Music* 5, no. 3 (Fall 1974): 91.

Green, Melanie. "'The Whistling Wife': Women and Popular Song in the Postbellum American South." M.M. thesis, West Virginia University, 2015.

Greene, Janet W. "Strategies for Survival: Women's Work in the Southern West Virginia Coal Camps." *West Virginia History* 49 (1990): 37–54. Republished at http://www.wvculture.org/history/journal_wvh/wvh49-4.html. Accessed May 7, 2019.

Gregory, James N. *The Southern Diaspora: How the Great Migrations of Black and White Southerners Transformed America*. Chapel Hill: University of North Carolina Press, 2005.

Hilliard, Emily. "'Written and Composed by Nora E. Carpenter': Song Lyric Scrapbooks, Home Recordings, and Self-Documentation." *Southern Cultures*. http://www.southerncultures.org/article/written-composed-nora-e-carpenter/. Accessed April 14, 2017.

Honey, Maureen. *Creating Rosie the Riveter: Class, Gender, and Propaganda during World War II*. Amherst: University of Massachusetts Press, 1984.

Huber, Patrick. "'A Blessing to People': Dorsey Dixon and His Sacred Mission of Song." *Southern Cultures* 12, no. 4 (2006): 111–31.

Hymnary.org. http://www.hymnary.org. Accessed June 13, 2017.

Kessler-Harris, Alice. *Out to Work: A History of Wage-Earning Women in the United States*. New York: Oxford University Press, 1982.

Kimber, Marian Wilson. *The Elocutionists: Women, Music, and the Spoken Word*. Urbana: University of Illinois Press, 2017.

Kirshenblatt-Gimlett, Barbara. "Objects of Memory: Material Culture as Life Review." In *Folk Groups and Folklore Genres: A Reader*. Ed. Elliott Oring, 329–38. Logan: Utah State University Press, 1989.

La Chapelle, Peter. *Proud to Be an Okie: Cultural Politics, Country Music, and Migration to Southern California*. Berkeley: University of California Press, 2007.

Lange, Jeffrey J. *Smile When You Call Me a Hillbilly: Country Music's Struggle for Respectability, 1939–1954*. Athens: University of Georgia Press, 2004.

LeMaster, J. R., ed. *Jesse Stuart on Education*. Lexington: University Press of Kentucky, 1992.

Lewis, Ronald L. *Transforming the Appalachian Countryside: Railroads, Deforestation, and Social Change in West Virginia, 1880–1920*. Chapel Hill: University of North Carolina Press, 2000.

Lowe, Melanie. "Colliding Feminisms: Britney Spears, 'Tweens,' and the Politics of Reception." *Popular Music and Society* 26, no. 2 (June 2003): 123–40.

McCoy, H. Virginia, Diana Gullett Trevino, and Clyde M. McCoy. "Appalachian Women: Between Two Cultures." In Kathryn M. Borman and Phillip J. Obermiller, ed., *From Mountain to Metropolis: Appalachian Migrants in American Cities*, 33–48. Westport, CT: Bergin & Garvey, 1994.

Meade, Guthrie T., Richard K. Spottswood, and Douglas S. Meade. *Country Music Sources: A Biblio-Discography of Commercially Recorded Traditional Music*. Chapel Hill: Southern Folklife Collection, University of North Carolina at Chapel Hill Libraries, 2002.

Montrie, Chad. "Continuity in the Midst of Change: Work and Environment for West Virginia Mountaineers." *West Virginia History*, new series, 1, no. 1 (Spring 2007): 1–22.

Pecknold, Diane. *The Selling Sound: The Rise of the Country Music Industry*. Durham, NC: Duke University Press, 2007.

Pinson, Bob. "Introduction." *Journal of Country Music* 5, no. 4 (Winter 1974): 134.

Poole, H. Randall. "From Black to White: The Transition of Bluefield State College from an Historically Black College to a Predominantly White Institution." PhD diss., University of Maryland at College Park, 1989.

Russell, Tony. *Country Music Records: A Discography, 1921–1942*. New York: Oxford University Press, 2008.

Sharpless, Rebecca. *Cooking in Other Women's Kitchens: Domestic Workers in the South, 1865–1960*. Chapel Hill: University of North Carolina Press, 2013.

Smith, Barbara Ellen. "De-Gradations of Whiteness: Appalachia and the Complexities of Race." *Journal of Appalachian Studies* 10, no.1/2 (Spring/Fall 2004): 38–57.

"Southern Folklife Collection Song Folios, circa 1882–1983." Southern Folklife Collection, Wilson Library, University of North Carolina at Chapel Hill Libraries. http://finding-aids.lib.unc.edu/30006/. Accessed January 15, 2017.

Specht, Joe W. "Put a Nickel in the Jukebox: The Texas Tradition in Country Music, 1922–50." In *The Roots of Texas Music*, ed. Lawrence Clayton and Joe W. Specht, 79–87. College Station: Texas A&M University Press, 2003.

Spence, Robert Y. *The Land of the Guyandot: A History of Logan County*. Detroit: Harlo, 1976.

Stoddart, Jess. *Challenge and Change in Appalachia*. Lexington: University Press of Kentucky, 2002.

Tams, W. P., Jr. *The Smokeless Coal Fields of West Virginia: A Brief History*, 2nd ed. Morgantown: West Virginia University Press, 2001.

Thomas, Jerry Bruce. *An Appalachian New Deal: West Virginia in the Great Depression*. Lexington: University Press of Kentucky, 1998.

Tribe, Ivan L. *Mountaineer Jamboree: Country Music in West Virginia*. Lexington: University Press of Kentucky, 1984.

Trotter, Joe William, Jr. *Coal, Class, and Color: Blacks in Southern West Virginia, 1915–32*. Urbana: University of Illinois Press, 1990.

Tucker, Susan. *Telling Memories among Southern Women: Domestic Workers and Their Employers in the Segregated South*. Baton Rouge: Louisiana State University Press, 1988.

UCLA Sheet Music Consortium. http://digital2.library.ucla.edu/sheetmusic/. Accessed June 15, 2017.
Union Carbide Corporation. "History." http://www.unioncarbide.com/History. Accessed March 7, 2017.
Waltz, Robert B., and David G. Engle. "Down Among the Budded Roses." In *The Ballad Index*. http://www.fresnostate.edu/folklore/ballads/RcDATBR.html. Accessed July 2, 2017.
Waltz, Robert B., and David G. Engle. "Foggy Mountain Top." In *The Ballad Index*. http://www.fresnostate.edu/folklore/ballads/CSW042.html. Accessed July 2, 2017.
Weiner, Deborah R. "From Shtetl to Coalfield: The Migration of East European Jews to Southern West Virginia." In Ken Fones-Wolf and Ronald L. Lewis, ed., *Transnational West Virginia: Ethnic Communities and Economic Change, 1840–1940*, 73–112. Morgantown: West Virginia University Press, 2002.
West Virginia: A Guide to the Mountain State. New York: Oxford University Press, 1941.
Whitburn, Joel. *The Billboard Book of Top 40 Country Hits: 1944–2006*. 2nd ed. New York: Billboard Books, 2006.
Wilkinson, Christopher. *Big Band Jazz in Black West Virginia, 1930–1942*. Jackson: University Press of Mississippi, 2012.
Williams, John Alexander. *West Virginia and the Captains of Industry*. Morgantown: West Virginia University Press, 1976.
Wolfe, Charles. "Up North with the Blue Ridge Ramblers: Jennie Bowman's 1931 Tour Diary." *Journal of Country Music* 6, no. 3 (Fall 1975): 136–45.

Chapter 9

Finding Hidden Women in the Feminist Narrative: Candie Carawan and Music in the Civil Rights Movement

—Kristen M. Turner

Historian, musician, and activist Bernice Johnson Reagon defines music in the civil rights movement as a force that "suspends the confusion and points to a higher order, sometimes long enough for you to execute the next step. Therefore singing will not set you free, but don't try to get free without it."[1] Protestors sang freedom songs at mass meetings, at demonstrations, during long days and months in jail, and even to pass the time on lengthy car rides between little rural towns in the Deep South. Many activists describe the music as their introduction to the civil rights struggle and one of the reasons they survived years of often traumatic and dangerous political work. Candie Carawan, who has spent her life in political advocacy, explains that music in the civil rights period was special because "there were literally hundreds of songs that were just springing up everywhere because of the situation, and people were singing them with just fantastic spirit. I've never experienced anything since that was anything like that group cohesion, and all expressed through song."[2] Music was an organizing tool, an instrument for education, a basis for unity within a political movement made up of people from disparate backgrounds, a source of comfort in the midst of racialized and politicized violence, and a symbol of activists' commitment to action.

Many women with musical skill became local and national leaders within the movement, including Bernice Johnson Reagon, Rutha Harris, Bettie Mae Fikes, and Fannie Lou Hamer, all of whom were talented singers and song leaders. They are part of a long history of women's civil rights political activism in the United States that stretches from abolitionism to Black Lives Matter.[3] Yet, early accounts of the civil rights movement contain little or no mention of women, and even assert "women all over the world are less active in politics than men."[4] Historians of the civil rights movement have struggled with the same weakness that still infects so much musicological scholarship—the reliance on a "Great Man" as the focus of the story with all others positioned as subordinates circling around the dominant male figure. As Kimberly Francis observes, in order to expose the true role of many women in music we must abandon this narrative and find another paradigm.[5] In civil rights scholarship, one approach to this issue has often been to find a way to redefine leadership in order to bring women and their actions to light.[6] The difficulty with this strategy for both music and civil rights studies, however, is that it still valorizes a central individual over the circle of support around that person. In this essay, I position the periphery over the center. I follow in Francis's footsteps and define Candie Carawan as a "cultural agent" who fits within Bourdieu's theory of the cultural field. A cultural agent, according to Francis's theorization, is someone who plays a role within the network of connections that produces a cultural field. In the case of the civil rights movement, the cultural field was created by the interactions between actors such as civil rights activists, song leaders, folk singers, composers, record-company executives, folklorists, and others. My goal is to offer a historical account that excavates Candie Carawan's activities during the civil rights movement by understanding her role within a larger network of musicians and cultural workers in the movement. She exerted influence within a group of song leaders, folk musicians, protesters, and scholars, some of whom were white like her, who defined the freedom song repertoire and encouraged activists to engage with Black culture through music. I seek to situate her historical erasure in terms that look beyond traditional stories of scholarly oversight or the minimization of women's contributions by patriarchal organizations, in favor of honoring the decisions and life circumstances that led Candie Carawan to work within prevailing social structures and take on a supporting role in the movement. Rather than wishing for more from her, I seek to uncover all that she did.

JOINING THE MOVEMENT

Carolanne Anderson Carawan was born on December 27, 1939, in Los Angeles, California and grew up in the area.[7] In 1957, she began her studies at Pomona College in Claremont, California, eventually majoring in art. Raised in a politically progressive family, Carolanne (usually known as Candie) became interested in the civil rights movement in high school. During her sophomore year at Pomona, Candie lived with Marietta Dockery, a Black student from Nashville's Fisk University who was participating in an exchange program between Pomona (a predominantly white college established in 1887) and Fisk (a historically Black institution also founded soon after the Civil War). The following year, in January

1960, Candie moved to Nashville to attend Fisk for the spring semester.[8] Candie wanted to go to Fisk because she "was just really intrigued with the whole idea of nonviolent resistance and the fact that the South was segregated but that there were people willing to work on it."[9] By this time, her former roommate Marietta Dockery was also back at Fisk, and she facilitated Candie's quick entry into a group of politically active students as soon as Candie arrived in Tennessee. On February 1, 1960, four Black students from North Carolina A&T sat in at the Woolworth's lunch counter in Greensboro, touching off a wave of sit-ins that quickly engulfed the South. Students from Fisk and other schools in Nashville began sitting in at downtown lunch counters on February 13, forcing Candie to decide whether to take part in the demonstrations within weeks of her arrival in the city. Ultimately, Candie was one of a handful of white students who chose to join the sit-ins.[10] On February 27, Nashville police officers arrested Candie and other protesters during a sit-in at McClellan's drugstore. According to Candie, her subsequent experience with the judicial system in Nashville, which supported racist politics at the expense of the truth, forever changed her understanding of America and propelled her into a life of political advocacy.[11]

Although Candie's decision to become an activist was transgressive, within the context of her family and social set it was not particularly revolutionary. Unlike so many other people who faced familial and social disapproval (even expulsion from school) when they joined political work, Candie's parents were progressives who supported her choices.[12] Her friends were also politically aware if not always activists themselves. In some respects, it would have been more rebellious if she had chosen not to participate in the sit-in because so many of her acquaintances at Fisk were already involved in civil rights work. Even so, Candie considered her options carefully because she was aware that her presence at demonstrations could inflame an already tense situation. She told me in an interview I conducted with her in 2010 that "I was worried that it might make people madder to see white participants.... On the other hand, I thought that this movement is about everybody. It's not just something that we're doing for Black people. We're trying to create a more just society here, and I have a stake in that as well."[13] Many white civil rights activists agreed with Candie and identified the injustice and immorality of segregation as a moral cancer at the center of American life that affected everyone no matter their race.

BEGINNING A NEW CHAPTER: HIGHLANDER AND GUY CARAWAN

During the weekend of April 1–3, 1960, Candie attended a workshop for college-age activists at the Highlander Folk School in Tennessee. In 1932 Myles Horton, Jim Dombrowski, and Don West founded the school, now called the Highlander Research and Education Center, to train social and political activists.[14] The workshop Candie went to in 1960 was designed to bring together college-aged protesters from around the South who had been sitting in so that they could get acquainted, plan a coherent strategy, and talk about ways to be more politically effective.[15] Folk singer Guy Carawan (1927–2015), the volunteer music director, was among the Highlander staff members working at the meeting.[16]

Like Candie, Guy was born in Los Angeles. After graduating from Occidental College, he began working as a folk singer, forging a close friendship with Bess Hawes, a folklorist and political activist who was an important figure in the folk music scene in Southern California. At her suggestion, he spent a month with Alan Lomax (Hawes's brother) in England during the summer of 1957.[17] This was the beginning of one of the most important connections in Guy's professional life. He was deeply influenced by Lomax's ideas about rural music, the study of folklore, and the possibilities of music's use in political work.[18] By the time Candie met him in 1960, Guy had been living in the South intermittently since 1953 and had been volunteering at Highlander since the late 1950s.[19]

At the College-Age Workshop, Guy introduced the participants to songs such as "We Shall Overcome" and "We Shall Not Be Moved."[20] He also attended a meeting two weeks later at Shaw University in Raleigh, North Carolina, at which the Student Nonviolent Coordinating Committee (SNCC) was organized, and once again led the students in songs that would become movement standards.[21] The students present at these two meetings took the songs with them all over the South, as well as the idea that communal performance of music based upon African American spirituals and traditional music could be a powerful component of the movement.[22] Guy and Candie started dating after the April 1 meeting, and Guy spent at least two months in Nashville during that semester. Certainly, he had professional reasons to be there—he sang at mass meetings and recorded a documentary album about the experiences of the activists—but Candie's presence was an equally strong motivation to visit the city.[23] The student leaders in Nashville, including Marion Barry, John Lewis, Diane Nash, Chuck Neblett, and Cordell Reagon became some of the most important political leaders and singers during the movement, and Guy's concentrated attention to that area at the beginning of their activist careers must have had an impact on their perception of music's value to political action.[24] Candie married Guy in California on March 17, 1961, walking down the aisle to "We Shall Overcome." After she graduated from Pomona a few months later, the couple moved to Atlanta.[25]

A PARTNERSHIP FORGED IN ACTIVISM

In an August 1959 letter addressed to the Friends of Highlander, Guy outlined an ambitious agenda designed to encourage music's use in the civil rights movement.

He planned to publish a book of "songs for integration," produce record albums devoted to this repertoire, and organize music festivals and training workshops for song leaders, educators, and folklorists.[26] By 1968 the couple had accomplished these objectives, along with another goal Guy added in 1961: documenting and studying the music of the movement as it developed throughout the South. Guy was well qualified to accomplish this task because he was a trained folklorist with a master's degree in sociology from the University of California at Los Angeles. In a memo to Myles Horton, Guy explained that, after a SNCC meeting in Jackson, Mississippi, in July 1961, he realized "there were . . . many good experienced singers who knew how to get freedom singing going and could do it much better than I."[27] He and Candie reasoned that the activists were too busy to document what they were doing, but both believed it important to preserve and disseminate the music of the movement.[28] This project would be one of their most lasting contributions to the civil rights struggle.

Between 1961 and 1965, Guy, often accompanied by Candie, traveled to all of what Candie called the "hot spots" to record mass meetings and demonstrations. Some of these field recordings were released as part of documentary albums Guy produced and issued through Folkways. These LPs were an important means of circulating songs and information about the movement to activists working in the South and to people throughout the United States who were interested in civil rights. In 1963, supported by a Newport Folk Foundation grant, the couple moved to Johns Island, South Carolina, to study the music and culture of the Gullah people, which ultimately bore fruit in a book and two albums. They saw their work in South Carolina as a corrective to earlier deeply racist scholarship on the area, as well as a way to connect their political goals with their interest in Black culture.[29] Their book, *Ain't You Got a Right to the Tree of Life? The People of Johns Island South Carolina*, highlights anti-racist work by local musicians, profiles people on Johns Island who collaborated with Highlander on political projects, and emphasizes the link between conditions on the island and segregationist governmental policies.

In addition to books and albums, the Carawans helped organize and lead several workshops on freedom songs and song leading.[30] While students learned new songs, the larger aim of the weekend courses was to introduce participants (many of whom came from urban, middle-class backgrounds) to rural Black culture and music. Candie primarily handled logistics and the inevitable paperwork related to marketing and running large workshops that attracted presenters and students from around the country. She did not take an active role as a leader in individual sessions.[31] During classes the facilitators, who included Guy and Black musicians from rural areas, argued that African Americans should understand and take pride in their history and culture as an act of resistance against white supremacy and racial oppression.[32] The salary Guy received for planning and teaching at these workshops are the only instances in which he was paid for his work in the movement during the 1960s.³³ Even though they always collaborated, the financial remuneration for the couple's work was invariably directed to Guy, while Candie's labor went uncompensated.

Candie took the lead in their writing partnership, drafting all the articles and books the couple published from the time of their marriage in 1961 until Guy's retirement from Highlander in the mid-1980s. In the years between 1962 and 1968, they released six albums and published two articles, two annotated freedom song books, and the book on Gullah culture. Guy published very little before they met, but became much more prolific afterwards, suggesting that Candie's writing skills and support were crucial to their output. According to Candie, "He [Guy] would always—we would talk through ideas and then I'd do a draft and then he'd critique the draft and it was endless revising. And I wish I'd recognized early on that Guy should continue to do his own writing because I think everything changed once we moved into that."³⁴ Early drafts of some of their written work showing their edits confirm her recollection.³⁵ Candie's regret that Guy's literary voice was silenced, or at least diminished, after their marriage indicates how much her involvement affected and changed Guy's writing style. Although she recognized that her participation was important, Candie also claims that it did not occur to her to ask that her name be included in their publications. In our interview she compared her duties to that of the wife who types up her husband's dissertation. It was Guy, according to Candie, who insisted that she be credited for their joint work.³⁶

When Candie met Guy, he had been working with Highlander since the late 1950s and was already a familiar figure to many activists. She was new to the movement and twelve years younger than Guy. Her college degree was in art, while Guy was a veteran folk singer. Candie fell naturally into what she described to me as a "helper" or "administrator" role within projects Guy had already initiated, not only because she was his wife but also because of her youth and inexperience compared to Guy. As Candie explained,

> But then once we got married and I—I didn't know that much—what I knew about folk music was who would come around to colleges and perform, right? I knew it was kind of interesting music and it was stylistically something I liked but I didn't really have a clue about the things that Guy ... [knew]. Or just his understanding of how important real community music is. So the first years we were married I was very much learning from him.³⁷

Candie functioned within multiple societal norms inside the movement and in the larger culture during the civil rights years. Activist Joan C. Browning maintains that many women played an "unsung nurturing role" in the movement by providing meals, a comfortable place to stay, and a sympathetic ear to civil rights workers.[38] Additionally, Ella Baker's example as an insider who performed logistical and administrative work was a powerful one for Candie and others. Baker began her political career with the National Association for the Advancement of Colored People, then provided the administrative expertise behind Martin Luther King Jr.'s Southern Christian Leadership Council, and mentored many students in SNCC. Candie explained in 2003 that Baker was

> an inspiration . . . to women who entered the Civil Rights Movement, because she always valued the contribution they could make and, you know, you didn't have to be a charismatic out-front person with a golden tongue. There were so many jobs in the Movement, and women were often very good at those jobs . . . she just was the person that gave a lot of women the courage and strength to know, "We can be part of this. We can do things."[39]

While there were many activists as young as Candie in the movement, most were frontline demonstrators who put their bodies on the line in marches and field organizing. After they married, however, the Carawans spent most of their time teaching, researching, and documenting music in the movement, which required a level of expertise that Candie was only just developing. Although Guy seems to have been more respectful of Candie's work than many men were in the 1960s, even Guy admitted in an interview that in 1964 "I had still been acting, you know I was like a strong male leader."[40] Candie would have been socialized by the era's gender roles as well as expectations within the movement to join her husband in his efforts rather than continuing on her own path.

One way to frame their work is as unequal partners. Guy, always out front in the spotlight, and Candie, at home, helping him when she was not otherwise occupied with caring for their son, Evan, who was born in 1962. Indeed, in one audiotape of an interview the couple conducted for *Ain't You Got the Right to the Tree of Life?*, Candie is involved in the discussion, but is also clearly in charge of Evan, who sometimes gets a bit disruptive as he plays.[41] In this scenario, she becomes the victim of the patriarchy, her impact minimal and later erased because of societal biases, which ensured that Guy received full credit for work they did together. This interpretation lacks nuance because it does not consider the full context of their lives together or their personalities. In a 1982 interview, Guy explains that their working method evolved to take advantage of their individual strengths. He called her clearly the better writer, but he did not mind doing a lot of the telephoning, for example.[42] Immediately after they married, Candie took on the duties that fit her life experiences at that time. Her actions must have been shaped in part by a society that reinforced that she should take on a "helper" role, but her personal humility, preference for behind-the-scenes administrative tasks, inexperience as a song leader or researcher, and her strong writing skills also explain her decisions. When Highlander hired her as a paid staffer in the late 1970s, she took on a more public role as an activist, educator, and musician. By that time, she had gained experience and confidence through years of experience with various political and social causes.

The Carawans' approach to their activism and marriage was not unique for the time. In a 1978 study of forty-one married white women involved in the civil rights movement, Rhoda Lois Goldstein concluded that even in couples who both performed political work outside of the home, "the division of labor was, nonetheless, fairly traditional in most cases; the women took active charge of the children and household during the day and usually did not hold full-time jobs."[43] The study also found that pairs "were aware of their different strengths and weaknesses, and the roles that each tended to play in organizations. Not only did they discuss civil rights, but they also had close partnerships within the home."[44] Like the people Goldstein studied, the Carawans participated equally in their civil rights work, but Guy was the primary wage earner, while Candie cared for their home and child.

Although Candie's omission from the civil rights narrative can be attributed to unconscious bias on the part of historians who simply overlooked her name on the Carawans' joint publications, Candie's reluctance to publicize her involvement is another reason for her erasure. As white people participating in a Black-led movement, the couple always defined their contributions carefully so as not to overemphasize their actions at the expense of African Americans who were crucial in developing and circulating civil rights music. Guy's long decline before his death forced her to take the lead in many of the interviews the two granted in the twenty-first century. Candie's loyalty to Guy, as well as her own modesty, meant that she revealed her individual actions only when prompted by the questioner. Thus, an endless loop formed around Candie's accomplishments that removed her from the narrative. Historians did not ask about her work, and she only described her activities if asked. If either the interviewers or Candie had stepped out of this dynamic, her role probably would have come to light more fully.

Candie's endeavors fit into Francis's concept of the "cultural agent" in two ways.[45] First, Candie was a member of the civil rights movement's cultural field. Music was, in part, such an important aspect of the movement because over time it became as much a cultural movement as a political one. While activists advocated for legislation that would end segregation and voting rights abuses, they were equally dedicated to a vision of a more equitable American society that acknowledged and celebrated Black culture. The spirituals and folk songs that were the basis of so many freedom songs were part of a musical heritage that had long been derided by some members of the Black intelligentsia and urban middle class who believed that the music was a reminder of enslavement and poverty. For example, when recording some freedom songs for Guy's first documentary album *Nashville Sit-in Story: Songs and Scenes of Nashville Lunch Counter Desegregation (by the Sit-In Participants)* (1960), Candie remembers that African American activist Angeline Butler told Guy, "Now, don't make us sound like some down country n-----s."[46] Even as late as 1964, in a report on that year's Sing for Freedom Workshop, which the Carawans organized, Josh Dunson observed, "The older singers wondered if by all that 'shouting' the 'kids' were not going to ruin their voices, and the 'kids' in some cases seemed ashamed of the 'down home' and 'old time' music. To a significant number, though by no means to all, the slave songs seemed out of place at a 'sing for freedom.'"[47] As historians as well as curators of that civil rights cultural marketplace, the Carawans were part of a network of activists, musicians, and scholars who worked to promote music as part of the Black Nationalist project. Second, her and Guy's work recording, transcribing, publishing, and teaching freedom songs helped establish a central repertoire for the civil rights movement. Song leaders taught new music to Guy and Candie, and they, in turn, transmitted the music to the public, song leaders, and performers. This labor placed them within a "cycle of consecration" whereby certain songs (and even verses of songs) were lifted above others to become part of the canon of freedom songs. Shana L. Redmond correctly argues that the Carawans' whiteness accorded them the privilege to travel freely around the South collecting songs, as well as the credibility with white publishers and record executives that gave them ready access to modes of circulation for their work that were more difficult to access for Black participants in the civil rights cycle of consecration.[48]

In March 1960, the freedom song repertoire did not exist as a coherent and circumscribed set of songs used in demonstrations, mass meetings, and fundraising concerts. In the late 1950s, when activists sang, they turned to music they already knew, such as hymns, camp songs, and popular rock 'n' roll tunes. By the end of 1961, in part due to the Carawans' efforts, most activists and song leaders had adopted a group of songs, including "We Shall Overcome," "Ain't Gonna Let Nobody Turn Me 'Round," and "This Little Light of Mine," as the core of the freedom song repertoire which continued to grow throughout the 1960s. As cultural agents, the Carawans were a significant part of a larger network that developed and canonized the freedom song repertoire between Highlander's College-Age Workshops in April 1960 and the fall of 1961. In addition to Guy's song leading at the College-Age Workshop and the meeting when SNCC was founded, the students at Guy and Candie's earliest song workshop (which the couple planned before their marriage and held at Highlander between August 29 and September 3, 1960) assembled an informal mimeographed songbook that Guy distributed at subsequent civil rights meetings and demonstrations.[49] SNCC leaned heavily on these songs to recruit and organize its members.[50] Many of the early leaders of SNCC were from Nashville and had close contact with Guy's song leading and his ideas about music. After the 1959–60 school year was over, they fanned out to different areas in the South, bringing freedom songs with them. Additionally, a core group of demonstrators who participated in the Freedom Rides were jailed during the summer of 1961 in Mississippi. Singing together helped the Freedom Riders endure the harsh conditions at the Mississippi State Penitentiary (also known as Parchman Farm). They cultivated a group of songs that they taught to others after their release.[51]

Much of the music came from the rich tradition of hymns and spirituals used in Black churches with the lyrics and even melodies modified as needed to make them relevant and useful in the movement. A smaller set of freedom songs, including "Which Side Are You On?" and "We Shall Not Be Moved," originated earlier in the twentieth century in the labor movement but migrated (often with modified texts) to the civil rights struggle. Most freedom songs have melodies and lyrics that can be memorized easily and quickly taught to a group for participatory performance. The texts often focus on the goal of integration or create community through a recounting of shared experiences or dreams for the future.

"THEY GO WILD OVER ME" AND THE STRUGGLE FOR CIVIL RIGHTS

Many songs that appear in early mass meeting programs and Guy and Candie's first field recordings did not appeal to the activists enough to spread throughout the movement. "They Go Wild Over Me" is a good example of the experimentation that took place in 1960 and early 1961 as activists tried out different types of songs with a wider range of styles than is represented in what would become the canonical freedom song repertoire. Candie wrote civil rights lyrics for this song in late February or March 1960 soon after her arrest at a sit-in at a Nashville lunch counter. The text shows how Candie moved within the gendered expectations of the era in general and the movement in particular.[52]

"They Go Wild Over Me" appears in the Carawans' first civil rights songbook, *We Shall Overcome: Songs of the Southern Freedom Movement*.[53] The tune was originally a popular Tin Pan Alley song recorded at least three times in 1917, by Eddie Cantor, Billy Murray, and Marion Harris.[54] The melody contains markers often associated with femininity in music—it is lighthearted but subdued, gently rhythmic but not marchlike. Quickly adapted by the Industrial Workers of the World (IWW) as the "Popular Wobbly," the song, now with new lyrics suitable for the labor movement, first appeared in the so-called *Little Red Songbook* in 1920.[55] Candie learned this version during the summer of 1959 from a roommate named Norma Hackleman.[56]

"They Go Wild Over Me" is different from a typical freedom song because it is derived from a fifty-year-old popular melody, tells a story, contains flashes of sly humor, and has lyrics too long and varied to be easily memorized and sung by a crowd. The verses recount a protester's experience. First the narrator of the song attracts the attention of a manager, then a judge throws the narrator in jail where he is locked in a "segregated cage." The next two stanzas are taken straight from the IWW version, with a new closing verse that specifically challenges Tennesseans to embrace justice and civil rights.

They Go Wild Over Me (lyrics as they appear in *Sing for Freedom*)

I'm as mild-mannered man as can be
And I've never done no harm that I can see.
Yet on me they put a ban
They would throw me in the can
They go wild, simply wild over me.

Oh the manager he went wild over me
When I went one afternoon and sat for tea.
He was breathin' mighty hard
When his pleas I'd disregard
He went wild, simply wild, over me.

Then the judge he went wild over me
And I plainly saw we never could agree.
So I let his nibs obey
What his conscience had to say
He went wild, simply wild over me.

Then the jailer he went wild over me
Well he locked me up and threw away the key.
In a segregated cage
I'd be kept, it was the rage
He went wild, simply wild, over me.

They go wild, simply wild, over me
I'm referring to the bedbug and the flea.
They disturb my slumber deep
They would rob me of my sleep
They go wild, simply wild, over me.

Will the roses grow wild over me
When I've gone into that land that is to be.
When my soul and body part

> In the stillness of my heart
> Will the roses grow wild over me?
>
> Will my children go wild or go free
> When it's time for them to go to town for tea.
> Will those bedsheet-wearin' whites
> Still yell "Down with civil rights"
> Or will justice have come to Tennessee?

Reprinted with permission from *Sing for Freedom* (NewSouth Books, 2007)

There are at least two extant recordings of "They Go Wild Over Me," both of which include Candie singing. The first is audio that appears on two Folkways recordings: *The Nashville Sit-in Story*, a documentary record Guy produced during the spring of 1960 to dramatize the experience of activists during a demonstration and their subsequent incarceration, and *American History in Ballad and Song, Vol. 2*.[57] This excerpt of the song begins on the second verse printed in *Sing for Freedom* and features Candie and another (unidentified) woman accompanied by guitar, probably played by Guy.

The second recording, at the Southern Folklife Collection at UNC-Chapel Hill, is a recording of a solo performance by Candie taped by the Carawans at a mass meeting on May 28, 1963, in Birmingham, Alabama, during the Children's Crusade.[58] Guy introduces Candie to the group as his wife, sharing with them that she joined the movement in Tennessee as an exchange student at Fisk in 1960 and was arrested during the sit-ins. Candie sings the entire piece to the assembled crowd while Guy accompanies her on guitar and occasionally adds vocal harmonization. Guy's acoustic guitar fingerpicking is completely unlike the ragtime accompaniment of the 1917 recordings of the original song and is unusual for freedom songs, which were generally performed a cappella or, less often, accompanied by Hammond organ or piano. While "They Go Wild Over Me" does not lend itself to group singing, the audience found other ways to participate in the performance. They responded to Candie with shouted interjections of "yes," a short-lived attempt to clap on the back beat, and loud laughter and applause when she sang of being jailed.[59] The crowd reacted strongly to that verse at least partly because many would have known that the couple had just been released from the county lock-up. Sheriff Eugene "Bull" Connor arrested them several days before when they tried to enter a mass meeting at the New Pilgrim Baptist Church. After that meeting was over, the crowd marched to the jail where Guy and Candie were being held, gathered outside, and sang to them.

The Birmingham performance is an example of Candie's work as a cultural agent because she was involved in memorializing the meeting by helping Guy to record it and contributed to it when she sang "They Go Wild Over Me." Given Guy's higher profile in the movement, it is doubtful that Candie would have been invited to perform that night had she been alone. Not only had he been involved with the movement longer, but Guy also always had a more public role than she did. As was true in the larger society in the 1960s, most people in the movement assumed that the man in a heterosexual couple was the more important member. Guy highlights the aspects of Candie's background that conveyed the most cultural capital with activists during his introduction—long-term commitment and time spent in jail. He informs the audience that she had been incarcerated in Nashville during the sit-ins, indicating that she had been involved in the movement since 1960 and that their weekend in Birmingham detention was not her first time behind bars.

Despite the breezy tone of the lyrics, the subject matter is serious, referencing two important topics. The first is the experience of activists who are arrested and jailed for (in this case) unnamed transgressions and silenced by the justice system. Just as happens to the narrator, real civil rights demonstrators cycled through the courts with little or no chance to defend themselves and were often confronted with "evidence" that obscured or misstated the true events. Candie faced this situation after she was arrested in Nashville. She remembers her testimony and that of other protesters being suppressed or ignored while police officers lied on the stand about what happened during the sit-ins.[60] White community leaders may have wished to make an example of demonstrators by incarcerating them, but at the same time they did not want to provide a forum for protesters to state their case.

The second subject is the challenge to Tennesseans (and by extension to all Americans) to take up the cause of freedom by asking if "justice [will] come to Tennessee?" Candie's explicit reference to the Ku Klux Klan ("bed-sheet wearin' whites") is unusual in freedom songs, particularly in lyrics written before 1964. Most freedom songs focus on the actions that society ("we") should undertake for justice, exhort activists to remain true to their purpose, or support integration. Many songs call out individual political leaders or police officers, such as Mississippi's governor Ross Barnett or Birmingham's Sheriff Connor, but few refer to the KKK or the faceless white majority. As a white woman in 1960, Candie may have felt safer evoking the terrorist group than would Black activists, who could easily imagine themselves becoming the Klan's targets. At around the same time Candie wrote her lyrics, African American civil rights attorney Z. Alexander Looby's Nashville home was bombed. Activists needed no reminder of the violence that stalked prominent civil rights supporters, but at this stage it was Black men such as Looby who attracted press attention and local notoriety who seemed most at risk from white supremacist terrorism. Later in the decade, after murders and attacks on white and Black men, women, and children, it became clear that no one in the movement was safe.

Although she wrote the lyrics and performed the music, Candie uses "man" to identify the narrator in both extant recordings of "They Go Wild Over Me." The beginning of the IWW version—"I'm as mild mannered as I can be / And I've never done them harm that I can see"—is almost identical to Candie's lyrics, aside from the change from "as *I* can be" to "as *man* can be."[61] Candie might have been taught the lyrics using "man," since the two versions are quite similar. Even so, she chooses not to refer to the narrator in the first person or as a woman, although she could easily have sung "gal" or "I." Perhaps Candie was simply nodding to societal assumptions that men were more likely to go to jail; these words, after all, date from early 1960, before the mass incarceration of women and even children. Her frame of reference would have been the criminal justice system, which imprisoned significantly more men than women. Moreover, the perception among many activists throughout the 1960s was that the police were more likely to arrest men and treated them more harshly than women, although Charles Payne and others have shown this was not the case.[62] In addition, Candie's deference to and comfort within the gendered norms of the time would have made it natural for her to use a male narrator, even though she wrote the lyrics and performed the song.

Whatever Candie's motivation, in 1960 it was not often that a "man" would have disclosed that a manager, a judge, and a jailer were all wild over him—people who would almost certainly have been men at the time. One way to read these lyrics is that "wild over me" suggests that society has lost its collective mind at the defiance presented by civil rights activists. Certainly, the violent responses protesters encountered is evidence of the fierce resistance mounted against them.[63] The magistrate verse could also have sexual connotations since he "was breathin' mighty hard / when his pleas I'd disregard."[64] With a male narrator, the interpretation in 1960 would more likely have been of breathing hard because of the manager's anger at the demonstrator, not sexual desire as might have been the case if a woman was the speaker. With Candie singing, however, it would have been easy to confuse the narrator's gender. Candie's performance, however, undercuts these interpretations. Her flirty, light vocal timbre and affect matches the equally fluffy but enticing tune. The text comes across as humorous; she's making fun of the officials' overwrought reactions rather than taking them seriously, while she floats above their abuses by pointing out how ridiculous the situation is. Her description of the Klan members wearing bedsheets denigrates them through gentle mockery instead of challenging their violence. When she wrote these lyrics, Candie had just participated in a series of demonstrations that were seeking to overthrow centuries of legalized oppression and brutality. She had also spent time in jail, a frightening experience for a young woman who never expected to see the inside of a cell. Yet, when she sang of the results, she diffused the tension and suppressed the fear with a sideways glance and a bit of fun. In other words, she performed the role that women were (and often still are) expected to play. She smoothed over, she placated, she laughed—but she also did not back down or modify her message of anti-racism. The song is an effective piece of political propaganda because she deftly universalizes the experience of activism. She is a woman taking on a man's persona, singing a tune and lyrics suffused with feminine signifiers but with a rigid determination more associated in the 1960s with masculinity.

CONCLUSION

In the opening seconds of a 2011 interview, Candie whispers to Guy, "Do you want to do a little of 'Tree of Life' again?" Guy launches into the song, while Candie softly sings backup.[65] This fleeting moment, barely caught on camera, epitomizes much about their relationship. He takes the showier position of singing lead and playing guitar, while she nudges him to the perfect song to begin the interview, and easily falls into a descant that she has clearly sung many times before. They share an intimacy and comfort with each other that only develops after long years together, each happy with the role they have carved out for themselves. Candie is one of many women who were rank-and-file civil rights workers who did not lead any projects, negotiate with community leaders, or speak to the press, but rather performed the labor required to keep the movement functional. She exemplifies an army of women who marched in demonstrations, attended to administrative details, toiled in the offices of civil rights organizations, and provided comfort for activists who needed a place to stay and a hot meal. The Carawans' role as cultural agents in the movement ensured not only a vital method of song transmission among activists through their workshops and recordings, but also that the music was documented for future generations. While her husband had been involved in the civil rights movement prior to their meeting, the increase in his productivity demonstrates that Candie's participation in their workshops and written output was vital to accomplishments that historians often credit to Guy alone. In telling Candie's story, it is important to note that she was not a rebel, even within a fight for freedom. Her preference for the background reflects the time in which she lived, but it was not a role she resented or felt forced to play. Her activities and music reveal that she, along with many other women, functioned effectively because of her comfort within the societal dictates of the time and the hierarchical structure of many movement organizations. Candie might not have had a great deal of agency, but she had the power to act. That was what was important to her and, as with many other women in the civil rights movement, what made her contributions possible.

NOTES

1. Bernice Johnson Reagon and others, "Oh Freedom: Music of the Movement," in *A Circle of Trust: Remembering SNCC*, ed. Cheryl Lynn Greenberg (New Brunswick, NJ: Rutgers University Press, 1998), 117.

2. "Collecting Material, Gullah Books," interview with Guy and Candie Carawan, 1979, Digital Library of Appalachia, http://dla.acaweb.org/cdm/ref/collection/Warren/id/2660.

3. There are many studies on Black women's activism on behalf of equal rights. Recent publications include Keisha N. Blain, *Set the World on Fire: Black Nationalist Women and the Global Struggle for Freedom* (Philadelphia: University of Pennsylvania Press, 2018); Bruce A. Glasrud and Merline Pitre, ed., *Southern Black Women in the Modern Civil Rights Movement* (College Station: Texas A&M University Press, 2013); Julia S. Jordan-Zachery and Nikol G. Alexander-Floyd, ed., *Black Women in Politics: Demanding Citizenship, Challenging Power, and Seeking Justice* (Albany: State University of New York Press, 2018); and Martha S. Jones, *Vanguard: How Black Women Broke Barriers, Won the Vote, and Insisted on Equality for All* (New York: Basic Books, 2020).

4. Donald R. Mathews and James W. Prothro, *Negroes and the New Southern Politics* (New York: Harcourt, Brace & World, 1966), 65 quoted in Charles M. Payne, *I've Got the Light of Freedom: The Organizing Tradition and the Mississippi Freedom Struggle*, 2nd ed. (Berkeley: University of California Press, 2007), 265.

5. Kimberly Francis, "Her-Storiography: Pierre Bourdieu, Cultural Capital, and Changing the Narrative Paradigm," *Women and Music: A Journal of Gender and Culture* 19 (2015): 170.

6. Belinda Robnett's concept of "bridge leaders" is an important contribution to decentering institutional leadership roles that tend to be filled by men. She argues that women often serve as bridges between formal organizations and local activists that are crucial in forming the alliances that allow national groups to mobilize grassroots political action. See *How Long? How Long? African-American Women in the Struggle for Civil Rights* (New York: Oxford University Press, 1997).

7. I will refer to Candie and her husband Guy by their first names to avoid confusion.

8. Guy and Candie Carawan, interview by Kristen M. Turner, June 28, 2010.

9. Guy and Candie Carawan oral history interview, 2003, transcript, Civil Rights Oral History Project, CROHPCarawanGC, Special Collections Division, Nashville Public Library, 9.

10. Candie discussed her decision to join the Nashville students in the February sit-ins in Guy and Candie Carawan, interview by Kristen M. Turner, June 28, 2010, and in a more contemporaneous interview for KSPC Radio (a college radio station serving Pomona College) that must have been recorded after she returned from Nashville, but before she married Guy in March 1961, "Candie Anderson on her Nashville Sit-in Experience," KSPC, n.d., FT-20008/9578, in the Guy and Candie Carawan Collection #20008, Southern Folklife Collection, Wilson Library, University of North Carolina at Chapel Hill.

11. "Candie Anderson on her Nashville Sit-in Experience," KSPC, n.d., FT-20008/9578.

12. Guy and Candie Carawan, interview by Kristen M. Turner, June 28, 2010.

13. Guy and Candie Carawan, interview by Kristen M. Turner, June 28, 2010.

14. On the history of Highlander, see Stephen A. Schneider, *You Can't Padlock an Idea: Rhetorical Education at the Highlander Folk School, 1932–1961* (Columbia: University of South Carolina Press, 2014).

15. An informational flyer about the workshop reports that the purpose was "to find a constructive approach to race relations and citizenship responsibilities as they affect young people of both races facing problems of the changing South." Tape recordings of sessions and notes from breakout groups during the workshop reveal wide-ranging discussions on many topics

including the goals of the movement, methods of protest, nonviolence, how to organize and communicate with students around the South, and whether to post bail after arrest. Records of the Highlander Folk School and Highlander Research and Education Center, microfilm, reel 43, 727–804, quotation from 731.

16. Highlander hired Guy as a full-time employee in 1975 and added Candie to the staff a few years later. They worked there for the rest of their careers. As of 2018, Candie still lived in a house they built next to the Center.

17. John Szwed, *Alan Lomax: The Man Who Recorded the World* (New York: Viking, 2010), 255, 322.

18. In a letter to Alan Lomax dated December 31, 1994, Guy tells him that "you are surely one of the key people who have influenced our lives and work in the most major and dramatic way." Folder 554 in the Guy and Candie Carawan Collection #20008, Addition of 2010, Southern Folklife Collection, Wilson Library, University of North Carolina at Chapel Hill. The Carawans frequently collaborated with Lomax, including inviting him to participate in the 1965 Sing for Freedom Festival and Workshop.

19. Joe Street, *The Culture War in the Civil Rights Movement* (Gainesville: University Press of Florida, 2007), 21.

20. For more information on Guy's involvement with Highlander during the civil rights years, see Peter J. Ling, "Developing Freedom Songs: Guy Carawan and the African-American Traditions of the South Carolina Sea Islands," *History Workshop Journal* 44 (Autumn 1997): 198–213; Street, *The Culture War in the Civil Rights Movement*, 15–39.

21. SNCC has been the subject of much scholarship. For some recent studies, see Sharon Monteith, *SNCC's Stories: The African American Freedom Movement in the Civil Rights South* (Athens: University of Georgia Press, 2020); Iwan Morgan and Philip Davies, ed., *From Sit-Ins to SNCC: The Student Civil Rights Movement in the 1960s* (Gainesville: University Press of Florida, 2012).

22. Josh Dunson, *Freedom in the Air: Song Movements of the Sixties* (New York: International Publishers, 1965), 42–43; Street, *The Culture War in the Civil Rights Movement*, 22.

23. Guy and Candie Carawan, interview by Kristen M. Turner, June 28, 2010.

24. Reagon and Neblett were founding members of the SNCC Freedom Singers; Barry and Lewis both served terms as chairman of SNCC (Lewis died in 2020 after a lifetime of civil rights leadership including thirty-three years in the US House of Representatives), and Diane Nash was the key organizer of the Freedom Rides and many other demonstrations. For more on the Nashville activists and their influence on SNCC and the civil rights movement, see Wesley Hogan, *Many Minds, One Heart: SNCC's Dream for a New America* (Chapel Hill: University of North Carolina Press, 2007).

25. Guy and Candie Carawan, interview by Sue Thrasher, January 28, 1982, transcript, Archives, Highlander Research and Education Center, New Market, TN.

26. Guy Carawan to Friends of Highlander, August 1959, Records of the Highlander Folk School and Highlander Research and Education Center, microfilm, reel 7, 338–39.

27. Guy Carawan memo to Myles Horton, 1965, Records of the Highlander Folk School, microfilm, reel 7, 350.

28. Guy and Candie Carawan, interview by Sue Thrasher, January 28, 1982.

29. Guy and Candie Carawan, *Ain't You Got a Right to the Tree of Life? The People of Johns Island South Carolina, Their Faces, Their Words and Their Songs*, revised and expanded ed. (Athens: University of Georgia Press, 1989), xi.

30. The workshops are: Sing for Freedom Workshop, August 28–September 3, 1960; Sing for Freedom Festival and Workshop, May 7–10, 1964; and Sing for Freedom Festival and

Workshop, May 6–9, 1965. A final workshop organized by Bernice Johnson Reagon at Highlander on October 1–3, 1965, and attended by the Carawans brought folklorists and professional folk singers together to discuss how to preserve and promote rural Black culture.

31. Guy and Candie Carawan, interview by Kristen M. Turner, June 28, 2010.

32. The discussions during workshops are preserved in recordings, transcripts, and reports in the Guy and Candie Carawan Collection #20008 in the Southern Folklife Collection, University of North Carolina at Chapel Hill.

33. During the 1960s, the Carawans' income largely derived from Guy's concert tours. Guy and Candie Carawan, interview by Kristen M. Turner, June 28, 2010.

34. Guy and Candie Carawan, interview by Kristen M. Turner, June 28, 2010.

35. Many of their working documents are accessible in the Southern Folklife Collection, University of North Carolina at Chapel Hill.

36. Guy and Candie Carawan, interview by Kristen M. Turner, June 28, 2010. I was unable to confirm some of Candie's account with Guy as age and disease had compromised his memory by the time I met them, nor do they discuss their working method in detail in other interviews I have consulted.

37. Guy and Candie Carawan, interview by Kristen M. Turner, June 28, 2010.

38. Joan C. Browning, "Shiloh Witness," in *Deep in Our Hearts: Nine White Women in the Freedom Movement* (Athens: University of Georgia Press, 2000), 76.

39. Guy and Candie Carawan oral history interview, 2003, Nashville Public Library, 27–28.

40. Guy and Candie Carawan, interview by Sue Thrasher, January 28, 1982.

41. William Saunders, interview by Guy and Candie Carawan, FT 20008/3612, in the Guy and Candie Carawan Collection #20008, Southern Folklife Collection, Wilson Library, University of North Carolina at Chapel Hill.

42. Guy and Candie Carawan, interview by Sue Thrasher, January 28, 1982.

43. Rhoda Lois Goldstein, "Wife-Husband Companionship in a Social Movement," *International Journal of Sociology of the Family* 8, no. 1 (January–June 1978): 104.

44. Goldstein, "Wife-Husband Companionship," 107.

45. Francis, "Her-Storiography," 174.

46. Guy and Candie Carawan, interview by Kristen M. Turner, June 28, 2010.

47. Josh Dunson, "Slave Songs at the 'Sing for Freedom,'" *Broadside* (May 30, 1964), in Records of the Highlander Folk School and Highlander Research and Education Center, microfilm, reel 31, 130.

48. Shana L. Redmond, *Anthem: Social Movements and the Sound of Solidarity in the African Diaspora* (New York: New York University Press, 2014), 174. In keeping with Candie's erasure, however, Redmond does not mention Candie's part in Guy's work with the civil rights movement, despite quoting from the *We Shall Overcome!* songbook that bears both of their names as authors.

49. Guy Carawan memo to Myles Horton, 1965, Records of the Highlander Folk School, microfilm, reel 7, 349–50.

50. Payne, *I've Got the Light of Freedom*, 147.

51. Bernice Johnson Reagon, "Songs of the Civil Rights Movement, 1955–1965: A Study in Cultural History" (PhD diss., Howard University, 1975), 124.

52. Candie performed the song at the College-Age Workshop, so she must have completed the lyrics by April 1, 1960.

53. Guy and Candie Carawan, ed., *We Shall Overcome! Songs of the Southern Freedom Movement* (New York: Oak Publications, 1963), reprinted in Guy and Candie Carawan, ed., *Sing for Freedom: The Story of the Civil Rights Movement Through Its Songs* (Montgomery, AL: NewSouth Books, 2007), 14–15.

54. These recordings are available on YouTube.

55. "The Popular Wobbly" was published in every edition of the IWW songbook (popularly known as the *Little Red Songbook* because of the color of the volume's cover and as a play on the Communist leanings of many of the union's early members) beginning in 1920.

56. Guy and Candie Carawan, interview by Kristen M. Turner, June 28, 2010.

57. *The Nashville Sit-In Story: Songs and Scenes of Nashville Lunch Counter Desegregation (by the Sit-In Participants)*, conceived and directed by Guy Carawan, Folkways Records, P. 1960, FH 5590. The recording is part of the "Jail Sequence" track. It is available on YouTube at http://bit.ly/2P6Mc9K; *American History in Ballad and Song, Vol. 2*, produced by Moses Asch, Folkways Records, 1962, FW05802.

58. Mass Meeting Held During the Southern Christian Leadership Conference's "Project C," May 28, 1963, Birmingham, AL, FT-20008/3645, in the Guy and Candie Carawan Collection #20008, Southern Folklife Collection, Wilson Library, University of North Carolina at Chapel Hill.

59. Guy and Candie Carawan, interview by Sue Thrasher, January 28, 1982.

60. Guy and Candie Carawan, interview by Kristen M. Turner, June 28, 2010.

61. T-Bone Slim, "The Popular Wobbly," *Songs of the Workers to Fan the Flames of Discontent*, 32nd ed. (Chicago: Industrial Workers of the World, 1968), 37, Internet Archive, http://bit.ly/2guxbOF.

62. Payne, *I've Got the Light of Freedom*, 269.

63. After I delivered a talk on this material on August 6, 2015, several members of the audience at the Feminist Theory and Musicology Conference held in Madison, Wisconsin, suggested this reading, and I thank them for the idea.

64. I thank Andrea Bohlman for this suggestion.

65. Guy and Candie Carawan, interview by Joseph Mosnier, September 9, 2011, Civil Rights History Project, American Folklife Center, Library of Congress, https://www.loc.gov/item/afc2010039_crhp0052/.

BIBLIOGRAPHY

Archives/Interviews

Carawan, Guy and Candie Collection. Southern Folklife Collection, Wilson Library, University of North Carolina at Chapel Hill.

Guy and Candie Carawan. Interview, 1979. Digital Library of Appalachia. http://dla.acaweb.org/cdm/ref/collection/Warren/id/2660.

Guy and Candie Carawan. Interview by Sue Thrasher. January 28, 1982. Transcript in the Highlander Research and Education Center Archive, New Market, Tennessee.

Guy and Candie Carawan Oral History Interview. Transcript. Civil Rights Oral History Project, CROHPCarawanGC, Special Collections Division, Nashville Public Library, 2003.

Guy and Candie Carawan. Interview by Kristen M. Turner, June 28, 2010.

Guy and Candie Carawan. Interview by Joseph Mosnier, September 9, 2011. Civil Rights History Project. American Folklife Center, Library of Congress. https://www.loc.gov/item/afc2010039_crhp0052/.

Records of the Highlander Folk School and Highlander Research and Education Center. Microfilm.

Recordings

Carawan, Guy. *The Nashville Sit-In Story: Songs and Scenes of Nashville Lunch Counter Desegregation (by the Sit-In Participants)*. Folkways Records, FH 5590, 1960.
Various artists. *American History in Ballad and Song, Vol. 2*. Folkways Records, FW05802, 1962.

Secondary Sources

Blain, Keisha N. *Set the World on Fire: Black Nationalist Women and the Global Struggle for Freedom*. Philadelphia: University of Pennsylvania Press, 2018.
Carawan, Guy. "The Living Folk Heritage of the Sea Islands." *Sing Out!* 14, no. 2 (April–May 1964): 29–32.
Carawan, Guy, and Candie Carawan. *Ain't You Got a Right to the Tree of Life? The People of Johns Island South Carolina, Their Faces, Their Words and Their Songs*, revised and expanded ed. Athens: University of Georgia Press, 1989.
Carawan, Guy, and Candie Carawan, ed. *Sing for Freedom: The Story of the Civil Rights Movement Through Its Songs*. Montgomery, AL: NewSouth Books, 2007.
Curry, Constance, and Joan C. Browning, et al. *Deep in Our Hearts: Nine White Women in the Freedom Movement*. Athens: University of Georgia Press, 2000.
Dunson, Josh. *Freedom in the Air: Song Movements of the Sixties*. New York: International Publishers, 1965.
Francis, Kimberly. "Her-Storiography: Pierre Bourdieu, Cultural Capital, and Changing the Narrative Paradigm." *Women and Music* 19 (2015): 169–77.
Glasrud, Bruce A., and Merline Pitre, ed. *Southern Women in the Modern Civil Rights Movement*. College Station: Texas A&M University Press, 2013.
Goldstein, Rhoda Lois. "Wife-Husband Companionship in a Social Movement." *International Journal of Sociology of the Family* 8 (January–June 1978): 101–10.
Hogan, Wesley. *Many Minds, One Heart: SNCC's Dream for a New America*. Chapel Hill: University of North Carolina Press, 2007.
Holsaert, Faith S., Martha Prescod Norman Noonan, Judy Richardson, Betty Garman Robinson, Jean Smith Young, and Dorothy M. Zellner, ed. *Hands on the Freedom Plow: Personal Accounts by Women in SNCC*. Urbana: University of Illinois Press, 2010.
Jones, Martha S. *Vanguard: How Black Women Broke Barriers, Won the Vote, and Insisted on Equality for All*. New York: Basic Books, 2020.
Jordan-Zachery, Julia S., and Nikol G. Alexander-Floyd, ed. *Black Women in Politics: Demanding Citizenship, Challenging Power, and Seeking Justice*. Albany: State University of New York Press, 2018.
Ling, Peter J. "Developing Freedom Songs: Guy Carawan and the African-American Traditions of the South Carolina Sea Islands." *History Workshop Journal* 44 (1997): 199–213.
Monteith, Sharon. *SNCC's Stories: The African American Freedom Movement in the Civil Rights South*. Athens: University of Georgia Press, 2020.
Morgan, Iwan, and Philip Davies, ed. *From Sit-Ins to SNCC: The Student Civil Rights Movement in the 1960s*. Gainesville: University Press of Florida, 2012.
Payne, Charles. *I've Got the Light of Freedom: The Organizing Tradition and the Mississippi Freedom Movement*. Berkeley: University of California Press, 2007.
Reagon, Bernice Johnson. "Songs of the Civil Rights Movement, 1955–1965: A Study in Cultural History." PhD diss., Howard University, 1975.

Reagon, Bernice Johnson, Sparky Rucker, Hollis Watkins, Charles Sherrod, Prathia Hall, Bernard Lafayette Jr., and Mendy Samstein. "Oh Freedom: Music of the Movement." In *A Circle of Trust: Remembering SNCC*, edited by Cheryl Lynn Greenberg, 110–26. New Brunswick, NJ: Rutgers University Press, 1998.

Redmond, Shana L. *Anthem: Social Movements and the Sound of Solidarity in the African Diaspora*. New York: New York University Press, 2014.

Robnett, Belinda. *How Long? How Long? African-American Women in the Struggle for Civil Rights*. New York: Oxford University Press, 1997.

Schneider, Stephen A. *You Can't Padlock an Idea: Rhetorical Education at the Highlander Folk School, 1932–1961*. Columbia: University of South Carolina Press, 2014.

Songs of the Workers to Fan the Flames of Discontent, 32nd ed. Chicago: Industrial Workers of the World, 1968.

Street, Joe. *The Culture War in the Civil Rights Movement*. Gainesville: University Press of Florida, 2007.

Szwed, John. *Alan Lomax: The Man Who Recorded the World*. New York: Viking, 2010.

Chapter 10

Come Go with Me to Freedom Land: Black Women Musicians and the Unexplored Sonic History of the March on Washington

—Tammy Kernodle

Let a new earth rise. Let another world be born. Let a bloody peace be written in the sky. Let a second generation full of courage issue forth; let a people loving freedom come to growth . . .

—Margaret Walker[1]

On the morning of August 28, 1963, actress and activist Ruby Dee walked across a stage erected near 15th Street and Constitution Avenue adjacent to the Washington Monument and began to recite Margaret Walker's poem "For My People." Published initially in 1937, the poem encapsulated the history of Black people in America. It captured the essence, spirit, and tenacity of people whose fight for freedom, equality, and opportunity was intricately tied to the mythologies promoted through the idea of America's exceptionalism. The words seemed a fitting prologue to the day's events, which by their end would draw over 250,000 people to the nation's capital. They came for different reasons: some to advocate for social justice, equality, and access to better economic opportunities, and others to aggressively protest the apathy of the Kennedy administration and its lack of action in the wake of the violence that plagued Blacks and activists in the South. Walker's words, especially the final stanzas that are the epigraph above, seemed prophetic as they called for the rise of a new generation to amplify the struggle.

Indeed, the rise of the generation of young Americans who propelled the civil rights struggle through a strategy of direct action that included sit-ins, pray-ins, marches, and the Freedom Rides seemed to embody Walker's call to action. This generation formed coalitions that consisted of varying ethnic/racial identities and ideological perspectives that spawned the social movements that transformed America's political and social milieu during the 1960s and 1970s.

The message of Walker's poem was punctuated by folksinger/guitarist Odetta, who soon after Ruby Dee recited the final stanza, entered the stage. She positioned herself at the microphone along with guitarist Bruce Langhorne. Following a short musical introduction, during which the two guitarists established the groove and overall ethos of the song, Odetta began singing the first stanza of the spiritual "Oh Freedom." It was the first song in what the singer called the *Spiritual Trilogy*. No doubt the songs that encompassed this medley were familiar to many in the audience. Those that attended Black churches throughout the South had heard and probably sung "Oh Freedom," "Come and Go with Me," and "I'm on My Way" as part of the congregational singing traditions and repertory that defined Black worship practices. Others, who had come to the South to take part in the direct-action campaigns, knew these as the freedom songs performed in the mass meetings and during moments of direct-action nonviolent resistance. Those that were alien to both probably knew them because the medley was featured on the singer's highly acclaimed debut album *Odetta Sings Ballads and Blues*.

By 1963 Odetta's *Spiritual Trilogy* and Walker's "For My People" were prominent examples of how Black women artists were advancing a type of radical cultural expression that was rooted in Black history, folk practices, and progressive/leftist ideology. Works such as these historicized the long struggle for civil rights in America, but also reflected how the experiences and perspectives of Black women framed important aspects of that struggle even if they were not always acknowledged or their struggles advanced through movement rhetoric. If we move beyond the materiality of Odetta's and Ruby Dee's performances, what becomes more evident is the underresearched aspects of the historic March on Washington for Jobs and Freedom and the depth and breadth of the cultural labor offered by Black women artist-activists during this seminal event.

The framing of this history began during the last quarter of the twentieth century and has increased exponentially during the first two decades of the twenty-first. This is due in part to the commemoration of the movement through public memorials, reunions, oral history projects, and a growing body of scholarship. This historiography includes monographs such as Charles Euchner, *Nobody Turn Me Around: A People's History of the 1963 March on Washington*, and William P. Jones, *The March on Washington: Jobs, Freedom and the Forgotten History of Civil Rights*;

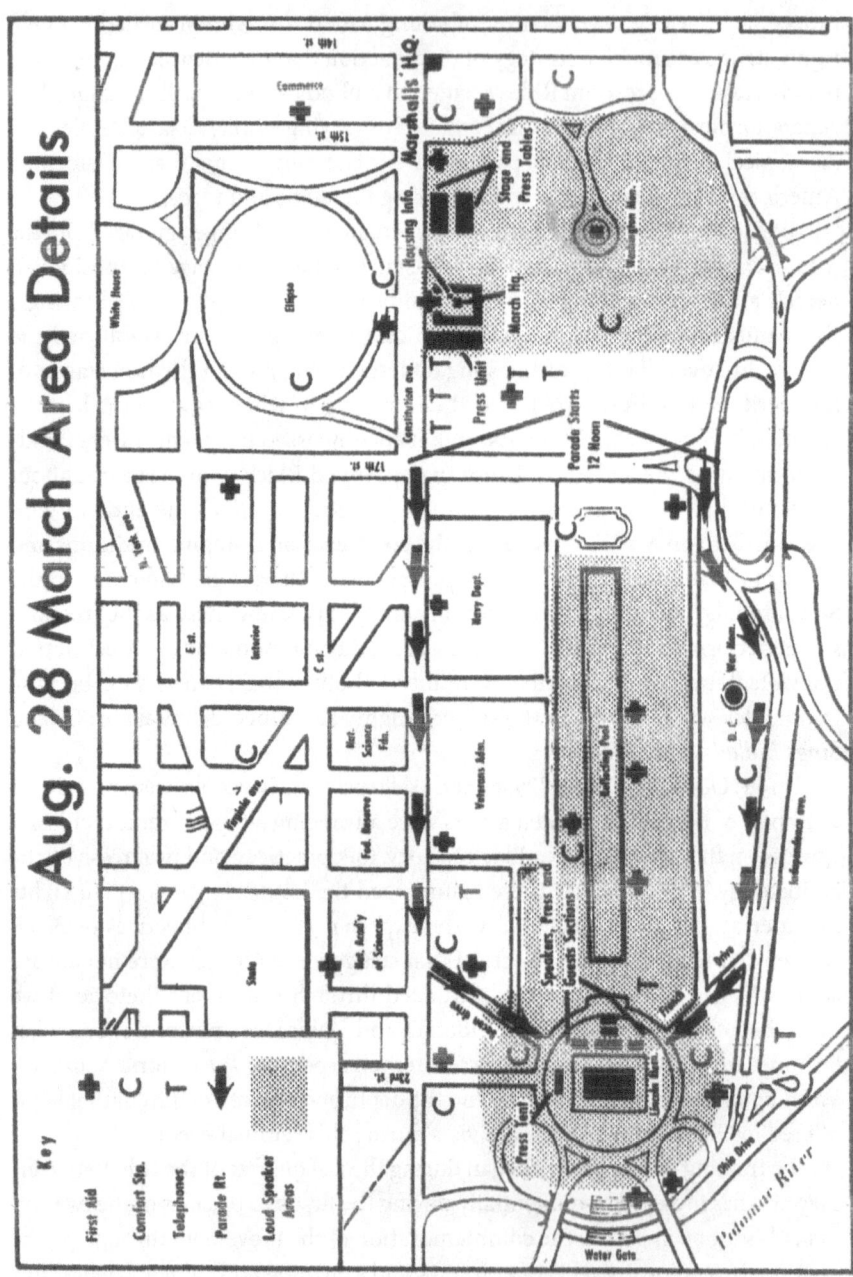

Fig. 10.1. Map of the MOW March.

documentary recordings like Smithsonian Folkways' *We Shall Overcome! Documentary of the March on Washington*; and a number of documentaries, including James Blue's iconic film *The March*. In addition to this body of work, the events of August 28, 1963, were also documented in magazines such as *Time*, and Black newspapers and periodicals like the *Pittsburgh Courier* and *Ebony*. Despite the richness and diversity of this body of work, the history and memory of the March on Washington (MOW) has been constructed around a limited array of musical and oratorical moments that took place only at the Lincoln Memorial.[2] This has also been influenced by the absence of available footage of the performances of Odetta, Camilla Williams, and the Eva Jessye Choir.

As a result, the existing framework ignores the larger geographic and musical footprint of the MOW. Figure 10.1 maps the spatial identity of the march, which encompassed four separate events situated in four different geographical spaces over a nine-hour period.[3] These events included a pre-march program at the Washington Monument, the march from the Washington Monument to the Lincoln Memorial, and a set of impromptu performances at Lincoln Memorial that preceded the formal march program.

In each of these locations, music was not only featured prominently, it also mediated the tensions that existed between movement factions, and challenged the exclusionary politics that muted the voices of women activists such as Dorothy Height and Ella Baker. The act of what scholar Stephen Stacks called freedom singing also factored heavily into the public relations strategy of promoting the march as not a protest.[4] While the repertory of freedom songs employed by white and Black activists during moments of nonviolent direct-action resistance drew from many different genres, the Negro spiritual became the focal point of the ideological and musical narrative scripted by the performances of Black women musicians during the MOW. Most important to this discussion is how the spiritual served as one of the central ways in which these women spoke themselves and their experiences into the frameworks of liberation, social change, and equality.

Through an examination of the performances of folksinger Odetta, concert artists Camilla Williams, Marian Anderson, and Eva Jessye, and gospel artist Mahalia Jackson at the MOW, this essay attempts to reclaim the unacknowledged and in some cases poorly documented aspects of the event in order to facilitate understanding of how Black women musicians and their curation and performance of specific song repertories shaped the liberation ideology and public relations strategy of the Black liberation movement.[5] It draws on the work of activist, historian, and singer Bernice Johnson Reagon in illuminating how Black women operate in the ritualized role of cultural worker who uses Black song traditions as a means of invoking the historical past in the present, while simultaneously nurturing the unrealized hope for the future.[6]

MUSIC AS THE PROMOTER OF IDEOLOGY AT THE MOW

The musical performances featured at the MOW were central in advancing a desire to draw the support of white, middle America to the movement. Bayard Rustin, the architect of the MOW, and the other march leaders viewed the event as a "performance" or opportunity to project to white, middle America an image of an integrated society. As figure 10.2 illustrates, this ideological approach was outlined strongly before the event. The pamphlet, sent to potential march participants, explained that the MOW was "conceived as an outpouring of the deep feeling of millions of white and colored American citizens that the time has come for the government of the United States of America and particularly for the Congress of that government to grant and guarantee complete equality in citizenship to the Negro minority of our population."[7] Absent from this were the radical protest strategies that fueled direct-action campaigns throughout the South. Instead, those who were called to gather on the nation's front lawn were urged to embody in dress, speech, and musical performances the ideologies of racial utopianism and Black exceptionalism that underscored the movement.

Racial utopianism was represented in the support offered by white celebrities such as Marlon Brando and the performances of white folksingers such as Bob Dylan, Peter, Paul and Mary, and Joan Baez. Their presence symbolized the relationship that had developed between the second wave of the folk song movement, white Hollywood, and movement organizations such as SCLC (Southern Christian Leadership Conference), SNCC (Student Nonviolent Coordinating Committee), and CORE (Congress of Racial Equality).

Black exceptionalism is terminology I use to frame the intersection of the ideology of racial uplift, Black progressive/leftist consciousness, and the narrative of American exceptionalism that was so heavily promoted in Cold War–era propaganda. This theoretical concept is rooted in the idea that incomparable achievement was evidence of Black America's adaptation of the dominant culture's core values.[8] While this generally focused on achievement in the areas of intellectual and civic labor, it also extended to the arts, especially to the classical music realm. Black exceptionalism underscored most of the cultural activism that was associated with the Harlem Renaissance in the years preceding World War II. However, in the decades following World War II, the Eurocentric ideals promoted by Renaissance-era Black intellectuals were rescripted through a lens that promoted Black vernacular expressive culture as the foundation for a progressive Black consciousness.[9]

The three concert artists featured during the formal program at the Lincoln Memorial precipitated the shift of mainstream American and European concert and operatic stages from spaces of segregation to integration during the 1940s and 1950s. Marian Anderson, Camilla Williams, and Eva Jessye achieved historic

Statement by the heads of the ten organizations calling for discipline in connection with the Washington March of August 28, 1963:

"The Washington March of August 28th is more than just a demonstration.

"It was conceived as an outpouring of the deep feeling of millions of white and colored American citizens that the time has come for the government of the United States of America, and particularly for the Congress of that government, to grant and guarantee complete equality in citizenship to the Negro minority of our population.

"As such, the Washington March is a living petition—in the flesh—of the scores of thousands of citizens of both races who will be present from all parts of our country.

"It will be orderly, but not subservient. It will be proud, but not arrogant. It will be non-violent, but not timid. It will be unified in purposes and behavior, not splintered into groups and individual competitors. It will be outspoken, but not raucous.

"It will have the dignity befitting a demonstration in behalf of the human rights of twenty millions of people, with the eve and the judgment of the world focused upon Washington, D.C. on August 28, 1963.

"In a neighborhood dispute there may be stunts, rough words and even hot insults; but when a whole people speaks to its government, the dialogue and the action must be on a level reflecting the worth of that people and the responsibility of that government.

"We, the undersigned, who see the Washington March as wrapping up the dreams, hopes, ambitions, tears, and prayers of millions who have lived for this day, call upon the members, followers and wellwishers of our several organizations to make the March a disciplined and purposeful demonstration.

"We call upon them all, black and white, to resist provocations to disorder and to violence.

"We ask them to remember that evil persons are determined to smear this March and to discredit the cause of equality by deliberate efforts to stir disorder.

"We call for self-discipline, so that no one in our own ranks, however enthusiastic, shall be the spark for disorder.

"We call for resistance to the efforts of those who, while not enemies of the March as such, might seek to use it to advance causes not dedicated primarily to civil rights or to the welfare of our country.

"We ask each and every one in attendance in Washington or in spiritual attendance back home to place the Cause above all else.

"Do not permit a few irresponsible people to hang a new problem around our necks as we return home. Let's do what we came to do—place the national human rights problem squarely on the doorstep of the national Congress and of the Federal Government.

"Let's win at Washington."

SIGNED:

Mathew Ahmann, *Executive Director of the National Catholic Conference for Interracial Justice.*

Reverend Eugene Carson Blake, *Vice-Chairman of the Commission on Race Relations of the National Council of Churches of Christ in America*

James Farmer, *National Director of the Congress of Racial Equality.*

Reverend Martin Luther King, Jr. *President of the Southern Christian Leadership Conference.*

John Lewis, *Chairman of the Student Nonviolent Coordinating Committee.*

Rabbi Joachim Prinz, *President of the American Jewish Congress.*

A. Philip Randolph, *President of the Negro American Labor Council.*

Walter Reuther, *President of the United Automobile, Aerospace and Agricultural Implement Workers of America, AFL-CIO, and Chairman, Industrial Union Department, AFL-CIO.*

Roy Wilkins, *Executive Secretary of the National Association for the Advancement of Colored People.*

Whitney M. Young, Jr., *Executive Director of the National Urban League.*

In addition, the March has been endorsed by major religious, fraternal, labor and civil rights organizations. A full list, too long to include here, will be published.

WHAT WE DEMAND*

1. Comprehensive and effective civil rights legislation from the present Congress—without compromise or filibuster—to guarantee all Americans

   access to all public accommodations
   decent housing
   adequate and integrated education
   the right to vote

2. Withholding of Federal funds from all programs in which discrimination exists.

3. Desegregation of all school districts in 1963.

4. Enforcement of the Fourteenth Amendment—reducing Congressional representation of states where citizens are disfranchised.

5. A new Executive Order banning discrimination in all housing supported by federal funds.

6. Authority for the Attorney General to institute injunctive suits when any constitutional right is violated.

7. A massive federal program to train and place all unemployed workers—Negro and white—on meaningful and dignified jobs at decent wages.

8. A national minimum wage act that will give all Americans a decent standard of living. (Government surveys show that anything less than $2.00 an hour fails to do this.)

9. A broadened Fair Labor Standards Act to include all areas of employment which are presently excluded.

10. A federal Fair Employment Practices Act barring discrimination by federal, state, and municipal governments, and by employers, contractors, employment agencies, and trade unions.

*Support of the March does not necessarily indicate endorsement of every demand listed. Some organizations have not had an opportunity to take an official position on all of the demands advocated here.

Fig. 10.2. MOW pamphlet.

firsts on concert and operatic stages during the first half of the twentieth century, and their talents illustrated how the intellectual labor of Black women countered primitivist readings of Black musical culture. They were all also significant in promoting the arranged spiritual as a form of protest culture in Cold War–era American and European concert halls. Their professional successes embodied the notion of Black exceptionalism.

The same can be argued regarding Mahalia Jackson and Odetta; both shifted from the insularity of grassroots music scenes to mainstream popularity in the years following World War II. They were acclaimed by their peers—white and Black—and eventually bore the appellation of "queen" within their respective musical circles. They also reflected how the spiritual, in its organic form and as part of the repertory of songs associated with the gospel aesthetic, became the foundation of a form of movement culture that accompanied the direct-action campaigns of the early 1960s. The remainder of this essay will focus on the performances of Black women musicians at the MOW and what they reveal about the role of Black women in widening the scope of the ideology of Black liberation through their interpretations of Black song traditions.

I'M ON MY WAY TO FREEDOM LAND

The March on Washington began with a pre-march program near the Washington Monument that was designed to rally demonstrators prior to the beginning of the scheduled march. The program consisted of a series of musical performances and short speeches that spotlighted the coalition that had developed between Hollywood celebrities, prominent folk singers, and movement organizers. The coupling of these groups in the early 1960s mirrored the type of coalition that defined the Popular Front during the 1940s and early 1950s. Odetta was one of the key figures who traversed the spheres that surrounded the second wave of the folk song movement, Hollywood, and the civil rights movement. Although she had followed the push for social change since the 1950s, Odetta did not become more directly involved until the early 1960s. She augmented her touring schedule to include performances on Black college campuses, which exposed her to the young activists who sustained direct-action campaigns.

Like a number of other musicians and celebrities, she began working on behalf of the movement, donating her talent and celebrity whenever needed. When asked years later about how she became involved in the movement, Odetta remarked, "People heard about this little nappy headed girl that was talking about the history and whatever. So, whenever they needed attention on what they were focusing on or to draw monies to [their cause] they would call upon me to do the benefits. So, it was like we were all developing at the same time."[10]

By 1963 Dr. King was regularly referring to her publicly as the "Queen Mother of the Folk Movement"; and Rosa Parks, the matriarch of the modern civil rights struggle, when asked by reporters which songs meant the most to her, replied "all of the songs Odetta sings."[11] Odetta became the first "voice" of the civil rights struggle, a distinction that was held by a few artist-activists during the 1960s. The appellation symbolized for movement leadership those artists that genuinely captured the spirit and ideologies of their efforts. Odetta's performance on a stage assembled in the shadow of a monument celebrating the general who commanded colonial militias in the effort that led to the decolonizing of America and its development into an independent nation magnified the duplicity between this legacy and Black America's continuous struggle for equal rights.

THE SPIRITUAL TRILOGY

Odetta's performance of the Spiritual Trilogy at the MOW reflected the competing perspectives regarding protest that enveloped the march. Many of the young activists who served on the front lines of the direct-action campaigns viewed the event as an opportunity to voice dissatisfaction with the Kennedy administration. The three songs that made up the Spiritual Trilogy—"Oh Freedom," "Come Go with Me," and "I'm on My Way"—aligned with and captured the radical protest narratives that galvanized this younger faction and the calls for unity that mirrored the coalition politics promoted by Dr. King and his associates. Although this performance is not featured in its entirety on the extant documentary recordings, it was documented by the Educational Radio Network, the early predecessor to National Public Radio that broadcast the march in its entirety.[12]

On this occasion the medley began as it always did, with the song "Oh Freedom." However, as she shifted into the second song "Come Go with Me," the performance took a surprising turn. Folksinger Josh White, inspired by the emotion of Odetta's singing, joined her on stage and began harmonizing the melody. Initially White's singing and playing matched that of Odetta, but as the song progressed, his emotions and singing heightened. He soon shifted from singing with Odetta to augmenting her vocals by repeating certain phrases, wailing, and elongating others.

By the time the performance moved into the last song "I'm on My Way," the singing and playing of both singers had intensified in volume and emotion. Both continued to grow as balladeer Lonnie Sattin, folksingers Peter, Paul and Mary, and the SNCC Freedom Singers joined in the singing. As the song entered the last stanza—"I'm on my way and I won't turn back"—the emotional level, volume, and polyphony of voices had risen to a level that mirrored the energy of the mass meetings. White continued his loud responses to Odetta's lead vocals, while Peter,

Paul and Mary and the SNCC Freedom Singers provided harmonized background vocals. In an instant, Odetta and the other performers had shifted the energy of the moment away from the muted expressions of resistance Rustin envisioned to a more animated form that energized all who witnessed this moment.

When the performance ended, the audience cheered and clapped so loudly that the master of ceremonies, actor Ossie Davis, called Odetta back to the stage to perform an encore. Noting the importance of the moment and the need to be strategic in her song selection, she chose the spiritual "No More Auction Block for Me." Like "Oh Freedom," "No More Auction Block for Me" provided an example of how the Negro spiritual nested the defiant nature and anger of the enslaved African. Odetta's interpretation was simple but powerful. She sang a cappella and moved through the text in a slow and deliberate manner.

> No more auction block for me. No more. No more.
> No more auction block for me. Many thousand gone.
> No pint of salt for me. No more. No more.
> No more pint of salt for me. Many thousand gone.
> Oh it's freedom bound I am. Oh yes, my Lord.
> Oh it's freedom bound I am. Many thousand gone.

There is very little ornamentation of the melody, and the resonant qualities of Odetta's voice grows stronger as she moves through each verse. There are a few instances where she inserted some of the timbral or harmonic inflections that were signatures of her style. It was in these moments that she moved beyond musical performance and began drawing on Black sermonic traditions by linking familiar themes of resistance, empowerment, and racial pride into a cohesive narrative. After a return to the first stanza, "No more auction block for me," Odetta transitioned into the spiritual "Child of God." The more up-tempo melody marked a shift not only in mood of the performance, but also in message.

> Anybody ask you who you are.
> Who you are. Who you are.
> Anybody ask you who you are.
> You tell 'em you're a child of God.

The crowd once again reacted enthusiastically. All of these performances considered together reveal how important Odetta was in recapturing the protest narratives embedded in Black folk traditions. They also show how she served as a musical and ideological bridge between the Old Left and the New Left.

Josh White, who turned her solo performance into a group sing, represented the generation of musician-activists that emerged out of the first wave of the folk song movement through the Popular Front. Odetta's relationship with White extended back to the early years of her career, when he would call her to the stage for impromptu performances. Like Robeson, Odetta credited White with not only advancing her knowledge of Black folk traditions but also the formation of her political consciousness. When other first-wave folk artists demonized and shunned White after his testimony before the House Committee on Un-American Activities in 1950, Odetta remained a faithful friend and supporter. Thirteen years later, White was still persona non grata to many and his career was lagging. His performance at the MOW, which was not captured in the commercial recording, archival radio broadcast, or film footage, was one of the hallmarks of the last years of his life.[13]

Joan Baez, Bob Dylan, and Peter, Paul and Mary, who joined White and Odetta on stage, represented the generation of white folk revivalists that propelled the second wave of the folk song movement and linked it with the struggle for racial equality in the early 1960s. Joan Baez's performance of the spiritual "O Freedom," just before Ruby Dee's recitation, is emblematic of the influence the Spiritual Trilogy had on this generation. Bob Dylan, one of the rising stars of the sixties folk scene at the time of the march, credits Odetta's debut album with sparking his interest in folk music.[14] The performances of these artists at the MOW reflected the racial coalition that had developed between the second wave of the folk song movement, direct-action campaigns, SNCC, and CORE.

The last group of musicians who joined Odetta on stage during this performance, the SNCC Freedom Singers, emerged from the front lines of the direct action campaigns. The group's performance of song repertories birthed out of these campaigns signified how Odetta's promotion of Black folk song practices had translated into a practical and usable form of verbalized protest for these young people. Much like Odetta's Spiritual Trilogy and her performance of the medley of "No More Auction Block"/"Child of God," the SNCC Freedom Singers' performances at the MOW consisted of an array of freedom songs that weaved a message of protest, resistance, and perseverance through the melodies of Negro spirituals, blues, and folk songs. Their repertory reflected a premise that Paul Robeson and Josh White first advanced and Odetta later projected: that Black folk songs provided a usable and tangible foundation for a type of radical Black cultural expression.

POST-MARCH PROGRAM AT THE LINCOLN MEMORIAL

As the program at the Washington Monument concluded, the mass audience gathered there began marching toward the Lincoln Memorial. The actual march encompassed the movement of two different groups that proceeded via two different routes. One group of participants, led by a contingent of female activists that included Rosa Parks, Daisy Bates, Gloria Richardson, and Diane Nash, marched up Independence Avenue. This has been identified in historical accounts as the "auxiliary march." While the "main march," led by the coalition of the March's board of directors, which included Dr. King, John Lewis, Roy Wilkins, and others, walked up Constitution Avenue. This movement was accompanied by moments of silence and song. As both groups of marchers met at the Lincoln Memorial, they encountered another set of musical performances that were programmed in real time to allow the official delegation time to reach the podium. One of these performances included celebrated opera diva Camilla Williams.

OH, WHAT A BEAUTIFUL CITY

The role of Black concert artists and composers in advancing the Black civil rights struggle has been underexplored in protest music scholarship. The link between the movement and this community strengthened in the early 1960s when a number of Black concert artists participated in concerts that benefited the NAACP and SCLC. In addition to the performers featured at the march, Coretta Scott King, who had aspired to be a concert singer before marrying Martin, also did a number of recitals that benefited the SCLC. Camilla Williams's rise to the operatic stage was emblematic of the rhetoric of Black exceptionalism that underscored the Black civil rights struggle. Born in Danville, Virginia, in 1919, Williams studied music at Virginia State College, a Black liberal arts institution located between Petersburg and Ettrick. Following graduation she returned to Danville, where she taught in the city's segregated school system and performed recitals whenever possible. In 1943, famed vocalist and teacher Madame Marion Szekely Freschl heard Williams sing during a performance in Philadelphia with the Virginia State College Choir. She encouraged the young singer to move there to further her study.

Williams studied with Freschl for three years, during which time she came to the attention of famed opera singer Geraldine Farrar and the conductor/impresario of New York City Opera, Laszlo Halasz. Their encouragement and support led to Williams becoming among the first Black women offered contracts with major American opera companies.[15] In 1946 Williams performed the role of Cio-Cio San in the New York City Opera production of *Madame Butterfly*. It was a first for a Black woman, but her performance was not without controversy.[16] The opera opened May 15, 1946, to a record audience that included a large Black contingency.[17] Like her mentor Marian Anderson, Williams became a symbol of Black pride and Black exceptionalism throughout the country. Her triumphant performance with the New York City Opera marked the opening of the breach that had excluded Black singers from the operatic stage. By 1963 Williams had garnered a significant career in opera, performing roles such as Mimi in *La Bohème*, Nedda in *Pagliacci*, Micaela in *Carmen*, Marguerite in *Faust*, and the title role in *Aida*.

Her experiences with Jim Crow on and off the stage inspired her work as a champion of civil rights. Long before it was fashionable, Williams performed at functions that benefited the NAACP and A. Philip Randolph's labor union, the Brotherhood of Sleeping Car Porters. During the summer of 1963, she returned to her hometown Danville to do a benefit concert to raise money for those jailed for participating in the large protest there.[18] Weeks before the MOW, Williams received a personal telegram from Roy Wilkins inviting her to perform the spiritual "Oh, What a Beautiful City." "I did not hesitate," recalled the singer years later. "I had always been supportive of Roy and the NAACP. Anything I could do to help in the fight for freedom and justice, I did. I grew up in the segregated South and had experienced prejudice even in New York, so I was eager to help."[19]

Edward Boatner's arrangement "Oh, What a Beautiful City" was one of several spirituals that Williams regularly featured during her recitals. Williams was among a number of well-known Black concert artists who popularized this version of the spiritual. Boatner's setting, which featured piano accompaniment, retained much of the spiritual's original melody. "Oh, What a Beautiful City" would have been known to most of the march's participants as it was still being sung in many of the southern Black churches. The song's lyrics represent the slave's vision of Heaven. The extant recording of the radio broadcast of the MOW only features a portion of the performance, as the correspondence shifts to a short interview with Marlon Brando. Even through the dialogue, one can still hear the resonant nature of Williams's voice as she moves through the spiritual. During the last stanza she sang several interval leaps. First from C_5 to F_5 followed by D_5 to F_5 on the text "twelve gates." The ending on the word "Hallelujah" featured an ascending three-note passage ending on B♭, which Williams extended in dramatic fashion. The response was immediate and enthusiastic.

Less than an hour later, she was once again called to the podium, this time to sing the national anthem.[20] "I was stunned when I heard my name announced three times," Williams recalled in her autobiography. "They wanted me to come up and sing in place of Marian Anderson. I ran up those many steps as quickly as I could and arrived at the microphone, breathless. I took a deep breath, prayed quickly, and sang it to the best of my ability. It was such a larger crowd, over 200,000 excited, exuberant, hopeful people. But I was not intimidated. I used what God gave me, my voice."[21] This performance marked the beginning of the official program and forever cemented Williams's connection with the march. A year later, when Dr. King was honored in New York for winning the Nobel Peace Prize, Camilla Williams was selected to perform. The presence of concert artists such as Williams during key moments of the civil rights struggle reflect how broadly movement organizations defined the notion of movement culture.

HE'S GOT THE WHOLE WORLD IN HIS HANDS

Contralto Marian Anderson (1897–1993) entered the national political spotlight in 1939 after the Daughters of the American Revolution (DAR) rejected her request to concertize at Constitution Hall in Washington, DC. Anderson became a lightning rod in the debate regarding segregation policies that governed America's concert halls and venues. Her cause drew the attention of First Lady Eleanor Roosevelt, who assisted in sponsoring a concert of Anderson at the Lincoln Memorial. Her subsequent hiring by the Metropolitan Opera Company in 1955 was considered a historic moment for Black America, despite occurring in the tension that surrounded Rosa Parks's arrest and the murder of Emmett Till.

In February 1963, she ended a fifteen-year self-imposed exile from performing in the South and embarked on an integrated tour of Texas. The tour dates, which took her to San Antonio, Dallas, Austin, and Houston, sold out and inspired newspapers as well as Vice President Lyndon B. Johnson to declare the tour a success in progressing race relations.[22] Months later, as the violence in Birmingham escalated, she supported the movement by hosting a benefit for the Danbury, Alabama, chapter of the NAACP. The event attracted more than 200 people and raised a significant amount for the Freedom Fund. A week later, the invitation to perform at the MOW arrived. The telegram read: "the entire committee unanimously decided that an invitation to sing *Star Spangled Banner* be extended to you for this historic occasion. Committee will consider it great honor if you will agree to do this."[23]

Anderson's performance at the MOW was both a recognition and commemoration of the historical and social significance of the 1939 concert. However, things did not go as planned. Delayed by the traffic surrounding the march, Anderson was unable to sing the anthem. One of her protégées, soprano Camilla Williams, performed in her absence. Anderson arrived at the platform minutes later in tears. As a consolation, the program committee decided to insert Anderson into the program. Aware of the importance of the moment, she decided to perform "He's Got the Whole World in His Hands." The arranged spiritual served as a primary component of Anderson's performance repertory. During her 1939 concert she performed three spiritual arrangements, and she was known for debuting new settings of spiritual melodies on most of her recitals. Many of these settings were written for Anderson and frame the relationship she cultivated with Black women composers, like Florence Price and Margaret Bonds. Anderson was central in popularizing the arrangements of Price in the repertory of Black concert artists.[24]

Dressed regally in a wide-brimmed hat, floral dress, and long white gloves, Anderson approached the main podium at the steps of the Lincoln Memorial and introduced her accompanant and the song title.[25] After a short piano introduction, Anderson's rich, resonant contralto voice entered. Her performance of the song bore all the hallmarks of the operatic interpretation, but also the importance of the moment. In extant footage, Anderson seems more and more to embody the words of the song as the performance progresses. She closes her eyes, gestures with her hands to emphasize certain words, and seems to spiritually transition to another space.

Like Odetta earlier in the day, Anderson took a performance stance that aligned her with the Black sermonic traditions that permeated many of the speeches given. She slowed the tempo of her singing at certain points to emphasize certain phrases, then returned to the original pulse in the next verse. Although not a long performance, Anderson's choice of verses was noteworthy. Like many preached sermons, the lyrical content moved from general references about universal experiences to more specific narrative tropes selected to draw listeners in and cement their emotional connection with the performer. In the first verse, Anderson manipulates the adjectives used to describe the context of the "world":

He's got the whole world in His hands.
He's got the big round world in His hands.
He's got the wide world in His hands.
He's got the whole world in His hands.

In the subsequent verses, the focus moves from the universality of the world to specific phenomena—wind and rain, moon and stars. In the third verse about the "little bitty babies," Anderson slowed the tempo to such a degree that it almost insinuated she was ending the song. More affectation in the voice is added at this moment and once again stress is placed on particular words. The next stanza, centered on the text "He's got you and me brotha, you and me sista," returns to the original tempo. The final stanza, which correlates with the emotional climax in sermonic practices, features increased dynamics as well as a dramatic ritardando where the words "He's got everybody in his hands" are heavily emphasized. The crowd, which was noticeably quiet during the performance, applauded enthusiastically. The moment, however unscripted, was poignant in that only a few years later, in 1965, Anderson retired from public performing.

FREEDOM IS A THING WORTH TALKING ABOUT: EVA JESSYE AND THE EVA JESSYE CHOIR

Very little has been written regarding Eva Jessye's role as the musical director of the MOW. It was her choir that served as the official chorus of the event and led the audience in the singing of "We Shall Overcome" following King's speech. However, along with the Hall Johnson Singers, the Eva Jessye Choir was among the earliest professional Black choruses in the United States. Jessye was the first Black woman to achieve international acclaim as a choral conductor. Born in 1895 in Coffeyville, Kansas, a former destination for escaping slaves, Eva Jessye's racial and political consciousness was formed in the cultural and political shadow of slavery and the failed politics of the Reconstruction era. From an early age she displayed considerable musical talent, which led to her studying music theory and choral music at Western University in Quindaro, Kansas. She graduated in 1914 and continued her studies at Langston University.[26] Following her graduation in 1919, Jessye taught for several years. She first came to prominence as a choral conductor when the regional choir she directed in Baltimore, Maryland, the Dixie Jubilee Singers, became regular guests on the *General Motors Hour* and other prominent radio shows during the late 1920s.

In 1926 she moved to New York to pursue a career in theater. During this period she met Will Marion Cook, who became her mentor and influenced her perspectives about the importance of Black folk practices. She was significant in creating a public context for "sonic Blackness" when she served as choral director for Gertrude Stein and Virgil Thomson's *Four Saints in Three Acts*, George Gershwin's *Porgy and Bess*, and MGM's 1929 film *Hallelujah*, the first talking film to feature an all-Black cast.

Jessye's engagement with the spiritual was not limited to live performance. In 1927 she published *My Spirituals*, a collection of spiritual settings for solo voice and piano. Unlike her contemporaries Harry T. Burleigh and Hall Johnson, she focused on lesser-known spiritual melodies and thus was significant in providing evidence of variant repertories of spirituals and expanding the performance repertory mined by Black concert singers such as Marian Anderson and Paul Robeson. Jessye's work with the spiritual also extended to the composition of choral settings. She was among the first arrangers to use authentic spiritual melodies in larger choral works.[27] Although several choral groups performed such works, Jessye's professional group of singers served as an important disseminator of this music. The group worked extensively during the 1940s and 1950s performing at churches, universities, and in support of wartime benefits.

Whenever possible, Eva Jessye used her performances as a platform for civil rights and social justice. She worked within progressive artistic circles, including the American Committee on Africa, which in time included Dr. King and Bayard Rustin. Founded in 1953, the American Committee on Africa was dedicated to supporting African liberation struggles.[28] Evidence of Jessye's involvement in the activities of this group date from 1959, when she organized a choir to perform for an African Freedom Rally that hosted Kenyan President Tom Mboya. A year later, she also performed in the Africa Freedom Day celebration at New York's Town Hall that benefited the Africa Defense and Aid Fund.

Eva Jessye's progressive politics extended to the repertory she performed and composed. Much like Odetta, she used her performances to illustrate the political and radical nature of Black folk song traditions. This can be heard in two of her most well-known works, the folk oratorios *Paradise Lost and Regained* and *The Chronicle of Job*. Jessye's choir also performed the choral works of other Black composers that contained a radical social justice theme, such as William Grant Still's *And They Lynched Him on a Tree*. By 1963 Jessye's work as a choral conductor and arranger aligned her with the growing cadre of Black female artist-activists who worked on behalf of the Black civil rights struggle. Dr. King personally invited her to serve as the musical director and the Eva Jessye Choir to serve as the official chorus of the MOW.

The group, conducted by Jessye, performed an original work that historians have referred to as *Freedom Is a Thing Worth Thinking About*. However, the piece was initially titled *Song of Freedom*, and a lyric sheet found in the Eva Jessye Collection at the University of Michigan reveals that she dedicated the work to the "whole of Africa."[29] This work is an example of Jessye's use of spiritual melodies as the basis for her larger choral works. She performed it twice before the MOW: first in 1944 for a Russian War Relief Program at Madison Square Garden called "Order of the Day," and at the 1959 African Freedom Rally. For the MOW, the choir was accompanied by trumpet, organ, and drums. The performance begins with a trumpet fanfare, followed by a short interlude during which a trio of voices and choir engage in antiphony that alternates between singing and spoken narrative. This is one of the markers of Jessye's arranging style and her larger choral works.

In this prelude, the choir sings in a slow and deliberate manner that attempts to set the ethos of the song's message. This is represented as follows:

TRIO SINGS IN HARMONY: "Freedom freedom"
CHOIR IN SPOKEN NARRATIVE: "Is a thing work thinking about."
TRIO SINGS: "This thing called freedom"
CHOIR RESPONDS: "Is a thing worth talking about."[30]

This choral prelude then shifts into the body of the work, which is centered on Jessye's reworking of the spiritual "Light Shine 'round the World." The spiritual melody remains largely in its authentic form, although it harmonizes in a way that mirrors the arranged spiritual tradition. The original text of the spiritual is replaced with a strong message of protest.

The chorus reads as follows:

Freedom's worth talking about.
Freedom is a thing worth singing about.
Freedom's worth shouting about.
Tell it all over the world.

The entrance of the chorus marks a shift in the ethos and rhythm of the song—more upbeat, joyous, and amplified by organ playing lightly and soft drumming.

The chorus is sung twice before shifting to the verses. What is notable on the extant recording of the performance is how the audience seems to start clapping during the second iteration of the chorus.

The verses that follow are sung by baritone Louis Andrew Fryerson. The choir responds to each statement or phrase with the refrain "freedom is a thing worth talking about."

> Let us counsel, you and me (Freedom is a thing worth talking about)
> The keynote is democracy (Freedom is a thing worth singing about)
> Send the message far and near (Freedom is a thing worth talking about)
> The time is now . . . the place is here (Tell it all over the world)

The second verse is a call to action for all Americans:

> Hasten, neighbor, why delay (Freedom is a thing worth thinking about)
> Take a stand for truth today (Freedom is a thing worth talking about)
> Join with hands across the sea (Freedom is a thing worth shouting about)
> United for liberty (Unity all over the world)

Following a return to the chorus, Fryerson shifts into a short vamp that disrupts the pattern. In many ways this portion of the song mirrors the oratory of Black sermonic practices. There are short phrases, and the rhythm of the response quickens; it is also in this section that similarity between the color of Fryerson's baritone voice and that of a male Black preacher becomes most evident.

> Scale the mountain (tell it all over the world)
> Span the desert (tell it all over the world)
> Bridge the ocean (tell it all over the world)
> To ev'ry nation (tell it all over the world)

This exchange is followed by the last iteration of the chorus, which is slowed for dramatic effect but also is noteworthy because it aligns with the radical ideology that Rustin attempted to mute at the MOW.

> Freedom's worth praying about.
> Freedom is a thing worth fighting about.
> Freedom's worth dying about.
> Tell it all over the world.

Like many of the other performers featured at the MOW, Jessye continued to work on behalf of the movement in subsequent months and years. In December 1963 she participated in a benefit for the Greenwood Mississippi Movement that was held in New York. A year later she and the choir performed at a memorial tribute in honor of W. E. B. Du Bois, who ironically passed on the morning of the MOW.

MY SOUL LOOKS BACK AND WONDERS HOW I GOT OVER

The last performer featured before Dr. King's speech had been from the beginning an ardent and steadfast supporter of this period of the Black civil rights struggle. Mahalia Jackson's role in the movement aligned the gospel music community in the struggle in more direct ways that go beyond repertory. Her musical and cultural influence is closely intertwined with the rise of Black gospel music in Chicago; Jackson's career began as a song demonstrator for the "Father of Gospel Music," Thomas Dorsey. Mahalia Jackson was one of a few female singers who traveled the country performing and selling the music of Dorsey. As Robert Darden outlines in *Nothing but Love in God's Water: Black Sacred Music from the Civil War to the Civil Rights Movement,* Jackson worked the "Gospel Highway" for many years, which exposed her more directly to the brutalities of segregation and racial intimidation. She did not have success as a recording artist until she recorded Rev. Herbert Brewster's "Move on Up a Little Higher" in 1947. The song reflected Brewster's progressive and radical political perspectives and linked gospel music with the ideology of racial uplift. It also reflected Jackson's political consciousness, which had been on display since the 1930s. Darden states that Jackson's activism began in 1948 when she was enlisted by US Representative William L. Dawson to aid the reelection campaign of President Harry S. Truman. Jackson started singing at campaign rallies in Chicago. After hearing the singer and gauging her influence over the crowds, Truman asked Jackson to accompany him on campaign stops throughout the Midwest. In return for her support, upon his reelection Truman invited Mahalia Jackson to sing at the White House.[31]

Jackson's popularity with white audiences grew throughout the 1950s. Much like Eva Jessye, who saw her concerts at various venues as being key to bringing races together, Mahalia Jackson began looking beyond the Gospel Highway and the church. In October 1950, she performed a sold-out concert at Carnegie Hall. She was the first gospel singer and the first Black artist since Duke Ellington's historic concert in 1943 to play the venue. She was featured on some of the major television variety shows of the day, which furthered her popularity with middle America. Jackson's relationship with the King-led wave of the Black civil rights struggle began in 1956, when Rev. Ralph Abernathy reached out to the singer in hopes she would perform for a fund-raising rally in Montgomery, Alabama. Initially Jackson was reluctant, but after visiting Abernathy and talking further she agreed to perform. Jackson's first performance in support of the movement took place on December 6, 1956, at the St. John A.M.E. Church in Montgomery.[32] It was the first of many that would align Jackson and the gospel music community with the movement.

Like the other performers discussed in this essay, Jackson was specifically invited by Dr. King to perform at the MOW. It should be noted that not everyone involved in the planning of the event agreed with this decision. Anna Hedgeman, who had argued vehemently for female representation on the podium, thought the singer did not project a representation of respectability for Black womanhood. For Hedgeman, a woman who had served as a dean at Howard University and embodied respectability politics, Jackson was "crude, unkempt, too large and ungainly."[33] However, Dr. King was insistent that Jackson perform, as she was one of the few singers capable of creating the environment that would connect him and the audience. In the years prior to the march, Jackson's singing had created the energy that fueled some of King's most celebrated oratory moments. She had an ability to—as we say in the Black Church—"set the atmosphere." Initially at Dr. King's request, Mahalia had planned to sing "Precious Lord, Take My Hand" at the march. But her manager Lou Mindling lobbied for something more upbeat. It is not clear how the song "How I Got Over" was selected, but its message resonated with the large crowd, who had stood through eight hours of speeches and musical performances.

Much like Jackson's first big hit "Movin' on Up a Little Higher," "How I Got Over" was representative of how the progressive politics of the postwar Black community had commingled with gospel music and Black liberation theology. Written by Clara Ward and recorded by the Ward Singers in 1951, the song's lyrics were inspired by a terrifying experience the group had while traveling through Georgia. Reflecting on the incident months later, Ward reworked an old spiritual from her childhood into the gospel song "How I Got Over." It bears all the hallmarks of the midcentury Black gospel song: the rhythm is set in the gospel waltz style with piano and organ accompaniment. Ward's lead vocals are set against the harmonized background vocals of the Ward Singers. Though not a fast song, Ward's rendition of the song has a little more lilt than Jackson's performance at the MOW. Jackson's interpretation was emblematic of how female gospel singers bridged the performative gap between preaching and gospel singing. It was fullthroated, simple, but nuanced. Noticeably absent were the vocal acrobatics that gospel singers sometimes employed. From the very beginning, it was clear that Jackson was speaking directly to the crowd, not performing. Rather than sing Ward's original lyrics, Jackson extrapolated various narrative strains that would have been familiar to many in the audience. She began with the song's chorus but moved lyrically between "I" and "we" in a manner that connected her experiences as a Black woman with those in the crowd. She emphasized in this moment the collective nature of the struggle for racial equality.

> How I got over. How did I make it over.
> My soul looks back and wonders how we made it over.
> Tell me how we got over. We had a mighty hard time coming on over.
> You know my soul looks back and wonder how I made it over.

Mahalia began the verses with the familiar Black gospel narrative tropes centered on her arrival in heaven and the type of praise she would engage in.

> Well, soon as I can see Jesus. The man that died for me.
> The man that bled and suffered. You know he hung on Calvary.
> I'm gonna thank him for how he brought me. I'm gonna thank God for how he taught me.
> Oh, thank my god for how he kept me. Oh, I'm gonna thank him 'cause he never left me.

The intensity of the polyphony of voice, organ accompaniment, and clapping heightened as the audience became drawn deeper into the song. Mahalia did not return to the chorus but continued the narrative of the verse.

> Then, I'm gonna thank him for old time religion.
> Yeah! I'm gonna thank God for giving me a vision.
> I'm gonna to join the heavenly choir.
> Yeah, I'm gonna to shout and never get tired.
> You know I'm gonna shout, somewhere 'round the altar.
> I'm gonna sing Glory Hallelujah.

By the time Jackson reached the last phrase, "You know I've got to thank him. Thank him for being... 'Cause God's been so good to me," vocally she had shifted fully into the shouting/preaching aesthetic. In that instant, Jackson shifted the atmosphere of the march, invoking the spirit and the emotion of the Black church and mass meetings to the National lawn. Before going into the next selection, Dr. King reportedly whispered to Jackson and her accompanist, Mildred Falls, that they should perform the spiritual "I Been 'Buked."

Coupled together, "How I Got Over" and "I Been 'Buked" constructed a narrative of reflection, praise, and resistance. Jackson's interpretation of the spiritual was slow and deliberate. Falls's accompaniment was subtle but substantial enough to allow Jackson to employ the full range and dexterity of her voice. The full-throated, shout/preaching style Jackson employed in "How I Got Over," gave way to a more nuanced reading of "I Been 'Buked." Jackson hummed, moaned, emphasized certain words and phrases by floating into falsetto. She emotionally wove a message that seemed directed at the detractors to the movement. This is most notable in the verse where she sang, "I'm going to tell my Lord, when I get home. Just how long you've been treating me so wrong." Lerone Bennett, covering the event for *Ebony*, described the performance:

> There is a nerve that lies beneath the smoothest of exteriors, a nerve 400 years old and throbbing with hurt and indignation. Mahalia Jackson penetrated the facades and exposed the nerve to public view. She was singing *I've Been Buked and I've Been Scorned* doing all the right things in the right way, and then, suddenly, it happened . . . A spasm ran through the crowd. The button-down men in front and the old women way back came to their feet, screaming and shouting. They had known that this thing was in them and that they wanted it touched. From different places, in different ways, with different dreams, they had come and, now, hearing this song, they were one.[34]

CONCLUSION

For years the musical history of the March on Washington for Jobs and Freedom was framed largely through film clippings and a commercial recording released by Folkways Records in 1964. As a result, public memory and the history of the event has been sanitized and the role Black women musicians played in advancing the political goals of the march and movement has been glossed over. It would be easy to ascribe the exclusionary politics that silenced the voices of Black women activists as the reasoning behind missing aspects of this musical history, but there is no evidence that this was the case. More than likely, copyright laws and contractual agreements framed what performances have been documented and made available for public consumption. These issues have significantly influenced the public dissemination of movement culture as evident in the recent redaction of the audio of Dr. King's speech in the 2008 remastering of James Blue's film *The March*.[35]

In the last two decades, the lens of Black civil rights movement historiography has expanded to include works like *Hands on the Freedom Plow: Personal Accounts by Women in SNCC* and *Freedom's Daughters: The Unsung Heroines of the Civil Rights Movement 1830 to 1970*, which reclaim the work and voices of women activists from the margins of civil rights history. This work seeks to add to this conversation by illuminating how the cultural labor of Black women musicians contributed significantly to formation movement culture. The performances of Odetta, Camilla Williams, Marian Anderson, the Eva Jessye Choir, and Mahalia Jackson at the March on Washington not only foster deeper understanding of this epoch and the act of freedom singing, but they also center these women within the ritualized contexts of Black life that involved the curation of Black song repertories as the means of shaping Black political thought and advancing a praxis of resistance.

NOTES

1. Margaret Walker, "For My People," *Poetry* 51, no. 2 (November 1937): 81–83.

2. This historiography also includes research that focuses on the role of music within the larger civil rights movement. For more information, see Bernice Johnson Reagon, "Let the Church Sing Freedom," *Black Music Research Journal* 7 (1987): 105–18; Shana Redman, *Anthem: Social Movements and the Sound of Solidarity in the African Diaspora* (New York and London: New York University Press, 2014); Brian Ward, "Sounds and Silences: Music and the March on Washington," *Bulletin of the German Historical Institute* S11 (August 2015): 25–48; Kristen Turner, "Guy and Candie Carawan: Mediating the Music of the Civil Rights Movement," MA thesis, University of North Carolina-Chapel Hill, 2011; Kerran Sanger, *"When the Spirit Says Sing!": The Role of Freedom Songs in the Civil Rights Movement* (New York: Garland, 1995).

3. Mimeographed page found in the Baynard Rustin Papers at the Library of Congress.

4. Stephen Stacks, "Headed for the Brink: Freedom-Singing in U.S. Culture after 1968," (PhD diss., University of North Carolina-Chapel Hill, 2019).

5. For more information on the public relation strategy of SNCC, see Vanessa Murphree, *The Selling of Civil Rights: The Student Nonviolent Coordinating Committee and the Use of Public Relations* (New York and London: Routledge, 2006).

6. Bernice Johnson Reagon, "African Diaspora Women: The Making of Cultural Workers," *Feminist Studies* 12, no. 1 (Spring 1986): 77–90.

7. "Statement by the heads of the ten organizations calling for discipline in connection with the Washington March of August 28, 1963," accessed September 8, 2016, http://www.libraries.wright.edu/community/outofthebox/files/2011/08/MLK_2.jpg.

8. Black exceptionalism draws on the different ideological perspectives that framed the politics of racial uplift and Black upward mobility in the late nineteenth and early twentieth centuries. While rooted in the theory of the Talented Tenth, first introduced by Henry Lyman Morehouse but more popularly attributed to W. E. B. Du Bois (in "The Negro Problem"), it also includes the Black feminism of Anna Julia Cooper (*A Voice from the South*) and the New Negro ideology promoted by Alain Locke (*The New Negro*) and other leaders of the Renaissance movement.

9. See Tammy L. Kernodle, "'When and Where I Enter': Black Women Composers and the Advancement of a Black Postmodern Concert Aesthetic in Cold War-Era America," in Colloquy: "Shadow Culture Narratives: Race, Gender, and American Music Historiography," *Journal of the American Musicology Society* 73, no. 3 (Fall 2020): 770–76.

10. Odetta quoted in the National Visionary Leadership Project, http://www.visionaryproject.org/gordonodetta/. Accessed April 4, 2012.

11. There are a number of sources that attributed this appellation to Dr. King. However, I have been unable to locate the primary source for this information. My use of it is based on the interview La Shonda Katrice Barnett conducted with Odetta for the book *I Got Thunder: Black Women Songwriters on Their Craft* (New York: Thunder's Mouth Press, 2007), 174.

12. Full audio clip of this performance and the encore is available at https://openvault.wgbh.org/catalog/A_3135488CBB9E467B9F0684BC930E6498#at_1943.953_s (starts at 32:45).

A short film clip of this performance is accessible at https://www.facebook.com/NMAAHC/videos/odetta-performing-at-the-1963-march-on-washington-for-jobs-and-freedom/593481824663407/, or "Odetta Performing at the March on Washington," https://www.gettyimages.com/detail/video/people-arriving-at-march-odetta-singing-im-on-my-way-news-footage/176452440.

13. For more information on Josh White, see Elijah Wald, *Josh White: Society Blues* (Amherst: University of Massachusetts Press, 2000).

14. Bob Dylan stated in a 1966 interview with *Playboy* magazine: "The first thing that turned me on to folk singing was Odetta. I heard a record of hers in a record store, back when you could listen to records right there in the store. That was in '58 or something like that. Right then and there, I went out and traded my electric guitar and amplifier for an acoustical guitar, a flat-top Gibson.... I learned all the songs on that record. It was her first." "Playboy Interview: A Candid Conversation with the Visionary Whose Songs Changed the Times," http://www.interferenza.net/bcs/interw/66-jan.htm. Accessed March 3, 2012.

15. Margalit Fox, "Camilla Williams, Soprano, Dies at 92; Achieved Oft-Overlooked Breakthrough," *New York Times*, February 3, 2012, A1.

16. Casting a Black woman in a role that served as the love interest of a white man was controversial in 1946, and there were public threats of violence. Halasz was pressured into staging another audition for the role months before the scheduled opening. With the help of makeup artist Eddie Sens, Williams was able to transform physically into a Japanese geisha and silenced critics as to whether she could effectively play the role.

17. Camilla Williams and Stephanie Shonekan, *The Life of Camilla Williams, African American Classical Singer and Opera Diva* (Lewiston, NY: Edwin Mellen Press, 2011), 86–87.

18. In relation to the other southern campaigns, the 1963 Danville effort is less well known. However, activists considered it one of the bloodiest and most violent. The paucity of information was a result of a media blackout implemented by city leaders. Even so, a number of activists have discussed their experiences in the city. By August, an estimated 600 persons had been jailed and charged in Danville. For more information regarding the Danville campaign, see http://nvdatabase.swarthmore.edu/content/pastors-and-students-lead-campaign-desegregate-danville-va-1963.

19. Williams and Shonekan, 155–56.

20. Williams's performance of the anthem is available at https://www.youtube.com/watch?v=fbc34YyhHTw.

21. Williams and Shonekan, 156.

22. For a full account of this tour, see Allan Keiler, *Marian Anderson: A Singer's Journey* (New York: Scribner, 2000), 308–9.

23. Keiler, *Marian Anderson: A Singer's Journey*, 309.

24. For more information on the relationship between Price and Anderson, see Alisha Jones, "Lift Every Voice: Marian Anderson, Florence B. Price, and the Sound of Black Sisterhood," https://www.npr.org/2019/08/30/748757267/lift-every-voice-marian-anderson-florence-b-price-and-the-sound-of-black-sisterh, accessed August 30, 2019.

25. Marian Anderson sings at the March on Washington video, https://www.gettyimages.com/detail/video/marian-anderson-introduced-and-sings-hes-got-the-whole-news-footage/176452495.

26. Source for information on Eva Jessye is Donald Fisher Black, "The Life and Work of Eva Jessye and Her Contributions to American Music," PhD diss., University of Michigan, 1986.

27. Black, "The Life and Work of Eva Jessye," 72.

28. This organization hosted a number of African leaders in the United States. Dr. King joined the organization in 1957 and served on the national committee formed by George Hauser and the other leadership.

29. "Freedom Is a Thing Worth Thinking About" lyric sheet, Eva Jessye Collection, University of Michigan, Ann Arbor, MI.

30. Eva Jessye Choir performance at the March on Washington [audio], https://www.youtube.com/watch?v=-WShHQv9kBc.

31. Robert Darden, *Nothing but Love in God's Water: Black Sacred Music from the Civil War to the Civil Rights Movement*, vol. 1 (University Park: Pennsylvania State University Press, 2014), 12. Darden talks about Jackson's performance at the MOW in *Nothing but Love in God's Water: Black Sacred Music from Sit-Ins to Resurrection City*, vol. 2 (University Park: Pennsylvania State University Press, 2016).

32. Darden, *Nothing but Love*, 130. For the full account of Jackson's interaction with Rev. Abernathy, see Laurraine Goreau, *Just Mahalia Baby* (Gretna, LA: Pelican, 1984): 218–21.

33. Charles Euchner, *Nobody Turn Me Around: A People's History of the 1963 March on Washington* (Boston: Beacon Press, 2010), 157.

34. Lerone Bennett, "Biggest Protest March: 250,000 Jam Washington for Huge Civil Rights Demonstration," *Ebony* (November 1963), 120–21.

35. This documentary film is available on YouTube, but viewers are warned in the summary comments about the redaction of the audio for King's speech.

BIBLIOGRAPHY

Barnett, La Shonda Katrice. *I Got Thunder: Black Women Songwriters on Their Craft*. New York: Thunder's Mouth Press, 2007.

Bennett, Lerone. "Biggest Protest March: 250,000 Jam Washington for Huge Civil Rights Demonstration," *Ebony* (November 1963), 120–21.

Black, Donald Fisher. "The Life and Work of Eva Jessye and Her Contributions to American Music," PhD diss., University of Michigan, 1986.

Blue, James. *The March*. https://www.youtube.com/watch?v=DQYzHIIIQ104&t=97s.

Cain, Michael Scott. *Folk Music and the New Left in the Sixties*. Jefferson, NC: McFarland, 2019.

Darden, Robert. *Nothing but Love in God's Water: Black Sacred Music from the Civil War to the Civil Rights Movement*, vol. 1. University Park: Pennsylvania State University Press, 2014.

Darden, Robert. *Nothing but Love in God's Water: Black Sacred Music from Sit-Ins to Resurrection City*, vol. 2. University Park: Pennsylvania State University Press, 2016.

Euchner, Charles. *Nobody Turn Me Around: A People's History of the 1963 March on Washington*. Boston: Beacon Press, 2010.

Fox, Margalit. "Camilla Williams, Soprano, Dies at 92; Achieved Oft-Overlooked Breakthrough." *New York Times*, February 3, 2012, A1.

Goreau, Laurraine. *Just Mahalia Baby*. Gretna, LA: Pelican, 1984.

Holsaert, Faith, Martha Prescod Norman Noonan, Judy Richardson, Betty Garman Robinson, Jean Smith Young, and Dorothy M. Zellner, ed. *Hands on the Freedom Plow: Personal Accounts by Women in SNCC*. Urbana and Chicago: University of Illinois Press, 2010.

Jones, Alisha. "Lift Every Voice: Marian Anderson, Florence B. Price, and the Sound of Black Sisterhood," https://www.npr.org/2019/08/30/748757267/lift-every-voice-marian-anderson-florence-b-price-and-the-sound-of-black-sisterh.

Jones, William P. *The March on Washington: Jobs, Freedom and the Forgotten History of Civil Rights.* New York: W. W. Norton, 2013.
Olsen, Lynne. *Freedom's Daughters: The Unsung Heroines of the Civil Rights Movement from 1830 to 1970.* New York: Touchstone Books, 2001.
Keiler, Allan. *Marian Anderson: A Singer's Journey.* New York: Scribner, 2000.
Kernodle, Tammy L. "'When and Where I Enter': Black Women Composers and the Advancement of a Black Postmodern Concert Aesthetic in Cold War-Era America." *Journal of the American Musicology Society* 73, no. 3 (Fall 2020): 770–76.
March on Washington, WGBH, https://openvault.wgbh.org/catalog/A_3135488CBB9E467B9F0 684BC930E6498#at_1943.953_s.
Murphree, Vanessa. *The Selling of Civil Rights: The Student Nonviolent Coordinating Committee and the Use of Public Relations.* New York and London: Routledge, 2006.
National Visionary Leadership Project. http://www.visionaryproject.org/gordonodetta/.
"Playboy Interview: Bob Dylan." http://www.interferenza.net/bcs/interw/66-jan.htm.
Reagon, Bernice Johnson. "Let the Church Sing Freedom." *Black Music Research Journal* 7 (1987): 105–18.
Reagon, Bernice Johnson. "African Diaspora Women: The Making of Cultural Workers." *Feminist Studies* 12, no. 1 (Spring 1986): 77–90.
Stacks, Stephen. "Headed for the Brink: Freedom-Singing in U.S. Culture after 1968." PhD diss., University of North Carolina-Chapel Hill, 2019.
Wald, Elijah. *Josh White: Society Blues.* Amherst: University of Massachusetts Press, 2000.
Walker, Margaret. "For My People." *Poetry* 51, no. 2 (November 1937): 81–83.
Ward, Brian. "Sounds and Silences: Music and the March on Washington." *Bulletin of the German Historical Institute* S11 (August 2015): 25–48.
Weissman, Dick. *Which Side Are You On? An Inside History of the Folk Music Revival in America.* New York: Continuum, 2006.
Williams, Camilla, and Stephanie Shonekan. *The Life of Camilla Williams, African American Classical Singer and Opera Diva.* Lewiston, NY: Edwin Mellen Press, 2011.

About the Contributors

Christina Baade is Professor and Chair of the Department of Communication Studies and Media Arts at McMaster University. Her current research crosses popular music, media, and sound studies, examining the performative work of women stars; the cultural impact of music broadcast and streaming; and cultural memory and national belonging in post–World War II Britain. Her publications include her award-winning book, *Victory Through Harmony: The BBC and Popular Music in World War II* (Oxford University Press, 2012), and three coedited collections: *Music and the Broadcast Experience: Performance, Production, and Audiences*, with James Deaville (Oxford University Press, 2016); *Music in World War II: Coping with Wartime in Europe and the United States*, with Pamela Potter and Roberta Montemorra Marvin (Indiana University Press, 2020); and *Beyoncé in the World: Making Meaning with Queen Bey in Troubled Times*, with Kristin McGee (Wesleyan University Press, 2021).

Candace Bailey received her PhD in Musicology from Duke University with a dissertation on English keyboard music of the seventeenth century. She has published and presented work on that subject and on topics related to women and music in the nineteenth-century southern United States. Her most recent publications include articles and essays in *Music & Letters* and the *Journal of the Society for American Music*, and she served as coeditor and contributor on *Beyond Boundaries: Music Circulation in Early Modern Britain* (Indiana University Press, 2017), for which she served as coeditor and contributor. In 2021, she published *Unbinding Gentility: Women Making Music in the Nineteenth-Century South* (University of Illinois Press, 2021), based on research supported by fellowships from the NEH and the National Humanities Center. Dr. Bailey currently serves as the secretary of the Society of American Music and as a Fulbright Specialist in American Studies.

Paula J. Bishop is on the faculty in the music department at Bridgewater State University in Massachusetts, where she teaches Western music history, music theory, country music, and other topics related to music of the United States.

She earned her PhD from Boston University with a dissertation on the Everly Brothers and has presented and published on the Everly Brothers, the Nashville songwriters Felice and Boudleaux Bryant, and feminism and country music. She is the coeditor of *Whose Country Music? Genre, Identity and Belonging* (Cambridge University Press, 2023).

Maribeth Clark, Professor of Music at New College of Florida, is writing a book exploring the cultural history of whistling in the United States. Her earlier scholarship focused on the importance of dance in the context of French grand opera. She and Davinia Caddy coedited *Musicology and Dance: Historical and Critical Perspectives* (Cambridge University Press, 2020). She has published articles in the *Journal of Musicology*, *Musical Quarterly*, and *19th-Century Music*, numerous reviews, and has contributed to two essay collections that focus on teaching information literacy.

Brittany Greening is a doctoral student in Communications and Media Studies at Carleton University. She holds a BEd in Secondary Music from the University of Alberta and an MA in Musicology from Dalhousie University. Her dissertation research examines the impacts of multilevel cultural policy on the lives and careers of Canadian musicians.

Tammy Kernodle is University Distinguished Professor of Music at Miami University, where she teaches in the areas of African American music and gender studies. Her scholarship concentrates on the spectrum of African American music, both classical and popular. It appears in a number of peer-reviewed journals and anthologies. She is the author of the biography *Soul on Soul: The Life and Music of Mary Lou Williams* (University of Illinois Press, 2020), which chronicles the life and music of Williams, whose career in jazz spans over six decades. Kernodle has worked with a number of educational institutions including the BBC, Rock and Roll Hall of Fame, and the National Museum of African American History and Culture and also appears in a number of award-winning documentaries.

Kendra Preston Leonard is a musicologist and music theorist whose work focuses on women and music in the twentieth and twenty-first centuries and music and screen history. She is the author of *Music for the Kingdom of Shadows: Cinema Accompaniment in the Age of Spiritualism*; *The Art Songs of Louise Talma*; *Music for Silent Film: A Guide to North American Resources*; *Louise Talma: A Life in Composition*; *The Conservatoire Américain: A History*; and *Shakespeare, Madness, and Music: Scoring Insanity in Cinematic Adaptations*. She is the Executive Director of the Silent Film Sound and Music Archive.

April L. Prince studied with the late K. M. Knittel at the University of Texas at Austin. Grounded in cultural and gender studies, her research focuses on nineteenth-century German concert culture, early twentieth-century country music and blues women, and music history pedagogy. She is currently a principal lecturer at the University of North Texas.

Travis D. Stimeling is professor of musicology at West Virginia University, where they also coordinate programs in Appalachian music and Appalachian studies. They have published widely on a number of topics with a primary focus in country music. Their most recent book is *Nashville Cats: Record Production in Music City* (Oxford University Press, 2020).

Kristen M. Turner teaches in the music and honors departments at North Carolina State University. She coauthored *Race and Gender in the Western Music History Survey: A Teacher's Guide* (Routledge, 2022) with Horace Maxile. Her research on American operatic culture and popular entertainment at the turn of the twentieth century has appeared in several journals, including the *Journal of the American Musicological Society* and the *Journal of the Society for American Music*, as well as a number of collected editions, including *Carmen Abroad: Bizet's Opera on the Global Stage* (Cambridge University Press, 2019), which received the 2021 RMA/Cambridge University Press Outstanding Edited Collection Book Prize.

Index

Acuff, Roy, 115, 150, 156, 157, 159
Agnes Woodward School of Whistling.
    See California School of Artistic
    Whistling
all-girl bands, 138, 140–43, 144nn13–15,
    146n60. *See also* girl groups
Anderson, Marian, 197, 198, 204, 206–7, 208,
    214, 216nn22–25
Arnold, Doris, 92, 95, 96
Atkins, Chet, 111, 118

Barbot, Hermine Petit, 12, 14–15, 16, 20, 21n7
bird sounds (imitations, songs, and
    whistling), 24–29, 31–42, 44n8, 44n11,
    45n23, 46n38, 47n56, 47n64, 48n83, 49n86
British Broadcasting Corporation (BBC), 88,
    90–98, 100–104, 105nn10–12, 105nn14–15,
    105nn17–20, 106n32, 106n34, 106n39,
    107n47, 107nn51–55, 107n58, 107n60,
    108n68, 108n73, 219, 220; Gramophone
    Department, 92; women's roles, 90–92,
    94, 96, 100–103
Bryant, Boudleaux, 111, 116–28, 220
Bryant, Felice, 7, 8, 111–28, 220
Burnett, Hazel, 53, 58, 60–62, 66–67

California School of Artistic Whistling,
    24–25, 29, 31–32, 34–36, 38, 42–43,
    45nn22–23, 45n28, 49n88
Carawan, Carolanne Anderson (Candie), 9,
    173–87, 188n2, 188nn7–13, 189n16, 189n18,
    189n23, 189n25, 189nn28–29, 190nn31–42,
    190n46, 190n48, 190nn52–53, 191n56,
    191nn58–60, 191n65, 215n2
Carawan, Guy, 175–82, 184–85, 187, 188n2,
    188nn7–13, 189n16, 189n18, 189n20,
    189n23, 189nn25–29, 190nn31–42, 190n46,
    190nn48–49, 190n53, 191nn56–60, 191n65,
    215n2
Carmen (opera), 63, 99, 205, 221
Carson, Fiddlin' John, 71, 83n17, 84n23, 85n41
Carson, Rosa Lee ("Moonshine Kate"),
    4, 7, 71–72, 74–75, 77–82, 82n2, 83n21,
    85nn36–38, 85nn40–41
Chaminade Clubs. *See* women's clubs
Charleston, South Carolina, 12, 14–15,
    21nn7–13
Chautauqua, 8, 26, 31, 34–35, 37–38, 40, 42, 43,
    45n27, 46n41, 47n54, 47n58, 47n61
class, 9, 11, 12–13, 16, 20n4, 21n9, 24–25, 63,
    72, 78, 81–82, 83n10, 91, 93, 94, 99, 106n28,
    106n32, 107n46, 113, 116, 126n7, 130–31,
    133–34, 137, 149–50, 152, 155–56, 159–61,
    165n19, 166n38, 167n43, 168n65, 177, 180
cues and cue sheets (silent film), 54, 58, 60,
    62–67, 69n24

Darlington, Margaret, 26, 41–42, 48n83,
    49n85
Decca Records, 102, 115, 129, 130, 139, 158
disc jockeys (DJs), 5, 88–92, 95–98, 100–104,
    104n3
Disney Bros., 41–42, 48n83
domesticity, 80, 83n10, 90–97, 101–2, 106n32,
    113, 132–33, 155

Epperson, Fay, 26, 36–37, 42, 47, 47n50, 47n58
Etude (magazine), 60–62

femininity, 7, 15, 19, 71, 73–74, 76–78, 81,
    84n23, 85n40, 90, 92, 95, 97, 102, 130–32,
    142, 143, 150, 182

feminism, 3, 8, 112, 131, 215n8, 220
Freedom Riders, 182, 189n24, 195
Freedom songs, 173–74, 177–78, 180–85, 187, 188n20, 195, 197, 214

girl groups, 135–37, 141–43, 145nn33–35, 146nn75–77, 146n83. *See also* all-girl bands
Goldie (singer). *See* Zelkowitz, Genya "Goldie" (Genya Ravan)
Goldie and the Gingerbreads, 4, 7–8, 129–31, 133–43

Hazelton, Frances, 26, 39–41, 45n30, 46nn39–40, 48nn73–82, 49n88
"He's Got the Whole World in His Hands" (song), 206–7
Hetherington, Carrie, 53, 58–60, 66–67, 69nn46–48, 70n49
Highlander Folk School (Highlander Research and Education Center), 175–78, 180–81, 188n14, 189nn15–16, 189n20, 189nn25–27, 190n47, 190n49
hillbillies, 72, 74, 78–79, 83n19, 84n21, 116, 156, 160, 168n64
Housewives' Choice, 88, 90, 102–3
"How I Got Over" (song), 211–13

"ideal woman," 114
Instone, Anna, 92
intimate public, 90–91, 93, 96–98, 100–101, 103–4, 105n8
"I've Been Buked" (song), 213–14

Jackson, Mahalia, 197, 200, 211–14, 217n32
Jay, Alice Smythe Burton, 53, 59–60, 62–67, 69nn39–44
Jessye, Eva, 197–98, 207–11, 214, 216n26, 217n29

King, Martin Luther, Jr., 179, 201, 204–5, 207–9, 211–14, 215n11, 217n28, 217n35
Kowalewski, Mariah Dillon, 12, 14–18, 20, 21n20, 21n22, 22n29
Ku Klux Klan, 185–86

Lewis, Margo, 131
Light Programme, 88, 92, 94, 96–99, 102–3, 106n39, 107n58, 107n60, 108n73

Lynn, Vera, 8, 88–93, 95–104, 104n1, 105nn21–22, 106n45, 107nn47–48, 107nn51–54, 107nn65–66, 108nn68–69, 108nn72–73

MacDonald, Carol, 131, 133–34, 138, 139
March on Washington for Jobs and Freedom, 194–215, 215n2, 215n7, 217n30
McKee, Margaret, 26, 31, 33, 35, 38–39, 42, 45n27, 47n66, 47nn69–70, 48n72
minstrelsy, 29, 55, 72, 75, 77, 84n23, 84n31, 85n38, 100, 159, 160, 168n58
Mobile Musical Association, 16–18
music: classical, 7, 13, 24, 26, 29, 32, 36, 55, 56, 62, 64, 65, 66, 92, 116, 131, 198, 216n17; country, 10n5, 71–74, 78, 82, 82n1, 83n15, 84nn21–22, 85n35, 111–15, 120, 121, 122–25, 126nn4–6, 127nn47–49, 145n30, 152, 156, 158, 160, 165n5, 165nn12–14, 166nn24–25, 167n47, 167n55, 168nn57–59, 168nn63–64, 168n67, 169n70, 219, 220, 221; folk, 55, 72, 77, 81, 82n4, 84n31, 85nn33–34, 114, 116, 123, 124, 150, 156, 174, 176, 177, 178, 180, 195, 197, 198, 200–203, 208–9, 216n14; gospel, 73, 156, 160, 197, 200, 211–13; jazz, 91, 95, 96, 99, 101, 106n39, 116, 145n30, 152, 160, 165n19, 166nn25–26, 168nn65–66, 220; Old-time, 7, 71–75, 77–82, 82n3, 84n21, 84n23, 85n41; opera, 15, 29, 38, 39, 59, 62, 63, 65–66, 198, 200, 204–7, 216n17, 218, 220, 221; popular, 8, 9, 24, 46n31, 57, 59, 61, 63, 64, 65, 66, 72, 73, 80, 81, 82n4, 84n32, 85n38, 89, 90–91, 95–96, 98, 99, 100, 102, 103, 105n10, 107n59, 125, 129–30, 132, 134, 135, 137–43, 144n17, 145n33, 145n50, 146n81, 150, 155–60, 164n3, 182, 191n55, 191n61, 219, 220, 221; rock and roll, 89, 91, 95–96, 97, 100–101, 104n5, 106n36, 108n76, 124, 129–44, 144nn1–4, 144nn13–15, 144nn17–18, 145n28, 145n30, 145n36, 145n42, 145nn57–58, 146n60, 146n65, 146n73, 181, 220; spirituals, 176, 180, 182, 195, 197, 200–203, 205–9, 212–13, 220; narrative, 5, 9, 32, 67, 72, 91, 93, 112–14, 120, 137, 140–42, 154, 161, 174, 180, 188n5, 197, 201, 202, 207, 209, 212, 213, 217n9

Nashville, Tennessee, 101, 111–12, 114, 117, 120–22, 124–26, 174–76, 182, 185, 189n24, 220, 221

New South, 72, 77–78, 81–82, 82nn5–6, 83n7, 83n10, 83nn12–14, 84n30
New Woman, 25, 43n7

"O What a Beautiful City" (song), 204–5
Odetta, 195, 197, 200–203, 207–8, 214, 215nn10–11, 216nn12–14
O'Grady, Carol, 129, 131–32
"Oh Freedom" (spiritual), 195, 201–2
Old South, 21n6, 72, 78, 82n5, 83n10
organists, 7, 11–20, 30, 45n23, 56–57, 59–60, 62, 68n4

Panebianco, Ginger, 129, 132–33
performance, 7, 28, 57, 61, 63, 64, 67, 69n34, 137
Peterman, Nancy, 131–32, 134
pianos, 21n18, 42; player, 57–58, 66, 70n51; sermonic, 203, 207, 210; social, 5, 8
Pillichody, Josephine Hutet, 12, 17–19, 22n32
practices: Black folk, 208; Black worship, 195; broadcasting, 91; gender and, 7, 131, 144nn7–8
Price, Florence, 54, 206, 216n24

Q, Shuggie, 132–33

race, 3, 4, 5, 10n4, 21n9, 54–57, 67n3, 68n15, 72–74, 80–81, 82n5, 83n15, 83n20, 84n23, 84n29, 85n35, 85n38, 90, 91, 94, 105n12, 105n14, 106n32, 107n62, 113, 114n9, 126n6, 130–31, 136, 137, 149, 150, 152, 155, 160, 166n36, 167n43, 168n58, 173, 175, 177, 188n15, 195, 198, 202–3, 206, 208, 211–12, 215n8, 215n9, 221
radio, 8, 38–39, 40–43, 47nn69–70, 48n80, 89–103, 104n3, 105nn7–8, 105n12, 105n16, 105n19, 106nn28–29, 106n31, 196n32, 196nn37–38, 106n40, 107n52, 107n56, 107n62, 107n64, 108n69, 108nn74–75, 115–16, 121, 152, 155, 160, 164, 168n67, 188n10, 201, 203, 205, 208
Ravan, Genya. *See* Zelkowitz, Genya "Goldie" (Genya Ravan)
Records at Six, 90–104
respectability, 84n21, 88, 93, 95–97, 99, 103, 130–31, 133–34, 152, 155, 159–60, 168n64, 212
Rolling Stone Magazine, 140–41, 142, 144n1

Rolling Stones (band), 140–41
Rustin, Baynard, 198, 202, 208, 210, 215n3

Sands, Fannie, 12, 15–19
sexuality, 10n4, 73, 130, 134, 137, 145n37, 146n81, 149
Shaw, Mrs. Alice J., 25, 43n6
SNCC Freedom Singers, 189n24, 201–3
songwriting, 7–8, 111–15, 117–19, 121–25, 126n14, 135–36, 142, 149, 215n11, 220
Southern Musical Journal, 16, 18–19, 22nn27–28, 22nn34–35
Spiritual Trilogy, 195, 201, 203
Stanley, Roba, 4, 7, 71–72, 74–77, 81–82, 83n21, 84n26
Student Nonviolent Coordinating Committee (SNCC), 176–77, 179, 181, 188n1, 189n21, 190nn23–24, 198, 201–3, 214, 215n5

"They Go Wild Over Me" (song), 182–86

vaudeville, 8, 24, 26, 31, 36, 38, 43, 45n24, 56, 57, 63, 85n38
Vera's Evening Record Album, 90, 97–98, 100–101, 103, 107n66

Whistling as an Art, 25, 27, 28, 40, 43n2, 44n9, 44n12
Williams, Camilla, 197–98, 204–6, 214, 216n15–21
women's clubs, 6, 8, 30, 31, 36–37, 39, 40, 42, 47n50, 47nn56–57, 47n72
Woodward, Agnes, 8–9, 24–43, 43nn2–3, 44nn9–10, 44nn12–17, 45n20, 45nn22–23, 45n27, 45n30, 46n36, 46nn39–40, 48n73, 49n88

Zelkowitz, Genya "Goldie" (Genya Ravan), 129, 131–35, 138–40, 143, 144n4, 144n16, 144nn20–23, 145n26, 145n32, 145n37, 146n59, 146n61, 146n67, 146nn89–90

www.ingramcontent.com/pod-product-compliance
Lightning Source LLC
Chambersburg PA
CBHW022014220426
43663CB00007B/1077